BASIC
RUSSIAN

Cover photo: Red Square, Moscow. (Courtesy of Sovfoto.)

Аме́рика

теа́тр

ра́дио

те́ннис

Ло́ндон

баскетбо́л

автомоби́ль

BASIC
RUSSIAN

MISCHA H. FAYER, Ph.D.

Head of the Russian Department, and
Director of The Russian School and
the Institute of Soviet Studies,
Middlebury College

PITMAN PUBLISHING CORPORATION

New York   •   Toronto   •   London

E. 0 **028019**^{1.2}

Associated Companies
SIR ISAAC PITMAN & SONS, LTD.
London   Melbourne   Johannesburg
SIR ISAAC PITMAN & SONS (CANADA), LTD.
Toronto

9999 051 610

PRINTED IN THE UNITED STATES OF AMERICA

INTRODUCTION TO THE STUDENT

Many Americans now realize that the importance of the study of Russian cannot be overestimated. That is why more and more schools in this country are adding the language to their curriculum. In the near future the teaching of Russian will be as widespread as that of Latin, French, or Spanish. Yet Russian is still regarded as something unusual and alien in our Western civilization.

The view that Russian is an extremely difficult language is often expressed by people who do not know it and have never attempted to learn it. This is natural because anything unfamiliar seems strange and difficult. And yet Russian is an Indo-European language like Greek, Latin, French, Spanish, Italian, German, and English, and has many common roots with them. It has similar sentence structure and inflection patterns, and it has borrowed many words from those languages. Its alphabet is different from the Latin, but not enough so as to require more effort than in learning the Greek or the Gothic alphabets. In some respects it is actually easier than the alphabets of many other European languages. Spelling and pronunciation are simple and easy—a real joy for one who has had to struggle with English or French as foreign languages.

Some aspects of Russian, on the other hand, are harder than anything one would encounter in either English, French, or Spanish. Let's face it: it is a highly inflected language, similar to Latin or German, and one must know the declensions of nouns, adjectives, and pronouns before getting into real conversation or reading. In the long run, however, one can progress as rapidly in Russian—and with no more effort—as in the other foreign languages commonly taught in American schools. Russian, in short, is neither so different nor so difficult as to discourage anyone from learning it.

Since Russian is a highly inflected language, it requires a different approach than the one that might be used in the beginning for French or Spanish, for instance. Some essentials of grammar must be mastered before one is ready for the type of conversation or reading that would appeal fully to an adult. Therefore, do not be impatient or in too big a hurry to attain your ultimate objectives. Your primary concern should be to achieve a solid foundation for future progress.   The man who builds a flimsy foundation for his house, because he is in a hurry to move into a completed dwelling, will never be a happy homeowner.   The student who has not mastered Russian declensions can hardly hope ever to use Russian correctly.

A foreign language is the key to a new, unfamiliar world.   Knowledge of Russian will open up to you a fascinating new area representing one sixth of the earth's land surface, and two and a half times the size of the United States.   It has been said that Russia is not merely a country, but a whole continent.   Russia, now known as the U.S.S.R., has emerged after World War II as the second world power.   It has made great strides in industry and in science, as demonstrated by the launching of the *Sputniks*.

Russian contributions in the nineteenth century in the realm of the arts are well known.   Enough to mention composers like Tchaikowsky in music, Tolstoy and Dostoevsky in literature, Stanislavsky in the theater, and Diaghilev in the ballet.   You, therefore, have many reasons for embarking on this exciting new venture —the study of Russian.

INTRODUCTION TO THE TEACHER

Objectives

The main objective of this text is to reduce all difficulties to the barest minimum and to present essentials simply, clearly, and as effectively as possible for the learning process. There is no intention, however, to avoid those principles of grammar or the idiomatic constructions which are indispensable for a solid foundation in the language. Further simplification of the grammar could only be achieved by the omission of important elements of grammar without which the student cannot hope to learn the language properly.

The stress is on aural comprehension, reading, and self-expression. No attempt is made, however, to impose a specific method on the teacher. The author believes that the best method is the one that the individual teacher considers most effective for the objective he has set for himself and his students.

For that reason, the material has been organized to provide maximum flexibility from the standpoint of teaching procedures. The teacher who prefers the oral approach can reduce written work to a minimum. Those who believe in written work will find a great abundance and variety of drills and exercises. Teachers who believe in the fourfold process for successful mastery of a foreign language will be able to combine aural drill, reading, and conversation with writing.

The pace is also left to the discretion of the teacher, but it is assumed that, under normal conditions, it will be possible to cover the text in one year or less, depending upon the level of instruction—high school or college.

Organization of the Material

The text contains twenty-eight units organized into five major sections. Each of these sections usually consists of six units, the last of which is a review of the material covered within the section as a whole. In two of the sections, there are five rather than six units, but in both these cases one of the units is expected to require twice the amount of time given to the others. Thus, each major section contains the equivalent of six units.

Supplementary material, including everyday expressions, short reading selections (with vocabulary), proverbs, and riddles are given in the Appendix for use in those classes in which an accelerated pace seems possible or desirable. In addition, the Appendix includes Russian songs, pronunciation charts, tables of declensions and conjugations, and comprehensive Russian-English and English-Russian vocabularies.

With respect to the plan of the individual units themselves, a few words are in order. Unit 1 is primarily intended to introduce the Russian alphabet, both as it is written and printed. Thereafter, each unit follows a standard pattern, with only slight modification in a few instances. This pattern is as follows:

1. The Basic Text—a connected reading selection with accompanying vocabulary.
2. A Разговóр (Conversation) or a second installment of the basic text, with vocabulary.
3. Произношéние—rules of pronunciation and phonetic drills (in the first ten lessons).
4. Граммáтика—rules of grammar.
5. Упражнéния—exercises for written or oral work.
6. Перевóд—translation exercises from English to Russian.
7. Вопрóсы—questions.

In effect, each unit contains seven parts through Unit 10, and six parts thereafter. It is easy, therefore, to assign one part of the unit, and in some cases two, for each daily assignment and thus cover one unit a week.

A brief description of the nature of the parts included in each unit will indicate how the book as a whole is organized.

Basic Text. The first part of the unit offers *connected* reading material, almost from the outset. Such material is more readily remembered than disconnected sentences given merely to introduce some point of grammar. It is also more helpful and interesting for the purposes of drill and conversation.

With respect to the presentation of vocabulary in conjunction with the basic text, Units 2–7 introduce a maximum of fifteen new words, of which four or five are cognates. This reduces the number of completely unfamiliar words to only about ten for each assignment. Beginning with Unit 8, a maximum of twenty new words is introduced. Vocabulary building is gradual, and new words and expressions are introduced on the basis of their frequency value or the immediate needs of classroom and other everyday situations. Occasionally, a word is introduced regardless of its frequency value because it makes the material more humorous or interesting. This is necessary, especially in the beginning, in order to present stimulating and connected narratives despite an extremely limited vocabulary. In addition, a number of proper names are given with the purpose of further enlivening the text. These are not considered essential to the students' functional vocabulary and thus need not receive the same attention.

Разговóр or Second Reading Installment. The second part of the unit reviews the new words given in the basic text and introduces some additional vocabulary. In Units 2–7, a maximum of seven simple new words are presented. Thereafter, between ten and fifteen new words are introduced, several of which are cognates.

Произношéние. The rules of pronunciation are presented with numerous illustrations and phonetic drills, and should be studied in conjunction with the reading selections for the most effective results. By distributing the material on pronunciation over the first ten units, it is possible to introduce the basic elements of pronunciation gradually. New words are introduced, not only with a view to their frequency value, but also to the new phonetic elements they involve. In the Appendix, complete pronunciation charts are offered, with cross references to the specific discussions in the text.

Граммáтика. The fourth part of the unit explains the new grammatical principles involved in the reading selections. The explanations are accompanied by examples, tables, and illustrations, and are sufficiently detailed to require only a minimum of class time, leaving the teacher more time for dictation, conversation, and blackboard work. In the advanced lessons, the grammar is presented in two installments, each of which is coordinated with one of the two reading selections. Thus it is possible to work on the first portion of the grammar in connection with the first reading selection, and separately on the second portion in connection with the other selection. Tables in the Appendix completely summarize the declensions and conjugations studied in the course of the text.

Упражнéния and Перевóд. The Упражнéния are exercises for written or oral work, which aim to fix the new material in the student's memory and make it functional. In a sense, they constitute a preparation for the Перевóд, the English-to-Russian translation exercises that follow; for they are simpler and easier than the latter.

Вопро́сы. The questions given in Russian at the end of each unit are intended as an oral drill, summary, and review of the material covered in the unit. This part should not be attempted before the students have mastered all the preceding parts of the unit. The questions, whether used for written assignments or oral work in class, should always be answered by the students with complete sentences so that they may obtain more practice in the language.

The five *Review Units* that appear at the end of each major section review the vocabulary and grammar covered in the preceding units by means of a variety of exercises. These are occasionally accompanied by tables that summarize and bring together the more important grammatical rules and inflection patterns.

In the *Appendix*, complete Russian-English and English-Russian vocabularies are given. In the case of the former, the perfective and imperfective forms of the verbs studied both appear, as well as irregular forms of nouns in the genitive singular, the nominative plural, and the genitive plural. In addition, cross references appear in these vocabularies, which enable the student to turn immediately to detailed explanations in the text.

This, then, describes the basic organization of the book. Its main virtue is that it comprehends all of the basic elements of good language instruction but at the same time allows the individual instructor great flexibility in his choice of approach. The teacher who wishes to stress the oral method of instruction may skip the presentation of the alphabet and the writing drills given in Unit 1 and begin with Units 2 and 3, which provide materials for oral practice. In addition, he can make use of the section on everyday expressions which appears in the Appendix. Because of the abundance of exercises and drills, teachers may omit some of them or assign them on an oral rather than a written basis. On the other hand, teachers who conduct their classes at a faster than average pace can draw on the supplementary materials in the Appendix and thus present a full year's work without recourse to another book.

In presenting the grammatical material and in selecting the vocabulary, idioms, and phrases, the author has relied on authoritative works of Russian scholars. He hopes that the gradual, systematic, and graphic presentation of grammar, the simple everyday vocabulary (largely based on Harry H. Josselson's *The Russian*

Word Count, 1953) and the connected and interesting reading matter will make the study of Russian an enjoyable experience for the student. The author feels that, with the aid of a carefully graded and organized text, the study of Russian will prove as easy and enjoyable as that of the other foreign languages taught in our schools.

ACKNOWLEDGMENTS

The author wishes to thank his friends and colleagues of the Middlebury College Russian Summer School and Institute of Soviet Studies who have offered many valuable suggestions and encouragement; and Dr. Stephen A. Freeman, Director of the Middlebury College Language Schools, whose helpful counsel on matters of methodology has proved very useful. He is also deeply grateful to the many high school and college teachers who, as students of the 1958 session of the Russian Summer School, shared their views and experience with the author and proved most encouraging and stimulating in his work. No one but the author, of course, is responsible for whatever shortcomings the book may have.

The author is especially indebted to his colleague in the Russian Department at Middlebury College, Mrs. Berthe O. Normano, for valuable suggestions and for reading the manuscript and proofs. Above all, he is indebted to his wife, Margaret W. Fayer, for helpful criticism, typing the manuscript, reading proof, and for her continued understanding and devoted help.

MISCHA H. FAYER

Middlebury, Vermont

CONTENTS

BASIC
RUSSIAN

U N I T 1

THE RUSSIAN ALPHABET

The Russian alphabet is called the *Cyrillic* alphabet after the monk St. Cyril, who lived in the ninth century and is reputed to have devised it. It contains many letters identical with or resembling Greek and Latin characters, and is therefore much easier to master than is generally assumed by beginners.

The alphabet consists of 31 letters (or 33 if the ё and й are counted as separate letters). The fact that there are more letters in Russian than in English actually makes spelling easier, because Russian sounds, with few exceptions, can thus be represented by individual letters instead of by various combinations of letters as, for example, in the English words *rough* or *beauty*.

The Written Alphabet

The written and printed alphabets closely resemble each other. Mastery of one will facilitate learning the other, regardless of which is learned first. If you wish to learn the *printed* alphabet before the *written* alphabet, turn to page 10.

The written alphabet is given first because (1) Russians ordinarily do not print, and (2) writing is faster and will save time. You can learn to write Russian in a short time with facility and speed if you form the proper writing habits. Observe these simple rules:

1. Make the capital letters larger than the small letters.
2. Keep the small letters equal in size.
3. Add no strokes, curves, or loops of your own to the letters. This only leads to confusion.

1

4. All strokes and loops should go as far below the solid line and as high above the dotted line as is indicated on the charts.

5. When forming each stroke, proceed in the direction of the arrow, as indicated in the charts. Do each stroke in numerical order.

Memorize the letters in groups of five using their Russian names, and remember their alphabetical order. To avoid confusion, never refer to them by their English equivalents.

Group I

a. How to pronounce 𝒜 𝑎 through 𝒟 𝜕

Written	Russian Name	Approximate English Sound	Examples
1. 𝒜 𝑎	ah	a in car	*Ánna*
2. 𝐵 𝑏	beh	b in book	*Báda*
3. 𝐵 𝑏	veh	v in visit	*Váza*
4. 𝒯 𝑟	gheh	g in glad	*Gazón*
5. 𝒟 𝜕	deh	d in do	*Dáma*

b. How to write 𝒜 𝑎 through 𝒟 𝜕.

Drill 1. Pronounce each letter aloud several times by its Russian name. Then write each capital and small letter several times. After you have learned to write them accurately, write the following combinations. (Do not link the letters in these exercises.)

Combinations :

Ba, Va, Ga, Da; Aa, Áda, Báda, Bára, Táda; Dba, Dad, Tab, Bag, Bára; Áda, Báda, Dána, Bába, Bab

Group II

a. How to pronounce *Е е* through *К к*.

Written	Russian Name	Approximate English Sound	Examples
6. *Е е*	yeh	*ye* in *yes*	*Éва*
7. *Ж ж*	zheh	*s* in treasure	*Жа́ба*
8. *З з*	zeh	*z* in *zone*	*Зо́на*
9. *И и*	ee	*ee* in see	*И́да*
10. *К к*	kah	*k* in *king*	*Кот*

b. How to write *Е е* through *К к*.

Drill 2. Practice writing and pronouncing the following syllables and words.   Do not attempt to learn the meanings of the words; they are given only for purposes of practice.

Syllables:

*Еж, Ез, Ек;   Иж, Из, Ик;   Аж, Аз, Ак;
Ке, Ки, Киз;   Кеж, Кез, Кед; Зек, Зик, Заг,
Гаж, Дак, Вик; Ика.*

Words:

*Как, Каба́к, Каза́к; Кино́, Каба́н, Вид;
И́да, Зо́на, Каби́на; Жа́ба, Ба́за, Éва;
Жа́жда, Изба́, Ва́нна.*

Group III

a. How to pronounce *Л л* through *П п*.

Written	Russian Name	Approximate English Sound	Examples
11. *Л л*	ell	*ll* in we*ll*	*Лóндон*
12. *М м*	em	*m* in ja*m*	*Мáма*
13. *Н н*	en	*n* in *n*arrow	*Нóта*
14. *О о*	aw	*o* in sp*o*rt	*Вóлга*
15. *П п*	peh	*p* in *p*ark	*Пáпа*

b. How to write *Л л* through *П п*.

Drill 3. Practice writing and pronouncing these syllables and words.

Syllables:

Ла, Ле, Ли, Ло; Мо, Ми, Ме, Ма; На, Не, Ни, Но; По, Пи, Пе, Па; Бал, Мел, Гин, Дон; Доп, Пон; Мик, Зим, Жак.

Words:

Дом, Пол, Кол, Пóлка, Пáлка; Вóлга, Вон, Лом; Зимá, Лéна, Заказáл, Дóма, Жáлко, Жáло, Жáлоба.

Group IV

a. How to pronounce *Р р* through *Ф ф*.

Written	Russian Name	Approximate English Sound	Examples
16. *Р р*	err	r in rose	*Ра́дио*
17. *С с*	ess	s in stop	*Стол*
18. *Т т*	teh	t in tip	*Тон*
19. *У у*	oo	oo in booty	*У́тро*
20. *Ф ф*	eff	f in fact	*Факт*

b. How to write *Р р* through *Ф ф*.

Drill 4. Practice writing and pronouncing these syllables and words.

Syllables:

*Ру, Су, Ту, Фу; Фа, Фе, Фи, Фо; Со, Си, Са;
То, Ти, Та; Фур, Тур, Сот, Сор; Фом,
Жеф, Тим, Жук, Стоп.*

Words:

*Уста́л, То́рмоз, Кусо́к, Уро́к; До́ступ,
Во́рон, Ваго́н, Фа́брика; Варва́ра,
Го́род, Сто́рож; Ду́ма, Двор, Фронт.*

Group V

a. How to pronounce *X x* through *Щ щ*.

	Written	Russian Name	Approximate English Sound	Examples
21.	*X x*	hah	*h* in *h*and (strongly aspirated)	*Хор*
22.	*Ц ц*	tseh	*ts* in fla*ts*	*Цвет*
23.	*Ч ч*	cheh	*ch* in *ch*eck	*Час*
24.	*Ш ш*	shah	*sh* in *sh*ort	*Школа*
25.	*Щ щ*	shchah	*shch* in fresh cheese	*Щи*

b. How to write *X x* through *Щ щ*.

Drill 5. Practice writing and pronouncing these syllables and words.

Syllables:

Ха, Хе, Хи, Хо, Ху; Цу, Цо, Ци, Це, Ца; Чу, Чо, Чи, Че, Ча; Шо, Ши, Ше, Шу, Ша; Ще, Щи, Щу, Що, Ща; Хуф, Цос, Шер, Час; Цап, Шоп, Шум, Хат.

Words:

Шапка, Папка, Хата, Мост; Хор, Сахар, Вахта, Бухта; Шкаф, Рука, Кузнец, Работница; Маша, Машина, Учебник; Щепка, Щит, Щука.

Group VI

a. How to pronounce ъ through Я я.

Written	Russian Name	Approximate English Sound	Examples
*26. ъ	(hard sign)	(has no sound)	Отъе́зд
*27. ы	yerih	y in syllable	Ры́ба
*28. ь	(soft sign)†	(has no sound)	Пальто́
29. Э э	eh	e in egg	Этáж
30. Ю ю	you	u in use	Ю́мор
31. Я я	ya	ya in yard	Я́лта

* These letters are never used at the beginning of a word; hence they have no written capitals.

† Indicates that the preceding consonant is pronounced soft.

b. How to write ъ through Я я.

ъ ы ь Э э Ю ю Я я

Drill 6. Practice writing and pronouncing these syllables and words.

Syllables:

Бы, Бэ, Бе, Бя; Вэ, Ве, Вю, Вя;
Ха, Шэ, Тю, Сэ, Мы, Яр.

Words:

Это, Я́ма, Сын, Шля́па; Ня́ня, Индю́к,
Бы́стро, Ю́ноша; Экзáмен, Гармóния,
Ты́ква; Ры́нок, Фру́кты, У́лица;
Соль, Боль, Мать, Спать, Читáть,
Конь, Ло́шадь.

Group VII

a. How to pronounce *Ё ё* and *Й й*.

Note: The two dots (called a *diaeresis*) over the *е* (*ё*) change the sound from *ye* to *yo* (as in *y*olk). The sign ⌣ over the *и* (*й*) shortens the sound from *ee* to *y* (as in bo*y*).

Written	Russian Name	Approximate English Sound	Examples
Ё ё	*yaw*	*yo* in *y*olk	*Ёлка*
Й й	short **и**	*y* in boy	*Чай*

Drill 7. Practice writing and pronouncing these syllables and words.

Syllables:

Аи, Ай; Ии, Ий; Ои, Ой; Уи, Уй; ыи, ый; Юи, Юй; Эи, Эй; Еи, Ей; Ёи, Ёй; Яи, Яй.

Words:

Мой, Твой, Тройка; Умей, Чайка, Яйца, Быстрей, Крайний.

Linking the Letters

Russian letters must be properly joined to avoid confusion and illegibility. Apply the following suggestions whenever you write in Russian.

a. Avoid any overlapping of letters.

right: *гражданин*

wrong: *гражданин*   —because the hook of

the *а* and the hook of the *ж* overlap. It is impossible to tell

where the *а* ends and the *ж* begins. Also note that in the last

two letters, the hook of the *и* fuses with the first stroke of the *н*,

which should be a straight line *н*.

b. Set off *л, м,* and *я* from preceding letters.

right: *тётя;*   right: *время;*

wrong: *тётя;*   wrong: *время;*

c. Make a break after *б* and *д*: *берег; дама.*

d. Make a break after *о* when it is followed by *л, м,* or *я*:

пол; потом; твоя.

e. Do not confuse *г* with *ч*, or *ш* with the English *w*:

год; что; шум.

Note: The first word below is illegible because:

Compare: { *Англия* }   *н* is not set off from *А*;

{ *Англия* }   *г* is not set off from *л*;

л lacks a loop at the bottom;

и and *я* overlap.

The Printed Alphabet

Memorize the letters in groups of five using their Russian names, and remember their alphabetical order. To avoid confusion, never refer to them by their English equivalents.

Russians ordinarily do not print. In the beginning, however, print the individual letters and words to remember them better. Later, use the Russian script exclusively.

Print uses mostly plain lines, whereas script uses curved lines and hooks. Straighten the curves, remove the hooks wherever possible, and note how little difference there really is between the written and printed letters.

Compare the script with the print and note the similarities.

SCRIPT	PRINT		SCRIPT	PRINT
1. *A a* = *A* =	A a	17. *C c* =	C c
2. *Б б* = *Б* =	Б б	18. *Т т*	Т т
3. *В в* = *В* =	В в	19. *У у* =	У у
4. *Г г* = *Г* =	Г г	20. *Ф ф* =	Ф ф
5. *Д д*	Д д	21. *Х х* =	Х х
6. *Е е* =	Е е	22. *Ц ц* = *Ц* =	Ц ц
7. *Ж ж* =	Ж ж	23. *Ч ч* = *Ч* =	Ч ч
8. *З з* =	З з	24. *Ш ш* = *Ш* =	Ш ш
9. *И и* = *И* =	И и	25. *Щ щ* = *Щ* =	Щ щ
10. *К к* = *К* =	К к	26. *ъ* =	ъ
11. *Л л* =	Л л	27. *ы* =	ы
12. *М м* = *М* =	М м	28. *ь* =	ь
13. *Н н* = *Н* =	Н н	29. *Э э* =	Э э
14. *О о* =	О о	30. *Ю ю* = *Ю* =	Ю ю
15. *П п* = *П* =	П п	31. *Я я* = *Я* =	Я я
16. *Р р* = *Р* =	Р р		

Group I

Printed	Russian Name	Approximate English Sound	Examples
1. **А а**	*ah*	*a* in c*a*r	А́нна
2. **Б б**	*beh*	*b* in *b*ook	Ба́ба
3. **В в**	*veh*	*v* in *v*isit	Ва́за
4. **Г г**	*gheh*	*g* in *g*lad	Газо́н
5. **Д д**	*deh*	*d* in *d*o	Да́ма

Drill 1. Pronounce each letter aloud several times by its Russian name.   Then print the following combinations several times.

Combinations : Ба, Ва, Га, Да; Аа, А́да, Ва́да, Ба́га, Га́да; Два, Даб, Гав, Баг, Ва́га; А́ба, Ба́ба, Да́га, Ва́ва, Бав.

Group II

Printed	Russian Name	Approximate English Sound	Examples
6. **Е е**	*yeh*	*ye* in *ye*s	Е́ва
7. **Ж ж**	*zheh*	*s* in trea*s*ure	Жа́ба
8. **З з**	*zeh*	*z* in *z*one	Зо́на
9. **И и**	*ee*	*ee* in s*ee*	Йда
10. **К к**	*kah*	*k* in *k*ing	Кот

Drill 2. Practice printing and pronouncing the following syllables and words.   Do not attempt to learn the meanings of the words; they are given only for purposes of practice.

Syllables : Еж, Ез, Ек; Иж, Из, Ик; Аж, Аз, Ак; Ке, Ки, Киз; Кеж, Кез, Кед; Зек, Зик, Заг; Гаж, Дак, Вик; Йка.

Words :   Как, Каба́к, Каза́к; Кино́, Каба́н, Вид; Йда, Зо́на, Каби́на; Жа́ба, Ба́за, Е́ва, Жа́жда, Изба́, Ва́нна.

Group III

Printed	Russian Name	Approximate English Sound	Examples
11. Л л	*ell*	*ll* in we*ll*	Ло́ндон
12. М м	*em*	*m* in ja*m*	Ма́ма
13. Н н	*en*	*n* in *n*arrow	Но́та
14. О о	*aw*	*o* in sp*o*rt	Во́лга
15. П п	*peh*	*p* in *p*ark	Па́па

Drill 3. Practice printing and pronouncing these syllables and words.

Syllables: Ла, Ле, Ли, Ло; Мо, Ми, Ме, Ма; На, Не, Ни, Но; По, Пи, Пе, Па; Бал, Мел, Гин, Дон; Доп, Пон, Мик, Зим, Жак.

Words: Дом, Пол, Кол, По́лка, Па́лка; Во́лга, Вон, Лом; Зима́, Ле́на, Заказа́л; До́ма, Жа́лко, Жа́ло, Жа́лоба.

Group IV

Printed	Russian Name	Approximate English Sound	Examples
16. Р р	*err*	*r* in *r*ose	Ра́дио
17. С с	*ess*	*s* in *s*top	Стол
18. Т т	*teh*	*t* in *t*ip	Тон
19. У у	*oo*	*oo* in b*oo*ty	У́тро
20. Ф ф	*eff*	*f* in *f*act	Факт

Drill 4. Practice printing and pronouncing these syllables and words.

Syllables: Ру, Су, Ту, Фу; Фа, Фе, Фи, Фо; Со, Си, Са; То, Ти, Та; Фур, Тур, Сот, Сор; Фом, Жеф, Гим, Жук, Стоп.

Words: Уста́л, То́рмоз, Кусо́к, Уро́к; До́ступ, Во́рон, Ваго́н, Фа́брика; Варва́ра, Го́род, Сто́рож; Ду́ма, Двор, Фронт.

Group V

Printed	Russian Name	Approximate English Sound	Examples
21. **Х х**	*hah*	*h* in *h*ard (strongly aspirated)	<u>Х</u>ор
22. **Ц ц**	*tseh*	*ts* in fla*ts*	<u>Ц</u>вет
23. **Ч ч**	*cheh*	*ch* in *ch*eck	<u>Ч</u>ас
24. **Ш ш**	*shah*	*sh* in *sh*ort	<u>Ш</u>ко́ла
25. **Щ щ**	*shchah*	*shch* in fre*sh ch*eese	<u>Щ</u>и

Drill 5. Practice printing and pronouncing these syllables and words.

Syllables: Ха, Хе, Хи, Хо, Ху; Цу, Цо, Ци, Це, Ца; Чу, Чо, Чи, Че, Ча; Шо, Ши, Ше, Шу, Ша; Ще, Щи, Щу, Що, Ща; Хуф, Щос, Шер, Час; Цап, Шоп, Шум, Хат.

Words: Ша́пка, Па́пка, Ха́та, Мост; Хор, Са́хар, Ва́хта, Бу́хта; Шкаф, Рука́, Кузне́ц, Рабо́тница; Ма́ша, Маши́на, Уче́бник; Ще́пка, Щит, Щу́ка.

Group VI

Printed	Russian Name	Approximate English Sound	Examples
26. **Ъ ъ**	(hard sign)	(has no sound)	Отъ<u>е́</u>зд
27. **Ы ы**	*yerih*	*y* in s*y*llable	Р<u>ы́</u>ба
28. **Ь ь**	(soft sign)*	(has no sound)	Паль<u>т</u>о́
29. **Э э**	*eh*	*e* in *e*gg	<u>Э</u>та́ж
30. **Ю ю**	*you*	*u* in *u*se	<u>Ю́</u>мор
31. **Я я**	*ya*	*ya* in *y*ard	<u>Я́</u>лта

* Indicates that the preceding consonant is pronounced soft.

Drill 6. Practice printing and pronouncing these syllables and words.

Syllables: Бы, Бэ, Бе, Бя; Вэ, Ве, Вю, Вя; Ха, Шэ, Тю, Сэ, Мы, Яр.

Words: Э́то, Я́ма, Сын, Шля́па; Ня́ня, Индю́к, Бы́стро, Ю́ноша; Экза́мен, Гармо́ния, Ты́ква; Ры́нок, Фру́к-ты, У́лица; Соль, Боль, Мать, Спать, Чита́ть, Конь, Ло́шадь.

Group VII

Note: The two dots (called a diaeresis) over the **e** (**ё**) change the sound from *ye* to *yo* (as in *yo*lk). The sign ˇ over the **и** (**й**) shortens the sound from *ee* to *y* (as in bo*y*).

Printed	Russian Name	Approximate English Sound	Examples
Е ё	*yaw*	*yo* in *yo*lk	Ёлка
Й й	short **и**	*y* in bo*y*	Чай

Drill 7. Practice printing and pronouncing these syllables and words.

Syllables: Аи, Ай; Ии, Ий; Ои, Ой; Уи, Уй, Ыи, Ый, Юи, Юй; Эи, Эй; Еи, Ей; Ёи, Ёй; Яи, Яй.

Words: Мой, Твой, Тро́йка; Уме́й, Ча́йка, Я́йца, Быстре́й, Кра́йний.

Произношéние (Pronunciation)

1-A. Hard and Soft Vowels

a. Russian vowels are divided into two groups: five *hard* and five corresponding *soft* vowels. Learn them in pairs, as this will help your pronunciation and your understanding of important grammatical principles.

hard: **а э о у ы**

soft: **я е ё ю и**

b. The first four *soft* vowels represent a combination of the *y* sound in *yes* and the corresponding *hard* vowels, thus:

$$y + \textbf{а} = \textbf{я}$$
$$y + \textbf{э} = \textbf{е}$$
$$y + \textbf{о} = \textbf{ё}$$
$$y + \textbf{у} = \textbf{ю}$$

c. When the hard vowels are pronounced, the tongue does not touch the roof of the mouth (the *palate*).

d. If the tongue is raised against the *palate* when **а, э, о,** or **у** is pronounced, the sound becomes softened or *palatalized*. **Я** is thus a palatalized **а**; **е**, a palatalized **э**; **ё**, a palatalized **о**; and **ю**, a palatalized **у**.

U N I T 2

КТО Э́ТО?

— Кто э́то? — Э́то я.*
— Кто э́то? — Э́то ты.
— Кто э́то? — Э́то он.   Э́то она́.
— Я профе́ссор.   Ты студе́нт.   Он то́же студе́нт.
— Кто э́то? — Э́то Ива́н.   Ива́н студе́нт.
— Кто э́то? — Э́то Ве́ра.   Ве́ра студе́нтка.
— Кто ты? — Я студе́нт.
— Кто он? — Он то́же студе́нт.
— Кто она́? — Она́ студе́нтка.
— Кто э́то? — Э́то А́нна.   Она́ то́же студе́нтка.

Слова́рь (Vocabulary)

кто who
э́то this
кто э́то? who (is) this?
я I
ты you (*fam. pron.*†)
он he
она́ she (pronounce the **o** like the *o* in *come*)

профе́ссор professor ‡ (*m.*) (*used for man or woman*)
студе́нт student ‡ (*m.*)
то́же also
Ива́н Ivan
Ве́ра Vera
студе́нтка student (*f.*)
А́нна Anne

* Dashes are used to distinguish the remarks of one speaker from those of another.
† All abbreviations are explained on p. 252.
‡ **Студе́нт** means *student of an institution of higher learning* and **профе́ссор** means *teacher* at such an institution.   The Russian words for *pupil* and *teacher* are harder to remember and pronounce, and will therefore be introduced at a later time.

16

Разгово́р (**Conversation**)

— Э́то студе́нт? — Да, э́то студе́нт.

— Э́то студе́нтка? — Да, э́то студе́нтка.

— Э́то профе́ссор? — Да, э́то профе́ссор.

— Э́то то́же профе́ссор? — Нет, э́то студе́нт.

— Ива́н профе́ссор? — О нет! Ива́н не профе́ссор. Он студе́нт.

— Ве́ра профе́ссор? — Нет, Ве́ра не профе́ссор. Она́ студе́нтка. Ива́н и Ве́ра студе́нты.

— Э́то Ве́ра? — Нет, э́то не Ве́ра. Э́то А́нна.

— Э́то студе́нт и́ли студе́нтка? — Э́то студе́нт.

— Э́то А́нна и́ли Ве́ра? — Э́то Ве́ра.

— Э́то профе́ссор и́ли студе́нт? — Э́то профе́ссор.

Слова́рь (**Vocabulary**)

да yes
нет no
не not
О oh

О нет! oh no!
и and
студе́нты (*pl.*) students
и́ли or

Произноше́ние (**Pronunciation**)

2-A. Stressed and Unstressed "a"

a. When the Russian **a** is stressed, it is pronounced like the English *a* in c*a*r. For example: Ива́н, она́.

b. When the **a** is unstressed, it is pronounced like the English *a* in cig*a*rette. For example: Ве́р**a**, студе́нтк**a**.

Phonetic Drill. Pronounce the following words aloud:

каранда́ш, кабине́т, салфе́тка, буты́лка, магази́н, фи́зика, а́тлас, газе́та, ка́рта, дра́ма, Во́лга.

2-B. Syllabification

a. A *syllable* consists of one or more letters and constitutes one unit of sound. There are as many syllables in a word as there are vowels. For example:

да (one vowel—one syllable)
Ве́-ра (two vowels—two syllables)

b. Syllabification means dividing words into syllables according to established rules. Correct syllabification is important both for pronunciation and for dividing a word at the end of a line.

c. Rules of syllabification.

1. Two consecutive vowels form two separate syllables:

ду-э́т, а́р-ми-я, э-го-и́ст

2. The semivowel **й** cannot be pronounced by itself and must always be used in combination with another vowel. It cannot, therefore, form a syllable by itself. For example:

ай, у-**ме́й**, ге-**ро́й**

3. A single consonant between two vowels forms a syllable with the following vowel. For example:

И-в**а́**н, Ве́-**р**а, о-**н**а́

4. When several consonants come between two vowels, the last one usually goes with the following vowel. For example:

жур-н**а́**л, сту-де́нт-ка

5. Only syllables can be "carried" from the end of one line to the beginning of the next.

Study Hints. To master new words with greater facility, pronounce the long ones by syllables at first, paying careful attention to the stress. Then pronounce the word as a unit until you can remember it.

Грамма́тика (Grammar)

2-1. Present Tense of "to be"

In modern Russian, the *present tense* of the verb *to be* is usually understood, but not stated.

Э́то студе́нт.   This (*is*) a student.

Ива́н не профе́ссор.   Ivan (*is*) not a professor.

2-2. Articles in Russian

There is no definite or indefinite article in Russian. Therefore, when a Russian sentence is being translated into English, the definite article *the* or the indefinite article *a* must be supplied according to the sense of the sentence.

Она́ студе́нтка.   She is *a* student.

2-3. The Pronoun "you"

Like other languages, Russian possesses two forms of the pronoun *you*. **Ты** (in French, *tu*; in German, *du*; in English, *thou*) is the *familiar singular* form of the pronoun *you*, and is used in addressing a close friend, a member of one's family, a child, or an animal. **Вы** (in French, *vous*; in German, *Sie*) is the *polite* form of *you*, and is used in all other circumstances. One would say "**Ты** студéнт" (you are a student) to a friend, but "**Вы** профéссор" (you are a professor) to his teacher.

2-4. The Nominative Case

The *nominative case* is used to express:

a. The subject of a sentence.

> **Я** профéссор.   *I* am a professor.

b. The predicate noun.

> Вéра **студéнтка**.   Vera is a *student*.

2-5. Intonation in Questions

A rise in *intonation* (that is, in the pitch of the voice) at the end of a sentence indicates a question.

> Это студéнт (*with a falling intonation*).   This is a student.
> Это студéнт (*with a rising intonation*)?   Is this a student?

2-6. The Use of нет and не

Do not confuse the words **нет** and **не**.   **Нет** means *no* and **не** means *is not*.   **Не** always stands before the word negated.

> **Нет**, это **не** Вéра.   *No*, this *is not* Vera.

Упражнéния (Exercises)

Replace the English words in parentheses with the appropriate Russian words.

1. Он (student). 2. Онá (student). 3. Он и онá (students).
4. Я (also) студéнт. 5. Ты (professor)? 6. (No), я (not) профéссор. 7. (You) и я (students).

Перевод (Translation)

Translate the following sentences into Russian, but omit words in parentheses.

1. Who (is) this?   2. (Is) this you?   (Use the familiar **ты**.)
3. Yes, it (is) I.   4. (Is) this Ivan or Vera?   5. Yes, it (is) Ivan and Vera.   6. (Is) Ivan (a) student (*m.*)?   7. Yes, Ivan (is a) student (*m.*).   8. (Is) Vera also (a man) student?   9. No, Vera (is) not (a man) student.   She (is a woman) student.   10. Vera and Ivan (are) students.   11. (Is) Anne (the) professor?   12. No, Anne (is) not (the) professor.

Вопросы (Questions)

Answer the following questions in Russian, using complete sentences.

1. Кто это?   2. Это студент?   3. Это студентка?   4. Он и она студенты?   5. Он студент или профессор?   6. Она студентка или профессор?   7. Это Анна или Вера?   8. Это он или она?   9. Ты профессор или студент?   10. Это Вера или Анна?

U N I T 3

ЧТО Э́ТО?

— Что э́то? — Э́то стол.

— Что э́то? — Э́то стул.   Э́то стол и стул.

— Что э́то? — Э́то ка́рта, а э́то карти́на.

— Где стол? — Стол тут.

— А где стул? — Стул там.

— Что на столе́? — На столе́ ка́рта.

— Что на сту́ле ? — На сту́ле карти́на.

— А где журна́л?   Он то́же на сту́ле?

— Нет, он не на сту́ле.   Он на столе́.

— Кни́га то́же на столе́? — Да, она́ то́же на столе́.

— Что на ка́рте?

— На ка́рте—*СССР.   Тут Москва́, а там Сталингра́д.

* The dash here means that the word *is* is understood, and that any other possible meaning is excluded.

Слова́рь (Vocabulary)

что (*pr.* **што**) what
стол table
стул chair
ка́рта map
а and
карти́на picture
где where
тут here
там there

на on, upon
на столе́ on the table (pronounce the **o** like the *o* in *come*)
журна́л magazine
кни́га book
СССР U.S.S.R.   (*pr.* **Эс Эс Эс Эр**)
Москва́ Moscow
Сталингра́д Stalingrad

21

Разговóр (Conversation)

— Э́то стол? — Да, э́то стол.

— Э́то тóже стол? — Нет, э́то не стол, а стул.

— Где кни́га? — Кни́га на сту́ле.

— Э́то карти́на? — Да, э́то карти́на.

— Э́то тóже карти́на? — Нет, э́то не карти́на, а ка́рта.

— Где на ка́рте Москва́ и где Сталингра́д?

— Москва́ тут, а Сталингра́д там.

— Где студéнты? Они́ в кла́ссе?

— Да, они́ в кла́ссе.

— А где Ива́н и Вéра? — Они́ тóже тут.

— Ива́н и Вéра, где вы? — Мы тут, в кла́ссе.

— А́нна, вы в кла́ссе? — Да, я в кла́ссе.

— Я профéссор? — Да, вы профéссор.

— Кто в кла́ссе? — Профéссор и студéнты в кла́ссе.

Словáрь (Vocabulary)

a but (**a** means *and*; after a negative, it means *but*)
Нет, э́то не стол, а стул No, this is not a table, *but* a chair
они́ they
класс class
в in (when used with the *prepositional*, **в** indicates *location* of an object; see
  ¶ 3-3)
вы you
мы we

Произношéние (Pronunciation)

3-A. Stressed and Unstressed "o"

a. The stressed **o** is pronounced like the English *o* in sport. For example: тóже, стол.

b. The pronunciation of the unstressed **o** depends upon its position in the word with respect to the stressed syllable.

1. When the **o** is *pre-tonic* (that is, when it immediately precedes a stressed syllable), it is pronounced like the *o* in *come*. For example: она́, Москва́.

2. When the **o** is *post-tonic* (that is, when it follows the stressed syllable) or when it appears in any other position, it has the indistinct sound of the *o* in *lemon*. For example: э́то, профéссор.

3-B. The Final "д"

Pronounce a final д like т.   Pronounce Сталингра́д as if it were written Сталингра́т.

3-C. В кла́ссе

Pronounce **в кла́ссе** as if it were spelled **фкла́ссе**.   That is, pronounce the **в** like **ф**, and say the phrase as if it were all one word.

3-D. Accent Marks

Since Russian vowels have different sounds, depending on whether they are stressed or unstressed, it is extremely important for good pronunciation to stress each word correctly.

Accent marks are not part of Russian spelling but are given throughout the book.   No accent mark appears on one-syllable words.

Phonetic Drill.   Pronounce the following words aloud:

окно́, пальто́, дрова́, но́вый, о́стрый, опя́ть, поня́ть, сад, град, рад, наза́д, пара́д.

Грамма́тика (Grammar)

3-1. Conjunctions: и   and   a

a. **и** is a *joining* conjunction:

Ива́н **и** Ве́ра студе́нты.   Ivan *and* Vera are students.

b. **a** is a *separating* conjunction:

А́нна тут, **a** Ве́ра там.   Anne is here, *and* Vera is there.

c. **a** is also used to express *difference* or *contrast*:

Он не профе́ссор, **a** студе́нт.   He is not a professor, *but* a student.

Note: After a negative, **a** means *but.*

3-2. Genders

There are three genders in Russian—masculine (*m.*), feminine (*f.*), and neuter (*n.*).

a. A *consonant* is the common ending for the *masculine*.   For example:

стол, студе́нт, Сталингра́д.

b. **-a** is the common ending for the *feminine*.   For example:

ка́рта, студе́нтка, Москва́.

c. **-o** is the common ending for the *neuter.*   For example:
перо́ (pen), окно́ (window).

3-3. The Prepositional Case

a. This case is called the *prepositional case* because it is used only with a preposition, such as **на** or **в**.   It is also referred to as the *locative case* because it is frequently used to indicate the *location* of an object.

Где карти́на?   Карти́на **на столе́**.   The picture is *on the table.*
Где студе́нты?   Они́ **в кла́ссе**.   They are *in class.*

Note: In the examples above, the prepositional is used to answer the question **где?** (where?).

b. To form the prepositional for a masculine noun, *add* the letter **-e** to the nominative singular form of the word.   To form the prepositional for a feminine noun, *replace* the nominative ending of **-a** with **-e**.   For neuter nouns, *replace* the nominative ending of **-o** with **-e**.   As the following table shows, the characteristic ending for the prepositional case is **-e**.

Case	Masculine	Feminine	Neuter
Nominative	стул стол	ка́рт**а** Москв**а́**	пер**о́** окн**о́**
Prepositional	сту́л**е** стол**е́**★	ка́рт**е** Москв**е́**	пер**е́** окн**е́**

★ Note the shift of stress.

3-4. Personal Pronouns

The personal pronouns, which have already been presented separately before, are given all together in the table below so as to distinguish between the first, second, and third persons in both the singular and plural.   Memorize them.

	SINGULAR			PLURAL	
1st person:	**я**	I		**мы**	we
2nd person:	**ты**	you (*fam.*)		**вы**	you (*pl.,* or *pol. sing.*)
3rd person:	**он** **она́** **оно́**	he she it		**они́**	they

Упражнéния (Exercises)

In place of the blanks, use suitable words to form a meaningful sentence:

1. Э́то не журнáл, а _____. 2. Э́то не стол, а _____. 3. Он не профéссор, а _____. 4. Онá не студéнт, а _____. 5. Студéнты в _____. 6. Сталингрáд тут, а Москвá _____. 7. Э́то картúна, и э́то _____ картúна. 8. Кáрта в _____. 9. Картúна на _____. 10. Москвá в _____.

Перевóд (Translation)

Omit the words in parentheses and include the words in brackets. Henceforth the present of the verb *to be* will not be enclosed in parentheses to indicate its omission in Russian.

1. The table is here, and the chair is there. 2. On the table (there is) a map, a picture, and a book. 3. On the chair (there is) a magazine. 4. Moscow is here, and Stalingrad is there. 5. We are students and they are students. 6. Is this Vera or Anne? This is Vera. Anne is in class. 7. Is Vera a professor? Oh no, she is not a professor, but a student. 8. Where is Stalingrad? Stalingrad is in the U.S.S.R. [в СССР]. 9. Is Moscow also in the U.S.S.R.? Yes, Moscow is also in the U.S.S.R. 10. The students are not in Moscow, but in Stalingrad.

Вопрóсы (Questions)

1. Что на столé? 2. Что на стýле? 3. Что на кáрте? 4. Москвá в СССР? 5. Сталингрáд тóже в СССР? 6. Кто в клáссе? 7. Профéссор тóже в клáссе? 8. А где Ивáн и Вéра?

ШКО́ЛА

Вот шко́ла. В шко́ле класс. В кла́ссе профе́ссор и студе́н-
ты.

Вот стена́. На стене́ доска́ и ка́рта. Тут стол и стул. На
столе́ журна́л, кни́га, и газе́та. На столе́ перо́ и каранда́ш.

Профе́ссор Петро́в чита́ет кни́гу, а Ива́н чита́ет газе́ту.
Ве́ра чита́ет журна́л.

А́нна сего́дня до́ма. Она́ не здоро́ва. Пётр сего́дня то́же
до́ма, но он здоро́в.

Слова́рь (Vocabulary)

шко́ла school	**кни́гу** *acc. of* **кни́га** (see ¶ 4-3)
вот here is, here are	**сего́дня** (*pr.* **сево́дня**) today
стена́ wall (see ¶ 4-A)	**до́ма** (*adv.*) at home
доска́ blackboard	**здоро́ва** (*adj., f.*) well, healthy
газе́та newspaper	**не здоро́ва** not well, sick
перо́ pen	**Пётр** Peter
каранда́ш pencil	**но** but (see ¶ 4-4)
Петро́в Petrov (*surname*)	**здоро́в** (*adj., m.*) well, healthy
чита́ет reads	

Разгово́р (Conversation)

— Э́то шко́ла? — Да, э́то шко́ла.

— Э́то то́же шко́ла? — Нет, э́то не шко́ла, а класс.

— Кто в кла́ссе? — Профе́ссор Петро́в и студе́нты в кла́ссе.

— Где стол? — Стол в кла́ссе.

— Что на столе́? — На столе́ журна́л, кни́га и газе́та.

— Что ещё на столе́? — На столе́ перо́ и каранда́ш.

— Что на стене́? — На стене́ доска́ и ка́рта.

— Что чита́ет господи́н Петро́в? — Господи́н Петро́в чита́ет кни́гу.

— А что чита́ют студе́нты? — Они́ чита́ют газе́ту.

— А́нна то́же чита́ет газе́ту? — Нет, она́ чита́ет журна́л.

— Пётр, что ты чита́ешь до́ма? — До́ма я чита́ю газе́ту и́ли журна́л.

— Ве́ра и Ива́н, что вы чита́ете до́ма?

— До́ма мы чита́ем газе́ту и́ли журна́л.

— Вы мно́го чита́ете? — Да, мы мно́го чита́ем.

— Э́то о́чень хорошо́!

Слова́рь (Vocabulary)

ещё (*adv.*) more
что ещё? what else ?
господи́н * Mr., gentleman
они́ чита́ют they read, they are reading
ты чита́ешь you (*fam. sing.*) read, you are reading
вы чита́ете you (*pl. or pol. sing.*) read, you are reading
мы чита́ем we read, we are reading
мно́го much (*colloq.* a lot)
о́чень very
хорошо́ well, good
э́то о́чень хорошо́! that (this) is very good!

* The word **господи́н** is now used only by Russians living abroad or by Soviet citizens in addressing foreigners.   In addressing each other, Soviet citizens use the words **граждани́н** and **гражда́нка** (*citizen, m. & f.*) or **това́рищ** (*comrade*).

Произноше́ние (Pronunciation)

4-A. Stressed and Unstressed "e"

a. A stressed .e at the beginning of a word or after a vowel is pronounced like *ye* in *yes*.   For example:

$$\text{Е́ва, е́сли, уе́хал, пое́л.}$$

b. An unstressed **e** in the pre-tonic position is pronounced like *e* in *event*.   For example:

$$\text{стена́, перо́, Петро́в.}$$

c. After **ж**, **ш**, or **ц**, the **e** is pronounced like *e* in *egg*.   For example:

$$\text{то́же, пи́шет.}$$

4-B. The Final "в"

At the end of a word, **в** is pronounced like **ф**.   For example:

здоро́в (*pr.* здоро́ф), Петро́в (*pr.* Петро́ф).

Phonetic Drill.   Если, Е́ва, чита́ет, река́, сестра́, стена́, есть, е́хать, едва́, дела́, несла́, вы́ше, ре́же, ни́же, полоте́нце.

Грамма́тика (**Grammar**)

4-1. Э́то, вот, тут, and там

Note the difference in the meanings of **э́то**, **вот**, **тут**, and **там**.

a. **Э́то** means *this is* or *it is*.   It is used to describe or define something.   For example:

Э́то шко́ла.   This is a school.

b. **Вот** usually means *there is* or *here is* when pointing out something or calling attention to something (in French, *voilà* and *voici*).   For example:

Вот шко́ла.   Here is the (or a) school.
Вот пальто́.   Here is the overcoat.

c. **Тут** means *here*, and **там** *there*; these words are used only to indicate the location of objects.

4-2. The First Conjugation.   Infinitive: чита́ть (to read)

a. Most Russian verbs have the ending **-ть** in the infinitive, and are conjugated in the present tense like **чита́ть** (*to read*).

b. To form the *present tense* of **чита́ть**, drop the ending **-ть** from the infinitive and add the personal endings to **чита-** (i.e., to the stem of the infinitive).

SINGULAR

я чита́**ю**	I read, I am reading
ты чита́**ешь**	you read, you are reading
он чита́**ет**	he reads, he is reading
она́ чита́**ет**	she reads, she is reading
оно́ чита́**ет**	it reads, it is reading

PLURAL

мы чита́**ем**	we read, we are reading
вы чита́**ете**	you read, you are reading
они́ чита́**ют**	they read, they are reading

Note: The *stem* is that part of an inflected word which remains unchanged throughout a given inflection. This applies to verbs, adjectives, nouns, and pronouns.

c. Memorize the present tense of **читáть** as well as the personal endings.

SINGULAR		PLURAL	
я	**-ю**	мы	**-ем**
ты	**-ешь**	вы	**-ете**
он онá ⟩ **-ет** онó		они́	**-ют**

d. There are two basic *conjugations* (i.e., patterns of endings) for Russian verbs. To determine which conjugation a verb belongs to, examine the ending of the second person singular. If the second person singular ending is **-ешь** (e.g., ты читá**ешь**), the verb belongs to the First Conjugation. The distinctive ending which characterizes the Second Conjugation will be discussed in ¶7-1. Henceforth in the vocabulary, we shall designate all verbs of the First Conjugation by the Roman numeral I.

4-3. The Accusative Case

a. The accusative case in Russian is used to express the *direct object* of a transitive verb. For example:

Вéра читáет **журнáл**.   Vera is reading a *magazine*.
Петрóв читáет **кни́гу**.   Petrov is reading a *book*.

b. Masculine and neuter nouns denoting *inanimate objects* are alike in the nominative and accusative singular.* For example:

nom.	журнáл	стул	Сталингрáд	перó
acc.	журнáл	стул	Сталингрáд	перó

c. Feminine nouns, *animate and inanimate*, change the ending **-a** to **-y** in the accusative singular.

nom.	кни́г**а**	Вéр**а**	Москв**á**
acc.	кни́г**у**	Вéр**у**	Москв**ý**

* For the accusative of masculine nouns denoting *animate objects*, see ¶10-3.

4-4. The Conjunction: но

Но, meaning *but*, states a fact contrary to the one logically expected.   Whereas **a** in the sense of *but* stresses difference or contrast, **но** shows contradiction.

Пётр дóма, **но** он здорóв.   Peter is home, *but* he is well.

Normally a schoolboy who is well would be in school, not at home.   Here the opposite is a fact.

In the sentence, "He is old but vigorous," the word *but* should be rendered by **но** in Russian, because vigor is not ordinarily associated with old age—quite the contrary.

Упражнéния (Exercises)

Supply the proper endings of **читáть** in the present tense, and replace the English words in parentheses with Russian ones in the proper cases.

1. Что на (the table), (a pen) и́ли (a pencil)?   2. Что ещё на (the table), (a map) и́ли (a picture)?   3. (The map) на (the wall), a (the picture) на (the table).   4. Я читá____ (a book). 5. А́нна читá____ (a magazine).   6. Студéнты мнóго читá____.   7. Что ты читá____ в (class)?   8. Они́ читá____ (the newspaper) дóма.   9. Что вы читá____ сегóдня?   Я сегóдня читá____ (a newspaper).   10. Петрóв читá____ óчень хорошó.

Перевóд (Translation)

1. Here is the professor, and here are the students.   2. Here is a blackboard, and there is a map.   3. The map is on the wall. 4. This is not a pencil, but a pen.   5. This is not a book, but a magazine.   6. I am home today.   I am not well.   7. Ivan is also home today, but he is well.   8. Is Anne well?   No, she is not well. 9. Where is Anne, at home or in school?   10. She is in school, but she is not well.   11. What is Mr. Petrov reading?   He is reading a newspaper.   12. What else is he reading?   He is reading a magazine.   13. What are the students reading today?   14. Peter, Vera, and Ivan are reading a book.   15. They are reading much, and that is very good.

Вопро́сы (Questions)

1. Где шко́ла?   2. Кто в шко́ле?   3. Что на стене́?   4. Где стол и стул?   5. Что на столе́?   6. Что ещё на столе́?   7. Что чита́ет господи́н Петро́в?   8. Он хорошо́ чита́ет?   9. Вы то́же хорошо́ чита́ете?   10. Где А́нна сего́дня?   11. Пётр то́же до́ма?   12. Кто здоро́в и кто не здоро́в?   13. Вы мно́го чита́ете до́ма?   14. Вы чита́ете хорошо́?   15. Кто о́чень хорошо́ чита́ет, Ива́н и́ли Ве́ра?

U N I T 5

МОЯ КО́МНАТА

Вот ко́мната. Э́то моя́ ко́мната. Она́ о́чень краси́вая. Тут окно́, а там дверь.

В ко́мнате но́вый стол. Э́то мой стол. На столе́ ла́мпа, бума́га, перо́ и каранда́ш. Мел то́же на столе́, но я пишу́ ме́лом то́лько на доске́ в кла́ссе. До́ма я пишу́ карандашо́м и́ли перо́м. Моё но́вое перо́ всегда́ на столе́. Я чита́ю по-ру́сски хорошо́, но пишу́ о́чень пло́хо.

Слова́рь (Vocabulary)

моя́ (*f.*) my
ко́мната room
краси́вая (*f.*) beautiful
окно́ window
дверь (*f.*) door
но́вый (*m.*) new
мой (*m.*) my
ла́мпа lamp
бума́га paper
мел chalk

я пишу́ I write (see ¶ 5-4)
ме́лом with chalk (see ¶ 5-5)
то́лько only
моё (*n.*) my
но́вое (*n.*) new
всегда́ (*pr.* фсегда́) always
по-ру́сски (*adv.*) Russian, in Russian (see ¶ 5-6)
пло́хо (*adv.*) badly, poorly

Memorize the nominative forms of the following words in their three genders:

	m.	*f.*	*n.*	
adj. & pron.	мой	моя́	моё	my, mine
adj.	краси́вый	краси́вая	краси́вое	beautiful
adj.	но́вый	но́вая	но́вое	new

32

Разгово́р (**Conversation**)

— Э́то ко́мната? — Да, э́то ко́мната.

— Э́то ва́ша ко́мната? — Да, э́то моя́ ко́мната.

— Где окно́ и где дверь в ко́мнате? — Окно́ в ко́мнате тут, а дверь там.

— Э́то ваш стол? — Да, э́то мой но́вый стол.

— Что на столе́? — На столе́ ла́мпа, бума́га, перо́ и каранда́ш.

— Ва́ша ла́мпа то́же но́вая? — Да, она́ но́вая и о́чень краси́вая.

— Чем вы пи́шете на доске́? — На доске́ я пишу́ ме́лом.

— А чем вы пи́шете на бума́ге? — На бума́ге я пишу́ перо́м и́ли карандашо́м.

— Как пи́шет ва́ше но́вое перо́ — хорошо́ и́ли пло́хо?

— Моё но́вое перо́ всегда́ пи́шет о́чень хорошо́.

— Вы уже́ чита́ете по-ру́сски?

— Да, я уже́ чита́ю по-ру́сски, но о́чень ме́дленно.

— А как вы пи́шете по-ру́сски?

— Я пишу́ по-ру́сски пло́хо и о́чень, о́чень ме́дленно, но по-англи́йски я пишу́ бы́стро и хорошо́.

Слова́рь (**Vocabulary**)

ваш, ва́ша, ва́ше (*adj. & pron.; pl. & pol. sing.*) your, yours
чем with what
как how
уже́ already
ме́дленно (*adv.*) slowly
по-англи́йски (*adv.*) English, in English (see ¶ **5-6**)
бы́стро rapidly, fast

Произноше́ние (**Pronunciation**)

5-A. The Sibilants : ж, ч, ш, and щ

a. When **ж, ч, ш**, or **щ** is pronounced, a hissing sound is produced. That is why these letters are called *sibilants*, from the Latin *sibilare* meaning *to hiss*.

b. **ю** can never be written after the sibilants **ж, ч, ш, щ**, and must be replaced by the corresponding hard vowel **y** (see ¶ **1-A**). This explains why, in **пишу́** (*I write*), the personal ending following the **ш** is **-y**, instead of the regular **-ю**, and in **пи́шут** (*they write*), **-ут** instead of **-ют**.

Грамма́тика (Grammar)

5-1. Agreement of Adjectives

a. An adjective agrees with the noun it modifies in gender, case, and number.

m.	мой стол	my table
	ваш стол	your table
f.	моя́ ла́мпа	my lamp
	ва́ша ла́мпа	your lamp
n.	моё окно́	my window
	ва́ше окно́	your window
m.	но́вый, краси́вый стол	a new, beautiful table
f.	но́вая, краси́вая ла́мпа	a new, beautiful lamp
n.	но́вое, краси́вое окно́	a new, beautiful window

5-2. Position of Adjectives

a. Attributive adjectives precede the noun they modify. For example:

но́вый стол   a *new* table
но́вая ла́мпа   a *new* lamp
но́вое окно́   a *new* window

b. Predicative adjectives follow the noun. The present tense of *to be* is then understood. For example:

стол **но́вый**   the table *is new*
ла́мпа **но́вая**   the lamp *is new*
окно́ **но́вое**   the window *is new*

c. When an adjective follows a noun, it can also be translated by adding the word *one* to its English equivalent. For example:

Стол но́вый.   The table is new   *or*   The table is a new *one*.
Ко́мната но́вая.   The room is new   *or*   The room is a new *one*.

5-3. Agreement of Personal Pronouns

Personal pronouns must agree in gender and in number with the nouns to which they refer. For example:

Где стол?   **Он** в ко́мнате.   Where is the table?   *It* is in the room.
Где Ива́н?   **Он** в шко́ле.   Where is Ivan?   *He* is in school.
Где бума́га?   **Она́** на столе́.   Where is the paper?   *It* is on the table.
Где А́нна?   **Она́** до́ма.   Where is Anne?   *She* is home.

Ва́ше перо́ но́вое?   Да, **оно́** но́вое.   Is your pen new (a new one)?   Yes, *it* is new (a new one).

Note: **он** and **она́** often mean *it* in English, depending on the gender of the word to which they refer.

5-4. Infinitive: писа́ть (I) *to write*

a. Present tense:

я пишу́	I write	мы пи́шем	we write
ты пи́ш**ешь**	you write	вы пи́ш**ете**	you write
он пи́ш**ет**	he writes	они́ пи́ш**ут**	they write
она́ пи́ш**ет**	she writes		
оно́ пи́ш**ет**	it writes		

b. **пиш-** is the *present stem* of **писа́ть**.   It is obtained by dropping the personal ending **-ешь** from the second person singular **ты пи́шешь**.

c. Many verbs form the present tense from the *present stem*, *not* from the *infinitive stem*.

Compare:

$$\text{чита́ -ть} \quad \begin{cases} \text{я чита́ -ю} \\ \text{ты чита́ -ешь} \end{cases}$$

$$\text{писа́ -ть} \quad \begin{cases} \text{я пиш -у́} \\ \text{ты пи́ш -ешь} \end{cases}$$

It is therefore important to memorize the *infinitive* as well as the *first* and *second person* singular of the present tense for every new verb.

5-5. The Instrumental Case

a. The instrumental case is used with or without a preposition, depending on the idea to be conveyed.

1. When used *without* a preposition, the instrumental indicates the *instrument* or *means* by which an action is performed, or the *agent* by whom it is performed.   Thus it answers the question **чем**? (*with what?*) or **кем**? (*by whom?*).   For example:

Профе́ссор пи́шет перо́м.   The professor is writing *with (by means of)* a pen.   (**Чем** он пи́шет?   *With what* is he writing?)

In the sentence "The book was written *by the professor*," the last three words are rendered in Russian by only one—**профе́ссором**.

In the question *"By whom* was the book written?" the first two words are rendered by **кем**.

2. For the use of the instrumental *with* a preposition, see **¶ 8-2**.

b. Masculine nouns ending in a consonant in the nominative singular add -**ом** to form the instrumental.*

nom.	мел	каранда́ш
instr.	ме́л**ом**	карандашо́**м**

c. Neuter nouns in -**о** add -**м**.*

nom.	перо́	окно́
instr.	пер**о́м**	окно́**м**

d. Feminine nouns in -**а** change the ending to -**ой** or -**ою**.*

nom.	ка́рта	Москва́
instr.	{ ка́рт**ой** { ка́рт**ою**	{ Москв**о́й** { Москв**о́ю**

5-6. По-ру́сски and по-англи́йски

По-ру́сски and по-англи́йски are adverbs, but are rendered in English as nouns. For example:

Я чита́ю по-ру́сски.	I read Russian.
Он пи́шет по-англи́йски.	He writes English.

Упражне́ния (Exercises)

A. Supply the appropriate personal pronoun for the following words. For example: студе́нтка **она́**.

1. мел _____. 2. ла́мпа _____. 3. дверь _____.
4. окно́ _____.   5. ко́мната _____.   6. класс
_____. 7. здоро́в _____. 8. здоро́ва _____.
9. Пётр _____. 10. Ве́ра _____. 11. стена́ _____.
12. Москва́ _____.   13. Сталингра́д _____. 14.
карти́на _____. 15. перо́ _____.

B. Supply an appropriate noun to agree with the following adjectives. For example: но́вая **кни́га**.

1. мой _____.   2. ваш _____.   3. моя́
_____. 4. ва́ша _____. 5. моё _____.
6. ва́ше _____. 7. краси́вый _____. 8.
но́вый _____. 9. но́вая _____. 10. краси́вое

* For exceptions, see **¶ 25-3b**.

_____.   11. новое _____.   12. краси́вая
_____.   13. _____ здоро́ва.

C. Supply the proper personal ending for the verbs and the appropriate case ending for the nouns. For example: Я пишу́ пер**о́м**.

1. Я сего́дня чита́___ кни́г___. 2. Кни́г___ тут. 3. Он чита́___ журна́л. 4. Она́ пи́ш___ мел___ на доск___.
5. Чем вы пи́ш___ до́ма? 6. До́ма мы пи́ш___ каранда́ш___ и́ли пер___. 7. Вы пи́ш___ и чита́___ по-ру́сски хорошо́?
8. Да, я чита́___ и пиш___ хорошо́, но о́чень ме́дленно.
9. Как студе́нты пи́ш___ и чита́___ по-англи́йски? 10. Они́ пи́ш___ и чита́___ о́чень бы́стро.

Перево́д (**Translation**)

Translate, omitting the words in parentheses.
1. Is this your room? 2. Yes, this is my room. 3. Is your room new? 4. Yes, it is new (a new one) and beautiful. 5. Where is the window? 6. The window is here, and the door is there.
7. What do you write with on paper? 8. On paper I write with a pen, and on the blackboard I write with chalk. 9. Do you already read Russian? 10. Yes, I read Russian, but very slowly. 11. English I read fast (rapidly). 12. Do you write Russian well or poorly? 13. I write Russian poorly and slowly. 14. And how do you read Russian? 15. I read Russian very fast.

Вопро́сы (**Questions**)

1. Э́то ва́ша ко́мната? 2. Где окно́ и где дверь? 3. Ваш стол в ко́мнате но́вый? 4. Что на столе́? 5. Как вы чита́ете по-ру́сски? 6. Как вы пи́шете по-англи́йски? 7. Чем вы пи́шете на бума́ге? 8. Чем вы пи́шете на доске́? 9. Чем профе́ссор Петро́в всегда́ пи́шет в кла́ссе? 10. Студе́нты чита́ют по-англи́йски бы́стро и́ли ме́дленно? 11. Вы чита́ете по-ру́сски то́лько в шко́ле? 12. До́ма вы всегда́ чита́ете по-англи́йски?

UNIT

REVIEW LESSON

Грамма́тика (Grammar)

6-1. Nouns: Table of Case Endings

Memorize the following table.

	MASCULINE	FEMININE	NEUTER
nom.	стул	ка́рта	перо́
	стол	Москва́	окно́
acc.	стул	ка́рту	перо́
	стол	Москву́	окно́
instr.	сту́лом	ка́ртой, -ою	перо́м
	столо́м	Москво́й, -о́ю	окно́м
prep.	сту́ле	ка́рте	пере́
	столе́	Москве́	окне́

Alphabet Review

A. Write the Russian script in alphabetical order; then check with the book for errors or omissions. Rewrite the alphabet until no errors occur.

B. Do the same with the printed alphabet.

Vocabulary Review

A. Write the Russian equivalent for each of the following words and indicate where the stress falls with an accent mark. If you are

38

not sure of the Russian word or its spelling, look it up in the English-Russian vocabulary.

1. who	13. at home
2. also	14. today
3. where	15. slowly
4. here	16. rapidly
5. there	17. Russian (in Russian)
6. more	18. English (in English)
7. very	19. already
8. much	20. only
9. well, good	21. always
10. well (healthy) (*m.*)	22. in
11. well (healthy) (*f.*)	23. on
12. or	24. how

B. Write the Russian equivalent for each of the following nouns, insert accent marks, and indicate the gender of each.   Underline the ending which shows the gender.   For example:

window—окно́ (*n.*)
paper—бума́га (*f.*)

1. professor	8. map	15. wall
2. student (girl)	9. picture	16. school
3. class	10. Moscow	17. newspaper
4. magazine	11. Stalingrad	18. room
5. book	12. pencil	19. paper
6. table	13. pen	20. lamp
7. chair	14. blackboard	21. door

C. Use one of the following adjectives in the proper gender with each of the above nouns.

1. мой, моя́, моё
2. краси́вый, краси́вая, краси́вое
3. ваш, ва́ша, ва́ше
4. но́вый, но́вая, но́вое

D. Use the vocabularies of Exercises A, B, and C in a spelling match.

Reading and Comprehension Drill

Read each of the following affirmative sentences aloud; then re-read them, changing your intonation to form questions (see ¶2-5).

Next, answer the questions both in the affirmative and the negative, using complete sentences.   For example:

> Вéра крас*и*вая студéнтка.   (affirmative)

Change to: Вéра крас*и*вая студéнтка?   (interrogative)

Possible answers:

> Да, онá крас*и*вая студéнтка.
> О да!   Онá óчень крас*и*вая.
> Нет, онá не крас*и*вая студéнтка.
> О нет!   Онá не крас*и*вая.

For another example:

> На стенé карт*и*на.   (affirmative)

Change to: На стенé карт*и*на?   (interrogative)

Possible answers:

> Да, на стенé карт*и*на.
> Нет, на стенé не карт*и*на, а кáрта.

1. Э́то студéнт.
2. Ивáн профéссор.
3. Пётр и Áнна студéнты.
4. Вéра тóже студéнтка.
5. Кáрта на столé.
6. На стенé доскá.
7. Пётр в Москвé.
8. Петрóв сегóдня дóма.
9. Студéнты в шкóле.
10. Áнна читáет кн*и*гу.
11. Студéнтка здорóва.
12. Он*и* читáют журнáл.
13. Господ*и*н Петрóв п*и*шет карандашóм.
14. Лáмпа нóвая и крас*и*вая.
15. Вáше перó всегдá на столé.
16. Вы хорошó читáете по-англ*и*йски.
17. Он*и* плóхо п*и*шут по-рýсски.
18. Ты ужé бы́стро читáешь.

Grammar Review

Supply the proper forms for the words in parentheses.   For example:

> Э́то (ваш) (room)—Э́то вáша кóмната.
> Петрóв (писáть) (with a pen)—Петрóв п*и*шет перóм.

1. Ваш стол в (room) (new).
2. Дóма вы всегдá (читáть) (Russian).
3. На (paper) я (писáть) (with a pen).
4. Э́то (my) кóмната.
5. Он*и* сегóдня (читáть) (a book).
6. Петрóв в (class).

7. (Но́вый) (краси́вый) ла́мпа.
8. (Your) окно́ (но́вый).
9. Они́ (чита́ть) (a magazine).
10. Он здоро́в, а она́ (sick).

Перево́д (Translation)

1. Who is this? 2. Yes or no? 3. Who is she? 4. Who are they? 5. What else? 6. This is my room. 7. I am not well (*m.*). 8. Here is a school. 9. The school is in Moscow. 10. The students are in class. 11. She is also a student. 12. That (this) is very good. 13. This is not a map, but a picture. 14. Vera is not a student, but a professor. 15. This is a table, and this is a chair. 16. The book is on the table. 17. The newspaper is on the chair. 18. Where is the magazine? 19. What is on the map? 20. Moscow is here and Stalingrad is there. 21. A blackboard and a map are on the wall. 22. A pen and a pencil are on the table. 23. With what are you writing—with a pen or a pencil? 24. What is she reading—a newspaper or a magazine? 25. Anne is home today, but she is well. 26. We write Russian poorly and slowly. 27. You read English well and fast (rapidly). 28. My window is very beautiful. 29. On the table is a beautiful new lamp. 30. I write with chalk on the blackboard.

МОЙ УЧИ́ТЕЛЬ

Я учени́к. Я уже́ чита́ю и пишу́ по-ру́сски. Я та́кже понима́ю по-ру́сски, но ещё не говорю́. Я хоро́ший учени́к.

Мой учи́тель — господи́н Петро́в. Он ру́сский. Он пло́хо говори́т по-англи́йски, потому́ что он то́лько оди́н год в Аме́рике. Но он о́чень хоро́ший учи́тель.

В кла́ссе господи́н Петро́в всегда́ стои́т. Он стои́т о́коло ка́рты, о́коло доски́, и́ли о́коло стола́. Тепе́рь он стои́т о́коло окна́.

Слова́рь (Vocabulary)

учи́тель (*m.*) teacher (man)
учени́к pupil (boy)
та́кже also, in addition
понима́ю I understand
понима́ть (I); понима́ю, -ешь, -ют to understand
ещё не говорю́ I do not yet speak
говори́ть (II); говорю́, -и́шь, -я́т to speak, to talk, to say
хоро́ший, хоро́шая, хоро́шее good
ру́сский (*noun & adj., m.*) Russian
потому́ что because
оди́н one
год year
Аме́рика America (*colloq.* the U.S.A.)
он то́лько оди́н год в Аме́рике he has been only one year in the U.S.A.
стои́т he stands
стоя́ть (II); стою́, -и́шь, -я́т to stand
о́коло (*requires gen. case*) near
тепе́рь now

УЧЕНИ́К И УЧЕНИ́ЦА (Разгово́р)

— Вы учени́ца? — Да, я учени́ца.

— Ива́н то́же учени́ца? — Нет, Ива́н не учени́ца, он учени́к.

— Вы хоро́шая учени́ца? — Да, я о́чень хоро́шая учени́ца, потому́ что я мно́го рабо́таю.

— Ива́н то́же хоро́ший учени́к? — О нет! Он о́чень плохо́й учени́к.

— Почему́ он плохо́й учени́к? — Потому́ что он ма́ло рабо́тает. В кла́ссе он ничего́ не чита́ет и ничего́ не пи́шет. Он то́лько говори́т и говори́т.

— Ва́ша учи́тельница, госпожа́ Ивано́ва, зна́ет, что он не рабо́тает и то́лько говори́т в кла́ссе? — Да, она́ о́чень хорошо́ э́то зна́ет.

Слова́рь (Vocabulary)

учени́ца pupil (girl)
хоро́шая (*f.*) good
рабо́таю I work
рабо́тать (I); рабо́таю, -ешь, -ют to work
плохо́й, плоха́я, плохо́е bad, poor
почему́ why
ма́ло little (not much)
ничего́ (*pr.* **ничево́**) nothing
ничего́ не чита́ет he reads nothing, he does not read anything
то́лько говори́т и говори́т he only talks and talks
учи́тельница teacher (woman)
госпожа́ Miss, Mrs.
Ивано́ва Ivanova
зна́ет knows
знать (I); зна́ю, -ешь, -ют to know

Sing this song in rounds to the tune of *Frère Jacques:*

Я не зна́ю,
Я не зна́ю,
    Ничего́!
    Ничего́!
Ничего́ не зна́ю,
Ничего́ не зна́ю,
    Хорошо́!
    Хорошо́!

Произноше́ние (Pronunciation)

7-A. Change of "ы" to "и" after Sibilants

The letter **ы** can never be written after the sibilants **ж, ч, ш**, or **щ** and must be replaced by the corresponding soft vowel **и** (see ¶ 1-A).   Hence the ending **-ий** in хоро́ший, instead of **-ый** as in но́вый.

7-B. The Gutturals : г, к, and x

a. Pronounce the letters **г, к**, and **x**, and note that they are pronounced in the throat.   They are therefore called *gutturals*, from the Latin *guttur* meaning *throat*.

b. The letter **ы** can never be written after the gutturals **г, к**, or **x** (or after the sibilants **ж, ч, ш**, or **щ**), and must be replaced by **и**. For example:

nom.	ка́рт**а**	кни́г**а**	доск**а́**	госпож**а́**
gen.	ка́рт**ы**	кни́г**и**	доск**и́**	госпож**и́** (see ¶ 7-3)

Грамма́тика (Grammar)

7-1. The Second Conjugation. Infinitive : говори́ть (to speak)

a. To form the present tense of **говори́ть**, add the personal endings to the present stem, that is, to **говор-**.

SINGULAR

я говор**ю́**	I speak, I am speaking
ты говор**и́шь**	you speak, you are speaking
он говор**и́т**	he speaks, he is speaking
она́ говор**и́т**	she speaks, she is speaking
оно́ говор**и́т**	it speaks, it is speaking

PLURAL

мы говор**и́м**	we speak, we are speaking
вы говор**и́те**	you speak, you are speaking
они́ говор**я́т**	they speak, they are speaking

b. Memorize the present of **говори́ть** as well as the personal endings.

	SINGULAR		PLURAL
я	**-ю**	мы	**-им**
ты	**-ишь**	вы	**-ите**
он }			
она́ }	**-ит**	они́	**-ят**
оно́ }			

Compare these personal endings with those of the First Conjugation (see ¶4-2) and commit them to memory.

c. The distinguishing mark of the Second Conjugation is the vowel **и** in the second person singular ending **-ишь** (ты говори́шь). This may be compared with the distinguishing mark of the First Conjugation, namely, the vowel **е** in second person singular ending **-ешь** (ты чита́ешь). Henceforth in the vocabulary, verbs of the Second Conjugation will be designated by the Roman numeral II, just as verbs of the First Conjugation are designated by the Roman numeral I. Verbs which do not fit either of these conjugations will be marked *irr.* (irregular).

7-2. The Verb in the Negative

a. The verb in the negative is formed by placing **не** before the affirmative. **Стоя́ть** (*to stand*) is conjugated both in the affirmative and the negative to illustrate this point.

AFFIRMATIVE	NEGATIVE	
я сто́ю	я **не** сто́ю	I do not stand, I am not standing
ты сто́ишь	ты **не** сто́ишь	you do not stand, you are not standing
он стои́т	он **не** стои́т	he does not stand, he is not standing
она́ стои́т	она́ **не** стои́т	she does not stand, she is not standing
оно́ стои́т	оно́ **не** стои́т	it does not stand, it is not standing
мы стои́м	мы **не** стои́м	we do not stand, we are not standing
вы стои́те	вы **не** стои́те	you do not stand, you are not standing
они́ стоя́т	они́ **не** стоя́т	they do not stand, they are not standing

b. To negate an action, **не** must precede the verb regardless of the presence of other negative words in the sentence.   For example:

> Он **ничего́ не** зна́ет.   He knows nothing.
> (*Literally:* He *nothing not* knows.)

7-3. The Genitive Case

a. The genitive denotes possession and corresponds to the *possessive* in English.   For example:

> стена́ шко́л**ы**   the wall *of* the school
> кни́га студе́нт**а**   the student*'s* book

The case ending in Russian performs the same function as the preposition **of** or the **'s** in English.

b. The genitive is also used with certain prepositions, such as **о́коло**.   For example:

> о́коло стол**а́**   near the table
> о́коло ка́рт**ы**   near the map
> о́коло окн**а́**   near the window

c. Formation of the genitive singular.

1. *Masculine* nouns ending in a *consonant* add **-a** to form the genitive:

nom.	студе́нт	учени́к	стул	стол
gen.	студе́нт**а**	учени́к**а́**	сту́л**а**	стол**а́**

2. *Feminine* nouns ending in **-a** change **-a** to **-ы**:

nom.	Ве́р**а**	ка́рт**а**	стен**а́**
gen.	Ве́р**ы**	ка́рт**ы**	стен**ы́**

Exceptions: Nouns whose stems end in **г, к**, or **х** (the gutturals), or in **ж, ч, ш**, or **щ** (the sibilants) take **-и** instead of **-ы**:*

nom.	кни́г**а**	доск**а́**	госпож**а́**
gen.	кни́г**и**	доск**и́**	госпож**и́**

3. *Neuter* nouns ending in **-o** change **-o** to **-a**:

nom.	пер**о́**	окн**о́**
gen.	пер**а́**	окн**а́**

---

* See ¶ **7-A** and **7-B.**

7-4. Subordinating Conjunctions: что and потому́ что

When **что** or **потому́ что** introduces a subordinate clause, it is separated by a comma from the main clause:

Она́ зна́ет, **что** он не рабо́тает.   She knows that he does not work.
Он ма́ло зна́ет, **потому́ что** он плохо́й учени́к.

He knows little because he is a bad pupil.

Упражне́ния (Exercises)

A. Supply the proper endings, accents, and meanings.   (Master
¶ 7-1 before doing this exercise.)

1. они́ пиш____	8. он говор____
2. вы рабо́та____	9. они́ сто____
3. мы говор____	10. я понима́____
4. он зна____	11. они чита́____
5. она́ понима́____	12. мы зна____
6. мы сто____	13. мы рабо́та____
7. я чита́____	14. вы пиш____

B. Give the genitive form for the following nouns, and supply the accents for both the nominative and the genitive.   (Master ¶ 7-3 before doing this exercise.)

1. студент	11. стена
2. студентка	12. окно
3. ученик	13. журнал
4. ученица	14. стул
5. господин	15. лампа
6. госпожа	16. бумага
7. профессор	17. доска
8. Анна	18. мел
9. Вера	19. карандаш
10. комната	20. перо

C. Supply the proper endings in the blanks, and replace the English words in parentheses with the Russian equivalent in the correct gender and case:

1. Она́ учени́____. 2. Она́ понима́____ (English). 3. Мы ещё не говор____ (Russian). 4. (My) учи́тельница (Mrs.) Ивано́ва. 5. Она́ ру́сск____. 6. Она́ о́чень (good) учи́тельница. 7. Она́ сто____ о́коло (table) и́ли о́коло (blackboard).

Перево́д (Translation)

Omit the words in parentheses and include the words in brackets.

Who Knows Why?

1. My teacher (*f.*) is Mrs. Ivanova.   2. She is Russian.   3. She is a very good teacher.   4. She says [**говори́т**] that I am a good pupil (*f.*).   5. I do not know why she is saying this [**э́то**], because I always work very little.   6. I read and write Russian only in class. 7. At home I read nothing and write nothing.   8. My teacher has been in America only one year, and she does not yet speak English very well.   9. She understands English, but in class we speak only Russian.   10. Mr. Petrov is also a teacher, and he is also Russian. 11. Mr. Petrov and Mrs. Ivanova are now in school.   12. They speak Russian very fast and I understand nothing.   13. Why do I understand nothing—because I am not a Russian, or because I am a bad pupil?   14. Who knows why?

Вопро́сы (Questions)

1. Кто вы?   2. Вы Ива́н и́ли Пётр?   3. Вы уже́ чита́ете по-ру́сски?   4. Как вы чита́ете по-ру́сски, бы́стро и́ли ме́дленно? 5. Вы та́кже говори́те по-ру́сски?   6. Как вы говори́те по-ру́сски, хорошо́ и́ли пло́хо?   7. Кто ва́ша учи́тельница? 8. Она́ ру́сская?   9. Она́ хоро́шая и́ли плоха́я учи́тельница? 10. Как она́ говори́т по-англи́йски?   11. Она́ в Аме́рике то́лько оди́н год?   12. Господи́н Петро́в то́же ру́сский учи́тель?   13. Он учи́тель Ива́на и Ве́ры?   14. Почему́ Ива́н ничего́ не зна́ет?   15. Господи́н Петро́в зна́ет, что Ива́н ма́ло рабо́тает?

U N I T 8

НА́ША СЕМЬЯ́

Сего́дня вся семья́ до́ма. Вот оте́ц. Он чита́ет газе́ту. Мать сиди́т на дива́не и чита́ет журна́л.

Мо́й оте́ц до́ктор. Он рабо́тает весь день, а ве́чером отдыха́ет. Мать учи́тельница, но она́ рабо́тает то́лько у́тром. А я ничего́ не де́лаю, потому́ что я не люблю́ рабо́тать.

Бори́с, мой ма́ленький брат, игра́ет с соба́кой. Ма́ша, моя́ сестра́, даёт соба́ке шокола́д. Оте́ц говори́т, что э́то не хорошо́, но на́ша соба́ка о́чень лю́бит шокола́д.

Слова́рь (Vocabulary)

на́ша (*f.*) our
семья́ (*f.*) family (see ¶ 10-B)
весь, вся, всё (*pr.* фcя, фcё; see ¶ 8-D) entire, whole
оте́ц father
мать (*f.*) mother
сиде́ть (**II**); **сижу́, сиди́шь, сидя́т** to sit
дива́н divan
до́ктор doctor
день (*m.*) day
весь день the whole day, all day
ве́чером in the evening
отдыха́ть (**I**); **отдыха́ю, -ешь, -ют** to rest
у́тром in the morning
де́лать (**I**); **де́лаю, -ешь, -ют** to do
я не люблю́ рабо́тать I do not like to work
люби́ть (**II**); **люблю́, лю́бишь, лю́бят** to love, to like
Бори́с Boris
ма́ленький, -ая, -ое (see ¶ 7-B) little, small
брат brother
игра́ть (**I**); **игра́ю, -ешь, -ют** to play

49

с (*with instr.*) with
собáка dog
с собáкой with the dog
Мáша Masha
сестрá sister
давáть (**I**); **даю́, даёшь, даю́т** to give
собáке (*dat.*) to the dog
наш, нáша, нáше our
шоколáд (*pr.* **шоколáт**; see **¶3-B**) chocolate

СЕМЬЯ́ ЖИВЁТ В ДЕРÉВНЕ (Разговóр)

— Где вы рабóтаете? — Я рабóтаю в гóроде.

— А где вы живёте? — Я живу́ в дерéвне.

— Вы рабóтаете в гóроде, но живёте в дерéвне. Почему́ вы не живёте в гóроде?

— Потому́ что я óчень люблю́ дерéвню. Там всегдá тúхо и я хорошó отдыхáю пóсле рабóты.

— Вáша семья́ тóже живёт в дерéвне?

— Да, вся нáша семья́ живёт в дерéвне.

— Что дéлает вáша мать? Онá тóже рабóтает?

— Да, онá рабóтает в магазúне, когдá онá здорóва.

— А где рабóтает вáша сестрá?

— Онá нигдé не рабóтает.

— Онá тóлько тепéрь не рабóтает?

— О нет! Онá никогдá не рабóтает и всегдá сидúт дóма.

— Что же онá дéлает дóма?

— Онá игрáет с собáкой, úли сидúт на дивáне и ничегó не дéлает.

Словáрь (Vocabulary)

жить (**I**); **живу́, живёшь, живу́т** to live, to dwell
дерéвня (*f.*) (*acc.* **дерéвню**) village, country
гóрод (*pr.* **гóрот**) town
тúхо quiet
пóсле (*with gen.*) after
рабóта work
магазúн store
когдá when
нигдé nowhere
онá нигдé не рабóтает she works nowhere, she does not work anywhere
никогдá never
сидéть дóма to stay home
же (*emphatic*) then, but
что же what then

Произношёние (Pronunciation)

8-A. Prepositions

Prepositions consisting of a single consonant, such as **в** (*in*) and **c** (*with*), are pronounced as part of the following word. For example:

в_кóмнате	*fkómnate*	(in the room)
c_собáкой	*ssobákoy*	(with the dog)

8-B. Hard and Soft Consonants

a. Pronounce the English words *do* and *dew*, or *pooh* and *pew*, and note the differences. The *d* in *do* or the *p* in *pooh* are hard, whereas in *dew* and *pew* they are soft.

b. A hard vowel (**a, э, o, y,** or **ы**) indicates that the preceding consonant is to be pronounced *hard*. For example:

нáша	(*n*asha)
шкóла	(sh*ko*la)

c. The **ь** (the soft sign) or a soft vowel (**я, e, ё, ю,** or **и**) indicates that the preceding consonant is to be pronounced *soft*. For example:

сегóдня	(sevod*n*ya)
студéнт	(stud*y*ent)
день	(dyen') (*cf.* **н** with *n* in *onion*)
читáть	(cheeta*t*')

8-C. Hard Consonants: ж, ш, and ц

a. The consonants **ж, ш,** and **ц** are always hard. Therefore, they can never be followed by a soft vowel sound.

b. When a soft vowel follows a hard consonant, it is pronounced like its corresponding hard sound. For example:

жить	is pronounced	жыть
центр	is pronounced	цэнтр
машúна	is pronounced	машы́на

8-D. The Diaeresis

A stressed **e** often becomes **ë**. In such cases, the *diaeresis* (the two dots over the **e**) indicates the stress, and the accent mark is not used.

Phonetic Drill.   Pronounce the following syllables and words.

a. Syllables:

ва-вя; во-вё; да-дя; ла-ля; ло-лё; лу-лю; ма-мя; мо-мё; му-мю; но-нё; на-ня; вэ-ве; дэ-де; лэ-ле; мэ-ме; тэ-те; ту-тю; та-тя.

b. Words:

лес, нет, газе́та, Ве́ра, мел, ме́дленно, дверь, мать, дива́н, чита́ть, писа́ть, игра́ть, тепе́рь, стоя́ть, де́лать, люблю́, ма́ленький, большо́й, день, тень, цирк, ци́фра, центр, офице́р, инжене́р, на́ция, револю́ция.

Грамма́тика (Grammar)

8-1. Typical Irregularities in the Present Tense

The following verbs contain some typical irregularities in the present tense.   Memorize them carefully, noting the exceptions.

a. Infinitive: **сиде́ть** (II) *to sit*

я сижу́	мы сиди́м
ты сиди́шь	вы сиди́те
он сиди́т	они́ сидя́т

Note: **д** changes to **ж** in the first person singular.   Remember that the *second person singular* regularly determines the inflection pattern of the present tense.

b. Infinitive: **люби́ть** (II) *to love, to like*

я люблю́	мы лю́бим
ты лю́бишь	вы лю́бите
он лю́бит	они́ лю́бят

Note: **л** is inserted in the first person singular, and the stress falls on the ending; in all other persons, the stress falls on the stem vowel.

c. Infinitive: **дава́ть** (I) *to give*

я даю́	мы даём
ты даёшь	вы даёте
он даёт	они́ даю́т

Note: In the present stem, the syllable **ва** of the infinitive disappears.   The **е** in the personal endings changes to **ё** and is stressed.

d. Infinitive: **жить** (I) *to live*

я живу́	мы живём
ты живёшь	вы живёте
он живёт	они́ живу́т

Note: The letter **в** is inserted after the stem, and **е** changes to **ё** in the personal endings.

8-2. The Instrumental Case with the Preposition c*

a. When used with the preposition **c**, the instrumental case often indicates association or mutual participation, and means *with*, *together with*, *along with*. For example:

Я живу́ с сестро́й в дере́вне.   I live with my sister in the country.
Я говорю́ по-ру́сски с бра́том.   I speak Russian with my brother.

b. With whom? is translated **с кем?**

С кем вы живёте?   With whom do you live?

8-3. The Dative Case

a. The dative in Russian expresses the *indirect object.*   It answers the question **кому́** (*to whom*) or **чему́** (*to what*).

b. The case ending performs the same function as does the preposition *to* in English.   For example:

Ма́ша даёт бра́ту кни́гу.   Masha is giving a book *to* her brother.
Кому́ она́ даёт кни́гу?   *To* whom is she giving a book?

c. Formation of the dative singular.

1. *Masculine* nouns ending in a *consonant* add **у** to form the dative:

nom.	стул	стол	брат
dat.	сту́лу	столу́	бра́ту

2. *Neuter* nouns ending in **-о** change **-о** to **-у**:

nom.	перо́	окно́
dat.	перу́	окну́

3. *Feminine* nouns ending in **-а** change **-а** to **-е**:

nom.	ка́рта	Москва́
dat.	ка́рте	Москве́

* See also ¶ 5-5.

Упражне́ния (Exercises)

A. Put the English words in the *dative* and the Russian words in parentheses in the *accusative*.

1. Я даю́ *brother* (кни́га). 2. Ты даёшь *Mr*. Петро́ву (ла́мпа).
3. Он даёт *sister* (ка́рта). 4. Мы даём *dog* (шокола́д). 5. Вы даёте *pupil* (стул). 6. Они́ даю́т *doctor* (карти́на).

B. Supply the proper equivalents for the words in parentheses.

1. Я живу́ (at home). 2. Ты живёшь в (town). 3. На́ша семья́ (lives) в (the country). 4. Мы (do not live) тут. 5. Вы всегда́ (live) с (sister). 6. Господи́н Петро́в и госпожа́ Петро́ва (live) в (Stalingrad).

C. Supply the personal verb endings and give the proper case endings to the words in parentheses. Indicate accents.

1. Я никогда́ не сиж____ на (стул). 2. Ты говор____ с (брат) и с (сестра́). 3. Они́ сто____ о́коло (дива́н). 4. Вы никогда́ не отдыха____ по́сле (рабо́та). 5. В (дере́вня) о́чень ти́хо. 6. Что ва́ша мать дела____ весь день? 7. Он зна____, что госпожа́ Ивано́ва сид____ до́ма ве́чером? 8. Почему́ Ма́ша да____ (соба́ка) шокола́д? 9. Моя́ ма́ленькая сестра́ нигде́ не рабо́та____. 10. Когда́ я в (го́род), я рабо́та____ в (магази́н).

Перево́д (Translation)

Omit the words in parentheses and include those in brackets.

1. I work in a store. 2. The store is in town, but I live in the country. 3. My whole [**вся моя́**] family lives in the country. 4. After work I do nothing. 5. I stay home and rest. 6. I never read anything [I never nothing not read] when I am home. 7. I only play with the dog. 8. My sister Vera does not work anywhere. 9. She does not like to work. 10. But she likes to read, and reads all day. 11. My father is a doctor and works in the morning. 12. In the evening he is always reading or writing. 13. Mother likes to sit on the divan when she is resting. 14. The dog is always near the divan when mother is in the room. 15. Mother likes the dog, and the dog knows it.

Вопро́сы (Questions)

1. С кем сестра́ игра́ет?   2. Что ещё она́ де́лает?   3. По-
чему́ брат ничего́ не де́лает?   4. Где мать рабо́тает?   5. Когда́
она́ не рабо́тает?   6. Где живёт ва́ша семья́?   7. Почему́ она́
живёт в дере́вне, а не в го́роде?   8. Что де́лает ваш ма́ленький
брат Бори́с?   9. Что вы де́лаете ве́чером по́сле рабо́ты?
10. Почему́ соба́ка стои́т о́коло дива́на, когда́ мать сиди́т на
дива́не?   11. Кому́ Бори́с даёт шокола́д?   12. Вы живёте с
сестро́й и́ли с бра́том?   13. Почему́ ва́ша сестра́ Ма́ша ещё не
говори́т по-ру́сски?   14. Вы всегда́ рабо́таете, когда́ же вы
отдыха́ете?   15. До́ктор зна́ет, что вы не отдыха́ете?   16. Что
же он говори́т?

UNIT 9

I

Я ПРЕДПОЧИТА́Ю ЖИТЬ В ГО́РОДЕ

Я живу́ и рабо́таю в го́роде.　У меня́ там ма́ленькая, некраси́вая ко́мната.　Пол в ко́мнате но́вый, но потоло́к о́чень ста́рый.

В ко́мнате у меня́ то́лько оди́н большо́й стол, два кре́сла и три сту́ла.　Больша́я ла́мпа стои́т на полу́ о́коло окна́.　О́чень ма́ленькая, ста́рая и некраси́вая ла́мпа стои́т на столе́.　Тепе́рь у меня́ есть но́вый дива́н, и я всегда́ предпочита́ю сиде́ть на дива́не.　Мой оте́ц не понима́ет, почему́ я хочу́ жить в го́роде.

Слова́рь (Vocabulary)

предпочита́ть (I); предпочита́ю, -ешь, -ют to prefer
у (*with gen.*) by, at
у меня́ I have (*lit.* by me)
у меня́ есть I have, I do have (*lit.* by me there is)
некраси́вый, -ая, -ое unattractive, ugly
пол floor
потоло́кᶠˡ ★ (*gen.* **потолка́**) ceiling (see ¶ 9-5)
ста́рый, -ая, -ое old
большо́й, больша́я, большо́е big
два (*m. & n.*) two
кре́сло armchair
три (*m., f., & n.*) three
на полу́ (*irr. prep. of* **пол**) on the floor
хоте́ть (*irr.*); **хочу́, хо́чешь, хотя́т** to want, wish (see ¶ 9-4)

★ The symbol ᶠˡ after a word in the Vocabulary indicates that the last **e** or **o** of the stem is dropped when the noun is declined.

56

II

Я ПРЕДПОЧИТА́Ю ЖИТЬ В ГО́РОДЕ (Continued)

У отца́ о́чень большо́й дом в дере́вне. В до́ме отца́ у меня́ больша́я и краси́вая ко́мната. Но я там никогда́ не могу́ рабо́тать, и́ли отдыха́ть.

У отца́ в до́ме живу́т: моя́ сестра́ Ка́тя и её муж Пе́тя, мой брат Фе́дя и его́ жена́ На́дя, дя́дя Ва́ня и тётя Та́ня. Де́душка и ба́бушка то́же живу́т у нас. Все говоря́т о́чень гро́мко и я никогда́ не могу́ чита́ть, рабо́тать и́ли отдыха́ть. Но оте́ц не понима́ет, почему́ я не хочу́ жить у него́ в дере́вне.

Слова́рь (Vocabulary)

оте́ц[fl] (*gen.* **отца́**) father (see ¶**9-5**)
у отца́ father has
дом house
мочь (**I**); **могу́, мо́жешь, мо́гут** to be able to, to be in a position to
Ка́тя (*f.*) Katya
её her
муж (*pr.* **муш**) husband (see ¶**9-A**)
Пе́тя (*m.*) Petya
Фе́дя (*m.*) Fedya
его́ (*pr.* **ево́**) his
жена́ wife
На́дя (*f.*) Nadya
дя́дя (*m.*) uncle
Ва́ня (*m.*) Vanya
тётя (*f.*) aunt
Та́ня (*f.*) Tanya
де́душка (*m.*) grandfather
ба́бушка grandmother
у нас at our house
все all, everybody
гро́мко loudly
у него́ (*pr.* **у нево́**) **в дере́вне** at his home in the village

Произношёние (Pronunciation)

9-A. Voiced and Voiceless Consonants

a. Pronounce the sound **ш**; then without changing the position of your tongue or lips, pronounce the sound **ж**. You will note that when you pronounce the **ж**, something vibrates in your throat. It is the vocal cords which produce the voice. Hence the **ж** is a *voiced consonant.* When you pronounce **ш**, the vocal cords remain inactive; that is, the **ш** is uttered by means of the breath, without participation of the voice. The **ш** is therefore a *voiceless consonant.*

b. For the sake of accurate pronunciation and spelling, it is important to remember the following *voiced* and *voiceless* consonants in pairs:

Voiced:	**б**	**в**	**г**	**д**	**ж**	**з**
Voiceless:	**п**	**ф**	**к**	**т**	**ш**	**с**

c. Under certain circumstances, voiced consonants are pronounced like the corresponding voiceless ones:

1. At the end of a word. For example:

клу**б**	(*club*)	is pronounced клу**п**
здоро́**в**	(*well*)	is pronounced здоро́**ф**
дру**г**	(*friend*)	is pronounced дру**к**
го**д**	(*year*)	is pronounced го**т**
му**ж**	(*husband*)	is pronounced му**ш**
гла**з**	(*eye*)	is pronounced гла**с**

2. When a voiced consonant precedes a voiceless one. For example:

всегда́	(*always*)	is pronounced **ф**сегда́
второ́й	(*second*)	is pronounced **ф**торо́й
во́**д**ка	(*vodka*)	is pronounced во́**т**ка
ска́**з**ка	(*tale*)	is pronounced ска́**с**ка
ло́**ж**ка	(*spoon*)	is pronounced ло́**ш**ка
тру́**б**ка	(*pipe*)	is pronounced тру́**п**ка

Phonetic Drill. хлеб, сад, рад, шокола́д, гара́ж, эта́ж, раз, без, из, ло́вко, бли́зко, францу́зский, за́втра, за́втрак, снег, всю́ду, Ки́ев, тру́бка, про́бка, вдруг, ска́зка, зуб, рука́в, встре́ча, сто́рож.

Грамма́тика (Grammar)

Part I

9-1. Personal Pronouns in the Genitive and Accusative

The personal pronouns in their various cases are used to form important idiomatic expressions. Therefore, learn the following inflections:

	SINGULAR				
nom.	я	ты	он	она́	оно́
gen.	меня́	тебя́	его́	её	его́
acc.	меня́	тебя́	его́	её	его́

	PLURAL		
nom.	мы	вы	они́
gen.	нас	вас	их
acc.	нас	вас	их

9-2. Possessive Phrases

a. **у**+*pronoun* or *noun* in the *genitive*.

1. The verb *to have* is most frequently rendered in Russian by the preposition **у**+*pronoun* or *noun* in the *genitive*:

у меня́	I have	у нас	we have
у тебя́	you have	у вас	you have
у него́	he has	у них	they have
у неё	she has		

у отца́	father has
у сестры́	sister has
у О́льги	Olga has

2. *At the home of* is also rendered by the preposition **у** + *pronoun* or *noun* in the *genitive*:

Де́душка живёт **у меня́**.	Grandfather is living at my home (house).
Дя́дя живёт **у тебя́**.	Uncle is living at your home (house).
Мы живём **у них**.	We live at their home.
Мой муж **у вас**?	Is my husband at your house?
Нет, он **у сестры́**.	No, he is at his sister's house.

3. The above construction is also used in place of possessives like **мой, ваш**, etc.:

У меня́ в ко́мнате большо́й стол.	In *my* room there is a big table.
у отца́ в до́ме	in *father's* house

4. **У кого́?** means *who has?* or *at whose house?*:

У кого́ моё перо́?	*Who has* my pen?
У кого́ живёт учи́тель?	*At whose house* does the teacher live?

b. **у** + *pronoun* or *noun* in the *genitive* + **есть**.

1. To emphasize possession in the sense of ability to make use of an object, **есть** (third person singular of **быть**, *to be*, in the present) is added.   Compare :

У кого деньги?	Who has *the* money? (In whose safekeeping is it? The banker may have it, but he cannot spend it.)
У кого **есть** деньги?	Who has some money (to spend)?
У кого автомобиль?	Who has *the* automobile? (In whose care is it at present? The garageman may have it, but only to grease it or fix it.)
У кого **есть** автомобиль?	Who has *an* automobile? (*I.e.*, to drive. Ability to use the car is here implied.)

2. **Есть** is also used in questions and answers:

У вас **есть** комната?	Have you a room?
Да, **есть**.	Yes, I have.

9-3. The Genitive with два, три, and четыре

After **два**, **три**, and **четыре** (four), the noun is in the genitive singular, not in the nominative plural.   **Два** is the form for the masculine and neuter, and **две** for the feminine.

два стула	two chairs (*lit.* two of a chair)
два кресла	two armchairs
две книги	two books
три стола	three tables
четыре девушки	four girls

9-4. Infinitive: хотеть (*irr.*) *to want, to wish*

PRESENT TENSE

я хочу	мы хотим
ты хочешь	вы хотите
он хочет	они хотят

Note: In the singular, the endings are those of Conjugation I; in the plural, those of Conjugation II.

Part II

9-5. Fleeting "o" or "e"

Many masculine nouns ending in **-ок**, **-ец**, or **-ень** drop the **o** or **e** when declined.   For example:

nom.	потоло́к	оте́ц	день
gen.	потолка́	отца́	дня
dat.	потолку́	отцу́	дню

9-6. Infinitive: мочь (I) *to be able* (*physically*), *to be in a position to*

PRESENT TENSE

я могу́	мы мо́жем
ты мо́жешь	вы мо́жете
он мо́жет	они́ мо́гут

9-7. Omission of the Possessive

When reference is to close members of the family, possessives like **мой**, **наш**, and **ваш** can be omitted.   For example:

Оте́ц не понима́ет, почему́ я не хочу́ жить у него́.
My father does not understand why I do not want to live at his house.

Упражне́ния (Exercises)

A. Translate.

1. I do not want to work.   2. You do not want to stay home.
3. He does not want to stand on the floor.   4. We do not want to read anything.   5. You do not want to live in town.   6. They do not want to live at his house; at her house; at their (somebody else's) house.

B. Translate the above sentences, substituting **мочь** for **хоте́ть**.

C. Replace the English words in parentheses with the appropriate expressions of possession, and supply the proper case endings for the Russian words in parentheses.   Include words in brackets.

1. (I have) в ко́мнате три (кре́сло).   2. (My sister has) в до́ме четы́ре (дива́н).   3. Мой дя́дя живёт (at our house). 4. Мы живём (at their house).   5. Её муж тепе́рь (at father's

house).   6. (Who has the) собáка?   7. (Who has a) [**есть**] собáка?
8. (Who has the) газéта?   9. (Who has a) [**есть**] газéта?   10. Две
(кни́га) у меня́ на столé.   11. Кни́га (is on his table).   12. (Father
has a) дивáн.   13. Егó женá (is at your house).   14. Её сестрá
(is at father's house).

D. Supply the proper form (in the present tense) of the verbs in
parentheses, and fill in the blanks with a suitable word.

1. Я (мочь) рабóтать _____, но не (хотéть).   2. Ты
óчень _____ (понимáть) по-ру́сски, но не (хотéть)
говори́ть.   3. Он (мочь) говори́ть, но не (хотéть).   4. Все
студéнты (писáть) по-англи́йски на _____.   5. Все
(давáть) собáке _____.   6. Дя́дя и тётя (говори́ть)
óчень грóмко в _____.   7. Мы (предпочитáть) жить
в _____.   8. Моя́ женá (предпочитáть) сидéть _____.
9. Большáя лáмпа (стоя́ть) на _____.   10. Мать всегдá
(сидéть) на _____, когдá онá читáет.

Перевóд (Translation)

Omit words in parentheses and include those in brackets.

1. Katya is at grandfather's.   2. Vanya is at (his) brother's.
3. My wife is at (her) sister's.   4. Only I am home.   5. Grandfather and grandmother, uncle Fedya and aunt Tanya are now in the
country.   6. When everybody [all] is home, they talk very loudly
and I cannot work.   7. When it is quiet in the house, I like to sit
on the divan and read.   8. My dog always sits on the floor near the
armchair.   9. The dog is very ugly, but I love her [**её**] and she
also loves me [**меня́**].   10. I have a big room.   11. The ceiling in
the room is old and the floor is also old, but the room is very
beautiful.   12. There are two divans and three armchairs in my
room [by me in the room].   13. Why do you not play with the dog?
14. I prefer to play with (my) brother and [with] sister.   15. (My)
mother does not understand why I prefer to live in town.

Вопрóсы (Questions)

1. Где вы живёте?   2. У вас там большáя и́ли мáленькая
кóмната?   3. Пол у вас нóвый и́ли стáрый?   4. А потолóк
тóже нóвый?   5. У вас в кóмнате два и́ли три крéсла?   6. Где
стои́т большáя лáмпа?   7. А где стои́т мáленькая лáмпа?

8. Больша́я ла́мпа краси́вая и́ли некраси́вая?   9. Где вы предпочита́ете сиде́ть, когда́ вы до́ма?   10. Оте́ц понима́ет, почему́ вы не хоти́те жить в го́роде?   11. Кто живёт у отца́? 12. Почему́ вы не мо́жете отдыха́ть в до́ме отца́?

U N I T 10

I

УРÓК

У нас тепéрь рýсский урóк. Мы изучáем рýсский язы́к. Учи́тель спрáшивает, а мы отвечáем. Мы все сегóдня отвечáем хорошó, потомý что урóк óчень интерéсный.

Учи́тель спрáшивает Ивáна: — Ивáн, когдá говоря́т "дóброе ýтро"?

Ивáн отвечáет: — "Дóброе ýтро" говоря́т ýтром.

— А когдá говоря́т "дóбрый день"?

— Днём говоря́т "дóбрый день".

Потóм учи́тель спрáшивает Вéру: — Вéра, что говоря́т вéчером?

Вéра хорошó знáет урóк и онá отвечáет: — Вéчером говоря́т "дóбрый вéчер".

— А когдá говоря́т "здрáвствуйте"?

— "Здрáвствуйте" говоря́т и ýтром, и днём, и вéчером и нóчью.

Вчерá Вéра тóже знáла урóк. Онá всегдá знáет урóк.

Словáрь (Vocabulary)

урóк lesson
изучáть (**I**); **изучáю, -ешь, -ют** to study (see ¶ **10-1**)
язы́к language
рýсский язы́к Russian (see ¶ **10-2**)
спрáшивать (**I**); **спрáшиваю, -ешь, -ют** to ask (questions) (used with *acc.* of person asked)

64

отвеча́ть (I); **отвеча́ю, -ешь, -ют** to answer
интере́сный, -ая, -ое interesting
Ива́на *acc. of* **Ива́н**
говоря́т one says, people say
до́брый, -ая, -ое good, kind
у́тро morning
до́брое у́тро good morning
днём in the daytime
пото́м then, afterwards
ве́чер evening
здра́вствуйте (*pr.* **здра́ствуйте**) how do you do?   hello!
и . . . и both . . . and
но́чью at night
вчера́ (*pr.* **фчера́**) yesterday
зна́ла (*f.*) knew

II

УРО́К (Continued)

Учи́тель пото́м спра́шивает Бори́са: — Бори́с, что вы говори́те хозя́йке до́ма, когда́ вы идёте домо́й?

Бори́с отвеча́ет: — Я говорю́ хозя́йке: "Я о́чень не хочу́ идти́ домо́й, но уже́ по́здно."

— А что говори́т хозя́ин до́ма, е́сли вы до́лго сиди́те у них?

— Хозя́ин говори́т: "Вы мно́го рабо́тали сего́дня, и за́втра у вас та́кже мно́го рабо́ты." А я отвеча́ю хозя́ину: "Да, я сего́дня мно́го рабо́тал, и за́втра у меня́ мно́го рабо́ты, но я лу́чше рабо́таю, когда́ ма́ло сплю."

Слова́рь (Vocabulary)

хозя́йка owner, mistress, hostess
хозя́йке до́ма to the hostess (to the owner of the house)
идти́ (I); **иду́, идёшь, иду́т** to go, to walk (see ¶ 10-7)
домо́й home, homeward (see ¶ 10-6)
о́чень не хочу́ идти́ домо́й I hate to go home
по́здно late
хозя́ин owner, master, host
е́сли if (**е́сли** never means *whether*)
до́лго (*adv.*) for a long time
вы рабо́тали you worked
за́втра tomorrow
мно́го рабо́ты much work (see ¶ 10-9)
лу́чше better
спать (II); **сплю, спишь, спят** to sleep

Произношéние (Pronunciation)

10-A. Stressed and Unstressed "я"

a. Stressed **я** is pronounced like *ya* in *yard*, only shorter.

b. Unstressed **я** is pronounced very much like the Russian unstressed **e**.   Thus, the **я** in **язык** sounds like the *ye* in *year*.

10-B. Separation Signs : "ь" and "ъ"

a. We have seen that a single consonant between two vowels is pronounced with the following vowel (see ¶2-B c-3).   However, when **ь** or **ъ** is inserted between the consonant and the vowel, the latter becomes separated from the consonant and is pronounced as if it were the first letter in the following syllable; i.e., the presence of the sound **й** (as the English *y* in *yes*) is thus indicated, and

$$
ь + \begin{cases} e \\ ё \\ я \\ ю \end{cases} \ or \ ъ + \begin{cases} e \\ ё \\ я \\ ю \end{cases} \ sound \ like \ \begin{cases} йе \\ йё \\ йя \\ йу \end{cases}
$$

For example:

отъ - éзд	(ot-*yéz*d)
объ - яс - нять	(ob-*yas*-niát')
семь - я́	(sem-*yá*)
нóчь - ю	(nóch-*yu*)

b. The **ь** can indicate both softness of the preceding consonant and its separation from the following vowel.   For example, the **м** in **семь - я́** and the **т** in **Тать - я́ - на** are both soft and separated from the vowels that follow them.

Phonetic Drill.   Pronounce the following words aloud:

Пять — пья́ница; сéмя — семья́; нюа́нс — óсенью; тётя — статья́; Кóля — кóлья; чей — чьей; отéц — отъéзд; сел — съел; обеща́ть — объéхать; идём — подъём.

Грамма́тика (Grammar)

Part I

10-1. Infinitive : изуча́ть (I) *to study*

The infinitive **изуча́ть** means *to study* something which requires a period of concentration.   For example:

Она **изучает** математику.   She *is studying* mathematics.
Мы **изучаем** русский язык.   We *are studying* Russian.

The object of study must *always* be stated with **изучать**.

10-2. Русский язык

The adjective **русский** cannot be used by itself to mean *Russian language*. The noun **язык** must therefore be added.

10-3. Accusative of Masculine Animate and Inanimate Nouns

a. Masculine and neuter inanimate nouns have the same endings in the accusative as in the nominative.

nom.	стол	перо
acc.	стол	перо

b. Masculine animate nouns that end with a consonant in the nominative have the same ending in the accusative as in the genitive.

nom.	доктор	отец	Иван
gen.	доктора	отца	Ивана
acc.	доктора	отца	Ивана

10-4. Accusative of Masculine Nouns Ending in -a

Masculine nouns that end in **-a** in the nominative change **-a** to **-y** in the accusative, just like regular feminine nouns.

nom.	дедушка
acc.	дедушку

10-5. Impersonal Expressions

The impersonal idea of *one, they, people* is conveyed by the third person plural of the verb in the present tense without the personal pronoun **они**. For example:

говорят   one says, they say, it is said

Part II

10-6. Adverbs: дома and домой

Дома and **домой** are adverbs that can both be translated as *home*. Note, however, the following distinction.

a. **Дóма** is used with verbs of rest and means *at home*:

> Я сижý **дóма.**   I am staying *home* (at home).

b. **Домóй** is used with verbs of motion and means *home, homeward*:

> Я идý **домóй.**   I am going *home* (homewards).

10-7. Infinitive: идти́ (I) *to go, to walk*

This verb denotes motion *on foot*, never in a conveyance.

PRESENT TENSE

я идý	мы идём
ты идёшь	вы идёте
он идёт	они́ идýт

10-8. The Past Tense

a. The past tense of most verbs is formed by dropping the ending **-ть** from the infinitive and adding to the stem:

-л   for the masculine
-ла   for the feminine } of all three persons in the singular
-ло   for the neuter

and **-ли** for any gender of all three persons in the plural.

b. Past tense of **чита́ть.**

	Singular			Plural
	m.	*f.*	*n.*	*m., f., n.*
я	чита́л	чита́ла		мы чита́ли
ты	чита́л	чита́ла		вы чита́ли
он	чита́л			
она́		чита́ла		} они́ чита́ли
онó			чита́ло	

c. Past tense of **говори́ть.**

я	говори́л	говори́ла		мы говори́ли
ты	говори́л	говори́ла		вы говори́ли
он	говори́л			
она́		говори́ла		} они́ говори́ли
онó			говори́ло	

10-9. The Genitive with Adverbs of Quantity

After adverbs of quantity, the genitive is used:

У меня́ мно́го **рабо́ты**.   I have much work.
У Ве́ры ма́ло **рабо́ты**.   Vera has little work.

Упражне́ния (Exercises)

A. Fill in the blanks with appropriate words.

1. Мы изуча́ем англи́йский _____. 2. Уро́к о́чень _____. 3. У́тром говоря́т _____. 4. Днём говоря́т _____. 5. Ве́чером говоря́т _____. 6. У нас сего́дня _____ рабо́ты. 7. У _____ есть соба́ка? 8. В ко́мнате у меня́ _____ дива́н, _____ сту́ла, и _____ кре́сла. 9. Ла́мпа стои́т на _____ о́коло _____. 10. Мы не хоти́м жить в _____. 11. Мы тепе́рь идём _____. 12. Вы всегда́ сиди́те в _____. 13. Де́душка и ба́бушка говоря́т о́чень _____. 14. Вы _____ сиди́те у хозя́ина.

B. Supply the proper forms of the words in parentheses.

1. Они́ (жить) _____ в (дере́вня) _____. 2. Ты (идти́) _____ домо́й. 3. Вы всегда́ (сиде́ть) _____ до́ма. 4. Она́ хорошо́ (отвеча́ть) _____ в (класс) _____. 5. Учи́тельница (спра́шивать) _____, а учени́ца (отвеча́ть) _____. 6. Она́ (спра́шивать) _____ (Ива́н) _____, а пото́м (Ве́ра) _____. 7. Вы (дава́ть) _____ (учени́ца) _____ шокола́д. 8. Мы ма́ло (спать) _____ но́чью.

C. Write the following verbs in the past tense, using this form:

	SINGULAR		PLURAL	
m.	я, ты, он	игра́л	мы	
f.	я, ты, она́	игра́ла	вы	игра́ли
n.	оно́	игра́ло	они́	

1. изуча́ть   5. дава́ть   9. сиде́ть
2. спра́шивать   6. хоте́ть   10. стоя́ть
3. отвеча́ть   7. де́лать   11. люби́ть
4. игра́ть   8. писа́ть   12. понима́ть

D. Supply the accusative of the following nouns.

1. уро́к	5. Ива́н	9. сестра́
2. хозя́ин	6. Бори́с	10. муж
3. у́тро	7. оте́ц	11. де́душка
4. хозя́йка	8. брат	12. соба́ка

Перево́д (Translation)

Omit the words in parentheses and include those in brackets.

1. They are studying English [the English language]. 2. Our lesson is very interesting. 3. We work long (for a long time) in the daytime. 4. The teacher is asking Ivan. 5. Ivan answers well. 6. I say "good day" to the hostess and "hello" to the host. 7. It is already late, but I do not want to go home. 8. I work better if I sleep a lot [much], but I cannot sleep. 9. Are you still [ещё] sleeping? It is already very late. 10. Of course [коне́чно (pr. коне́шно)] it is late, but I want to sleep.

Вопро́сы (Questions)

1. У нас тепе́рь ру́сский и́ли англи́йский уро́к? 2. Что вы изуча́ете? 3. Кто спра́шивает и кто отвеча́ет? 4. Почему́ все хорошо́ отвеча́ют сего́дня? 5. Кого́ (whom) учи́тель спра́шивает? 6. Почему́ он спра́шивает Ива́на, а не Ве́ру? 7. Когда́ говоря́т "до́брое у́тро"? 8. Когда́ говоря́т "до́брый день"? 9. Когда́ говоря́т "до́брый ве́чер"? 10. Когда́ говоря́т "здра́вствуйте"? 11. Вы мно́го рабо́тали сего́дня? 12. Вы хорошо́ спи́те но́чью?

U N I T 11

I

КУДА́ ВЫ ИДЁТЕ?

1. **Па́вел:** Здра́вствуйте, Никола́й.
2. **Никола́й:** До́брое у́тро, Па́вел.
3. **П.:** Как вы пожива́ете?
4. **Н.:** О́чень хорошо́, спаси́бо.
5. **П.:** Куда́ вы идёте?
6. **Н.:** Я иду́ в парк.   А вы куда́ идёте?
7. **П.:** Я иду́ в шко́лу.
8. **Н.:** О́чень жаль, что идёте в шко́лу, а не в парк.
9. **П.:** Почему́ жаль?   Я о́чень люблю́ шко́лу.
10. **Н.:** Я то́же люблю́ шко́лу, но сего́дня о́чень хоро́ший день, и я не хочу́ сиде́ть в кла́ссе.   Я предпочита́ю гуля́ть.
11. **П.:** А я предпочита́ю шко́лу и всегда́ люблю́ сиде́ть в кла́ссе.
12. **Н.:** О́льга то́же бу́дет в па́рке.   Вы зна́ете О́льгу? Она́ о́чень краси́вая де́вушка.
13. **П.:** Коне́чно зна́ю. Она́ краса́вица! Я то́же иду́ в парк!
14. **Н.:** О нет! Вы идёте в шко́лу. До свида́ния.

Слова́рь (Vocabulary)

куда́ where to, whither
куда́ вы идёте? where are you going?
Никола́й Nicholas
Па́велⁿ (*gen.* **Па́вла**) Paul

71

как вы поживáете? how are you?
поживáть (I); поживáю, -ешь, -ют to get on
спасúбо thanks, thank you
парк park
жаль it is a pity
óчень жаль it is a great pity, it is too bad
день^я (*gen.* **дня**) day
хорóший день a beautiful day
гуля́ть (I); гуля́ю, -ешь, -ют to walk (for pleasure), to take a walk
Óльга Olga
бýдет will be (see ¶ 11-2)
дéвушка girl
конéчно (*pr.* **конéшно**) of course, certainly
красáвица beauty, a beautiful girl
до свидáния good-bye

II

ÝМНЫЙ ЧЕЛОВÉК

1. **Николáй:** Аллó!
2. **Пáвел:** Аллó! Кто у телефóна?
3. **Н:** Говори́т Николáй Смирнóв. А! Это вы, Пáвел? Здрáвствуйте! Как поживáете?
4. **П.:** Спаси́бо, óчень хорошó. А вы, Николáй?
5. **Н.:** Я тóже хорошó. Где вы сейчáс, Пáвел?
6. **П.:** Я сейчáс в дерéвне у бáбушки, но зáвтра бýду в Нью-Йóрке.
7. **Н.:** Ах, как жаль! Зáвтра я éду в Вашингтóн.
8. **П.:** Как дóлго вы там бýдете?
9. **Н.:** Мóжет быть два дня, а мóжет быть и четы́ре.
10. **П.:** А что вы бýдете дéлать в Вашингтóне?
11. **Н.:** Пожáлуйста не спрáшивайте. Это покá ещё секрéт.
12. **П.:** А! Я знáю! Óльга живёт в Вашингтóне! Онá недáвно былá в Нью-Йóрке, и вы с ней гуля́ли в пáрке.
13. **Н.:** Вы óчень ýмный человéк, но пóмните, пожáлуйста, что всё это секрéт.
14. **П.:** Хорошó. Бýду пóмнить. До свидáния.

Словáрь (Vocabulary)

ýмный clever, smart
человéк man, person
аллó! hello!

телефóн telephone
кто у телефóна? who is on the phone?
Смирнóв Smirnov
сейчáс now, right now
бýду I shall be (see ¶ 11-2)
Нью-Йóрк New York
ax! oh!
éхать (I); éду, éдешь, éдут to go (by conveyance), to ride (see ¶ 11-4)
Вашингтóн Washington
как дóлго? how long?
мóжет быть perhaps
и *here:* even
что вы бýдете дéлать? what will you be doing?
пожáлуйста (*pr.* **пожáлуста**) please
не спрáшивайте do not ask
покá (*adv.*) for the time being
покá ещё as yet, still
секрéт secret
недáвно recently
былá was (*past tense of* **быть**: **был, былá, бы́ло, бы́ли**)
с ней (*instr. of* **онá**) with her
пóмнить (II); пóмню, пóмнишь, пóмнят to remember
всё э́то all this

Граммáтика (Grammar)

Part I

11-1. The Accusative with в and на

a. **в** or **на** + the accusative indicates motion toward a given object. For example:

Я идý **в шкóлу**.	I am going *to school*.
Я идý **на концéрт**.	I am going *to a concert*.

b. With verbs of motion, **в** means *into* and is used to indicate motion to the interior of an object (one having enclosed space):

1. Я идý **в шкóлу**   means "I am going to school" (*and am also going inside it.*)

2. With **концéрт** or **урóк**, **на** must be used because these nouns designate occasions, not objects which one can enter (go inside).

c. Useful Hints: When the sentence answers the question **где?** (*where?*), use the *prepositional* with **в** or **на**; when it answers the question **кудá** (*where to? whither bound?*), use the *accusative*.

Part II

11-2. Future Tense of быть (*irr.*) *to be*

SINGULAR

я бу́ду	I shall be
ты бу́дешь	you will be
он бу́дет	he will be

PLURAL

мы бу́дем	we shall be
вы бу́дете	you will be
они́ бу́дут	they will be

Note: The present tense endings of the First Conjugation are added to the stem **буд-** to form the future of **быть**.

11-3. Compound Future Tense

a. This tense is formed by adding the infinitive to the future of **быть**:

я бу́ду чита́ть	I shall read, I shall be reading
ты бу́дешь чита́ть	you will read, you will be reading
он бу́дет чита́ть	he will read, he will be reading
мы бу́дем чита́ть	we shall read, we shall be reading
вы бу́дете чита́ть	you will read, you will be reading
они́ бу́дут чита́ть	they will read, they will be reading

b. Only verbs denoting incompleted or repeated action can be expressed in the compound future tense. All verbs given thus far belong to this category.

11-4. Infinitive: éхать (I) *to go* (*by conveyance*)

This verb denotes motion by conveyance, never on foot.

PRESENT TENSE

я éду	мы éдем
ты éдешь	вы éдете
он éдет	они́ éдут

11-5. The Imperative

The imperative is formed from the stem of the present tense (see ¶5-4).

a. If the stem ends in a consonant, add **-й** for the singular and **-йте** for the plural:

PRESENT	PRESENT STEM	IMPERATIVE
ты идёшь	ид-	идѝ go! (*fam. sing.*) идѝте go! (*pl.*, or *polite sing.*)
ты лю́бишь	люб-	любѝ love! (*fam. sing.*) любѝте love! (*pl.*, or *polite sing.*)

b. If the stem ends in a vowel, add **-й** and **-йте**:

PRESENT	PRESENT STEM	IMPERATIVE
ты чита́ешь	чита-	чита́й read! (*fam. sing.*) чита́йте read! (*pl.*, or *polite sing.*)

Упражне́ния (Exercises)

A. Supply the verb endings and put the words in parentheses in the proper case.   Indicate accents.

1. Куда́ вы ид_____? 2. Я ид_____ в (школа). 3. Почему́ вы не ед_____ в (город)? 4. Я предпочита_____ сиде́ть в (класс). 5. Вы зна_____ кто буд_____ в (парк)? 6. Нет, не зна_____. 7. Вы не помн_____ (Ольга)? 8. Коне́чно помн_____. 9. Она́ неда́вно была́ в (Нью-Йорк). 10. Что вы бу́д_____ де́лать в (деревня)?

B. Give the familiar and polite forms of the imperative for the verbs in parentheses.

1. (Отвеча́ть) гро́мко. 2. (Писа́ть) ме́дленно. 3. (Жить) в дере́вне. 4. (Знать) уро́к. 5. (Рабо́тать) у́тром. 6. (Отдыха́ть) ве́чером. 7. (Спать) но́чью. 8. (Говори́ть) по-ру́сски в кла́ссе. 9 (Изуча́ть) ру́сский язы́к. 10. (Сиде́ть) на полу́. 11. Э́то секре́т. Пожа́луйста не (спра́шивать). 12. Не (рабо́тать) так мно́го.

C. Put the first ten sentences of Exercise B in the compound future, in different persons.

Перево́д (Translation)

Omit the words in parentheses and include the words in brackets.

1. Where are you going, Nicholas?   2. I am going to school. 3. It is too bad that you are not going to the park.   4. Olga will be walking (taking a walk) in the park.   5. She is a very beautiful girl.

6. They say that she is a beauty.   7. I am going to New York if you are also going.   8. Where shall we live and what shall we be doing there?   9. Please do not ask me [**меня**].   I do not as yet know.   10. What was your sister doing yesterday?   11. She stayed home and read all day.   12. How is she?   13. Thank you, she is well.   14. And how are (your) uncle and aunt?   15. They were recently in Washington; now they are in the country.

Вопро́сы (Questions)

1. Как вы пожива́ете сего́дня?   2. Как пожива́ет ваш де́душка? ва́ша ба́бушка, ваш дя́дя, ва́ша мать?   3. Что вы де́лали сего́дня?   4. Где вы за́втра бу́дете рабо́тать?   5. Где ва́ша сестра́ была́ вчера́?   6. А где была́ вся ва́ша семья́?   7. Где вы все бу́дете за́втра?   8. Вы предпочита́ете гуля́ть в па́рке и́ли сиде́ть до́ма?   9. О́льга краси́вая де́вушка?   10. Когда́ она́ была́ в Нью-Йо́рке?   11. Когда́ ваш оте́ц бу́дет до́ма?   12. Кто о́чень у́мный челове́к?   13. Почему́ он у́мный?   14. Где сейча́с Па́вел?   15. Как до́лго Никола́й бу́дет в Вашингто́не?

U N I T 12

REVIEW LESSON

Грамма́тика (Grammar)

12-1. Table of Regular Conjugations

The forms thus far covered of the two regular conjugations are
given below. Review them thoroughly before doing the exercises.

CONJUGATION I CONJUGATION II

INFINITIVE

чита́ть to read   **говори́ть** to speak

PRESENT TENSE

я чита́ю	я говорю́
ты чита́ешь	ты говори́шь
он чита́ет	он говори́т
мы чита́ем	мы говори́м
вы чита́ете	вы говори́те
они́ чита́ют	они́ говоря́т

PAST TENSE

я, ты, он чита́л	я, ты, он говори́л
я, ты, она́ чита́ла	я, ты, она́ говори́ла
оно́ чита́ло	оно́ говори́ло
мы, вы, они́ чита́ли	мы, вы, они́ говори́ли

COMPOUND FUTURE TENSE

я бу́ду	я бу́ду
ты бу́дешь	ты бу́дешь
он бу́дет	он бу́дет
мы бу́дем }чита́ть	мы бу́дем }говори́ть
вы бу́дете	вы бу́дете
они́ бу́дут	они́ бу́дут

IMPERATIVE

чита́й	говори́
чита́йте	говори́те

77

Verb Review

A. Conjugate the following regular verbs in all the forms given in ¶ 12-1 and indicate the stress throughout. In case of doubt, refer to the vocabularies of individual lessons or the vocabulary section at the end of the book.

1. поживáть	5. гуля́ть	9. изучáть
2. пóмнить	6. спрáшивать	10. отвечáть
3. понимáть	7. дéлать	11. предпочитáть
4. знать	8. игрáть	12. рабóтать

B. The following verbs deviate from читáть or говори́ть in some respect. Conjugate them in all forms as you did the regular verbs in Exercise A, and point out or underline the irregularities in the conjugations of these verbs.

Group I. The past tense is regular and has the stress on the stem in the three genders:

1. éхать	4. давáть
2. сидéть	5. хотéть
3. люби́ть	6. писáть

Group II. The past tense is irregular or has the stress on -á in the feminine:

1. идти́ (*past:* шёл, шла, шло, шли)
2. мочь (*past:* мог, моглá, моглó, могли́) (has no *future* and no *imperative*)
3. жить (*past:* жил, жилá, жи́ло, жи́ли)
4. спать (*past:* спал, спалá, спáло, спáли)

12-2. The Interrogative Pronoun: кто

a. The interrogative pronoun кто (*who*) refers to persons or animals, whereas что (*what*) refers to objects.

b. Memorize the declension of кто before doing the remaining exercises.

nom.	кто?	who?
gen.	когó?	of whom? whose?
dat.	комý?	to whom?
acc.	когó?	whom?
instr.	кем?	by whom?
prep.	о ком?	about whom?

Comprehension Drill

A. Translate the following sentences into idiomatic English.

1. Моя́ тётя неда́вно была́ у нас.   2. Её учи́тельница то́лько оди́н год в Аме́рике.   3. Все в до́ме говоря́т о́чень гро́мко.   4. Мы ещё не говори́м по-ру́сски.   5. Они́ сего́дня ничего́ не де́лают.   6. Ива́н никогда́ ничего́ не чита́ет.   7. О́чень жаль, что вы предпочита́ете ничего́ не де́лать.   8. Студе́нты изуча́ют ру́сский язы́к.   9. Говоря́т, что его́ сестра́ краса́вица.   10. Э́то пока́ ещё секре́т.

B. Translate the following questions into idiomatic English and answer them in Russian.

1. У кого́ мой каранда́ш?   2. У кого́ есть перо́?   3. У кого́ живёт ва́ша учени́ца?   4. Вы за́втра бу́дете рабо́тать весь день?   5. Кому́ (see ¶ 8-3) вы даёте карти́ну?   6. Вы сейча́с до́ма, и́ли в дере́вне?   7. Как пожива́ет ваш де́душка?   8. Как до́лго вы бу́дете в Вашингто́не?

Pronunciation Review

A. Pronounce the following words aloud, and explain why the bold-face vowels or consonants are pronounced as they are. Review preceding sections on pronunciation for correct answers.

1. оди́н   2. е́хать   3. бли́зко   4. да́же   5. пешко́м   6. му́ж   7. до́ма   8. домо́й   9. я́зык   10. за́втра   11. маши́на   12. жить   13. шокола́д   14. не зна́ю   15. с бра́том

B. Pronounce the following accurately.

1. сего́дня   2. здра́вствуйте   3. ничего́   4. семья́   5. вся   6. всё   7. ма́ленький   8. большо́й   9. день   10. но́чью

Grammar Review

A. Change the following sentences into the past and the compound future.

1. Она́ изуча́ет ру́сский язы́к.
2. Учи́тельница спра́шивает.
3. Хозя́ин говори́т с хозя́йкой.
4. Вы понима́ете уро́к.
5. Мой брат и его́ жена́ живу́т у нас.

6. Ты даёшь газе́ту отцу́.

7. Они́ стоя́т о́коло па́рка.

B. Supply the proper case endings for the nouns or pronouns in parentheses.

1. Я живу́ с (оте́ц) и с (сестра́) в (дере́вня).

2. Кому́ вы даёте (кни́га), (учени́к) и́ли (учени́ца).

3. У (ты) в (ко́мната) три (кре́сло).

4. Учи́тель спра́шивает (Ива́н) и (Ве́ра).

5. Муж говори́т с (жена́).

Перево́д (Translation)

A. Translate orally at sight.   Omit the words in parentheses and include the words in brackets.

1. I am a good pupil (*m*.).   2. She is a good teacher.   3. You have a poor [bad] pen.   4. The whole class is here today.   5. My mother worked all day today.   6. What will you be doing at home tomorrow?   7. Do not play with the dog!   8. Do not sit on the floor!   9. They have a very ugly room.   10. She loves (her) brother and (her) sister.   11. You are a very clever person.   12. When does one say "good evening"?   13. Her new armchair is at father's.

B. Write the following sentences.

1. We have been only one year in the U.S.A.   2. They do not as yet speak Russian.   3. We understand nothing when you speak fast.   4. My teacher (*m*.) is Russian, and of course speaks Russian very well.   5. I am going to the store after work.   6. We never work anywhere.   7. How long will you be in Moscow?   8. You stayed home very long.

U N I T 13 *

I

У МЕНЯ НЕТ АВТОМОБИ́ЛЯ

Мы живём далеко́ от го́рода, и я до́лжен ходи́ть в шко́лу пешко́м. Я о́чень не люблю́ ходи́ть, но у меня́ нет автомоби́ля. У отца́ есть автомоби́ль, но он до́лжен е́здить в конто́ру о́чень ра́но. Он рабо́тает в конто́ре ка́ждый день.

Моя́ сестра́ О́льга, коне́чно, то́же хо́дит в шко́лу пешко́м, но э́то ей нра́вится. Она́ да́же говори́т, что мы живём сли́шком бли́зко от шко́лы.

Слова́рь (Vocabulary)

у меня́ нет I do not have (see ¶ 13-1)
автомоби́ль (*m.*) (*gen.* **автомоби́ля**) automobile
у меня́ нет автомоби́ля I have no automobile (see ¶ 13-1)
далеко́ (*adv.*) far
от (*with gen.*) from
до́лжен, должна́, должно́ obliged to, have to, must
ходи́ть (**II**) *hab.*† ; **хожу́, хо́дишь, хо́дят** to walk (see ¶ 13-2 & 13-3)
пешко́м (*adv.*) on foot
ходи́ть пешко́м to go on foot
я о́чень не люблю́ I very much dislike
ра́но (*adv.*) early
е́здить (**II**) *hab.*; **е́зжу** (*pr.* **е́жжу**), **е́здишь, е́здят** to go (by conveyance), to ride (see ¶ 13-3)

---

* For the sake of clarity in presentation, the *actual* and *habitual* verbs are treated in one unit. The unit, however, is intended as a *double* unit, requiring approximately twice as much time as the average unit.

† *Hab.* designates *habitual* verbs.

контóра office
кáждый, -ая, -ое every, each
ей (*dat. of* **онá**) to her
нрáвится (*pr.* **нрáвица**) is pleasing
это ей нрáвится she likes it (*lit.* this is pleasing to her)
дáже even
слúшком (*adv.*) too (much)
блúзко (*adv. followed by* **от**) (*pr.* **блúско**) near

II

КАК ЖАЛЬ!

У нас в дóме живёт наш рýсский учúтель, господúн Смирнóв. У господúна Смирнóва есть нóвый, хорóший автомобúль, но он всегдá предпочитáет ходúть пешкóм в шкóлу. Сегóдня идёт дождь, но автомобúль господúна Смирнóва стоúт в гаражé, а господúн Смирнóв идёт в шкóлу пешкóм. Почемý он не éдет? Я не понимáю зачéм он купúл автомобúль!

Господúн Смирнóв знáет, что мне óчень нрáвится егó автомобúль, и он иногдá даёт егó мне. Одúн раз он дал мне автомобúль на четýре дня. Но мне нýжен автомобúль кáждый день! Сегóдня вéчером хочý éхать с Вéрой в теáтр, но у меня нет автомобúля. Как жаль!

Словáрь (Vocabulary)

как жаль! what a pity!
дождь (*m.*) rain
идёт дождь it is raining
гарáж garage
зачéм why, wherefore
купúл (*past of* **купúть**) bought
мне (*dat. of* **я**) to me
мне нрáвится I like
иногдá sometimes
егó (*acc. of* **он**) it, him
раз time (occasion)
одúн раз once
дал (*past of* **дать**) gave
четýре four
на четýре дня for four days
нýжен, нужнá, нýжно necessary

мне нýжен I need (see ¶ 13-6)
сегóдня вéчером tonight, this evening
теáтр theater

Грамматика (Grammar)

Part I

13-1. Possessive Phrases in the Negative

a. The present tense of the verb *to have* in the negative is rendered thus:

SINGULAR		PLURAL	
у меня нет		у нас нет	
у тебя нет	} + genitive	у вас нет	} + genitive
у негó нет		у них нет	
у неё нет			

b. Compare the negative construction with the affirmative:

AFFIRMATIVE (see ¶ 9-2)

У меня **есть** газéта.   I have a newspaper.
У меня **есть** автомобиль.   I have an automobile.

NEGATIVE

У меня **нет** газéты.   I have no newspaper. (I do not have any newspaper.)

У меня **нет** автомобиля.   I have no automobile. (I do not have any automobile.)

13-2. Verbs of Motion

a. Verbs of motion in Russian do not indicate direction. Direction is indicated by prepositions or by prefixes. For example:

Я идý **в** контóру.   I am *going* to the office.
                               (**в** = *into*)

Я идý **из** контóры.   I am *coming* from the office.
                               (**из** = *out of*)

Я **при**хожý* в контóру.   I *arrive* at the office.
                               (**при** = *arrival at*)

Я **у**хожý* **из** контóры.   I *leave* the office.
                               (**у** = *departure from*)

* In the grammar, unfamiliar words are used only as illustrations, and are not to be memorized.

b. The distinction is always made in Russian between motion on foot, and motion by means of a conveyance.   For example:

Я **иду́** в конто́ру.	I am going (*on foot*) to the office.
Я **е́ду** в конто́ру.	I am going (*not on foot*) to the office.

13-3. Actual and Habitual Forms of Verbs :

идти́ and ходи́ть
е́хать and е́здить

Verbs of motion have two distinct forms: the *actual* and the *habitual*.

a. The *actual* verb implies *actual* performance at a *given time*, not merely *possible* performance at unspecified times.   It is specific with regard to:

1. The *direction* of the motion.

Я е́ду в конто́ру	I am going (by conveyance) to the office. (I am bound for the office.)

2. The *time* the action *actually* takes place.

Я е́ду домо́й.	I am going home. (I am actually on my way home.)
Я за́втра е́ду домо́й.	I am going home tomorrow. (I will actually be on my way home tomorrow.)

b. The *habitual* verb implies *possible* performance at an unspecified time or at various times.   It is *general* and *indefinite* with regard to:

1. The direction of the motion.

Я хожу́, когда́ у меня́ нет автомоби́ля.	I walk when I have no car. (Walking could be in any direction, or aimless.)

2. Time of possible performance.

In the sentence above, the action takes place when no car is available.   But we do not know when this happens.   A car may always be available and the action may never actually take place, and only remain *possible* forever.

c. Present tense of $\begin{cases} \text{идти́ (I) — ходи́ть (II)} \textit{ to go (on foot)} \\ \text{е́хать (I) — е́здить (II)} \textit{ to go (by con-} \\ \qquad\qquad\qquad\qquad\qquad\qquad \textit{veyance)} \end{cases}$

ACTUAL	HABITUAL	ACTUAL	HABITUAL
идти́ (I)	**ходи́ть** (II)	**е́хать** (I)	**е́здить** (II)
я иду́	я хожу́	я е́ду	я е́зжу
ты идёшь	ты хо́дишь	ты е́дешь	ты е́здишь
он идёт	он хо́дит	он е́дет	он е́здит
мы идём	мы хо́дим	мы е́дем	мы е́здим
вы идёте	вы хо́дите	вы е́дете	вы е́здите
они́ иду́т	они́ хо́дят	они́ е́дут	они́ е́здят

Part II

13-4. Dative of Personal Pronouns

SINGULAR

nom.	*dat.*	*meaning*
я	мне	to me
ты	тебе́	to you
он	ему́	to him
она́	ей	to her
оно́	ему́	to it

PLURAL

мы	нам	to us
вы	вам	to you
они́	им	to them

13-5. "To like" in Russian

When the object liked is in the singular, the verb *to like* is rendered thus:

Мне нра́вится учи́тель.	I like the teacher (*lit.* the teacher is pleasing to me).
Тебе́ нра́вится моя́ сестра́.	You like my sister.
Им нра́вится наш дом.	They like our house.

Note: The direct object of the English sentence becomes the subject of the Russian sentence. Therefore, before translating into Russian such sentences as "I like the teacher," paraphrase it as "The teacher is pleasing to me."

13-6. Ну́жен, нужна́, and ну́жно

In constructions using **ну́жен, нужна́,** or **ну́жно** (meaning *necessary*), the subject of the English sentence must be expressed in the dative.   For example:

Мне ну́жен автомоби́ль.   I need a car (*lit.* to me, a car is necessary).

Бра́ту нужна́ соба́ка.   Brother needs a dog.

Тебе́ ну́жно перо́.   You need a pen.

Им нужна́ ко́мната.   They need a room.

Что **ему́** ну́жно?   What does he need (want)?

Note: In this construction, the gender of the thing needed determines the gender of the word for *necessary*.

Упражне́ния (Exercises)

A. Supply the opposites of the words and phrases given, and use them in sentences.   For example:

по́здно — Сего́дня я **ра́но** е́ду в парк.

1. далеко́ от   2. у неё есть   3. гро́мко   4. ме́дленно   5. краси́вое   6. но́вая   7. большо́й   8. всегда́   9. там   10. хорошо́   11. ма́ло   12. до свида́ния

B. Replace the words in parentheses with appropriate Russian equivalents.

1. У него́ есть (paper), но у него́ нет (pencil).   2. Она́ живёт (far), но у неё нет (automobile).   3. У нас нет (garage), но у нас есть (automobile).   4. У них нет (divan), но у них есть (armchair).   5. Мы ка́ждый день (go on foot) в (theater).   6. Куда́ ты тепе́рь (going on foot)?   7. Господи́н Смирно́в никогда́ не (walks) в (school).   8. (I need) газе́та, а (she needs) журна́л.   9. (We need) учи́тель, а (they need) учи́тельница.   10. (You need) кре́сло.   11. (Sister needs) рабо́та.   12. (Father needs) конто́ра.

C. Fill in the appropriate verb form.   Make sure that you are using the correct verb of motion.

1. Сего́дня мы _____ (on foot) в парк.   2. Они́ всегда́ _____ (by conveyance) в го́род.   3. Куда́ она́

теперь _____ (by conveyance)? 4. Они каждый день
_____ (on foot) в город? 5. Вы сегодня вечером
_____ (on foot) в театр. 6. Куда вы каждый день
_____ (by conveyance) так быстро?

D. Supply the personal pronoun in the proper case.

1. Он дал (me) _____ карандаш. Карандаш теперь
у _____. 2. Я даю (her) книгу. Книга теперь у
_____. 3. Вы даёте (them) _____ лампу. Лампа
теперь у _____. 4. Они дают (you, *fam.*) _____
бумагу. Бумага теперь у _____. 5. Мы даём (you, *pl.*)
_____ картину. Картина теперь у _____.
6. Они дают (us) _____ карту. Карта теперь у _____.

Перевод (Translation)

A. Omit words in parentheses and include those in brackets:

1. My uncle has to be in the store every day. 2. He works (a
great deal) [much], but he likes it. 3. He even says that his work
in the store is interesting. 4. He lives near [from] the store and
always walks [on foot]. 5. Why [wherefore] did you buy a car?
It stays [**стоит**] in the garage, and you walk. 6. I prefer to walk,
but it is raining today. What a pity! 7. Once you gave the car to
(your) brother for four days. 8. I need a car tonight because I am
going to the theater.

B. Omit words in parentheses and include those in brackets.
The corrected translation can be used for additional oral work—for
questions and answers, or as a dialogue between two students.

1. Where are you going (walking)?
2. I am going to the office.
3. Why aren't you riding?
4. I am not riding because I have no car.
5. I know that you (do) have a car. Where is it now?
6. My wife has it now. [It is now by (my) wife.]
7. It is raining now, but you are going on foot, and she is riding!
8. She always rides and I always walk.
9. I do not understand why you give her the car. It is your car.
10. It is my car, but she is my wife and I love her.
11. Does she love you too?
12. Of course!

13. Why then [**Почему́ же**] does she not walk?

14. You have no wife and you do not understand anything [you nothing not understand].

15. I have no wife, but I always have a car!

Вопро́сы (**Questions**)

1. Вы живёте далеко́ и́ли бли́зко от го́рода?   2. Вы хо́дите и́ли е́здите в шко́лу?   3. Вы предпочита́ете ходи́ть пешко́м и́ли е́здить?   4. Когда́ ваш оте́ц до́лжен е́здить в конто́ру?   5. Кто живёт у вас в до́ме?   6. Когда́ идёт дождь, господи́н Смирно́в хо́дит и́ли е́здит в шко́лу?   7. Вы понима́ете заче́м господи́н Смирно́в купи́л автомоби́ль?   8. Вам нра́вится автомоби́ль господи́на Смирно́ва?   9. Заче́м вам сего́дня ну́жен автомоби́ль?   10. С кем (see ¶ 8-2) вы е́хали в теа́тр вчера́?   11. Как ча́сто (how often) вы е́здите в го́род?   12. Заче́м вам ну́жен автомоби́ль ка́ждый день?   13. Кто вам дал автомоби́ль на четы́ре дня?   14. Автомоби́ль господи́на Смирно́ва сли́шком большо́й и́ли сли́шком ма́ленький?   15. Когда́ вы бу́дете рабо́тать в конто́ре?

U N I T 14

ДА́ЧА НА БЕРЕГУ́ МО́РЯ

1. — Где вы тепе́рь живёте?
2. — Я живу́ на да́че.
1. — Кто ещё там живёт?
2. — Вся на́ша семья́ там живёт.
1. — Когда́ вы живёте на да́че?
2. — Весно́й и ле́том.
1. — А где вы живёте о́сенью и зимо́й?
2. — О́сенью и зимо́й мы живём в го́роде.
1. — Вам нра́вится ва́ша да́ча?
2. — Она́ нам о́чень нра́вится, потому́ что она́ о́чень краси́вая и нахо́дится на берегу́ мо́ря.
1. — Кто купи́л э́ту краси́вую да́чу, вы и́ли ваш оте́ц?
2. — Оте́ц купи́л её.
1. — Како́го она́ цве́та?
2. — Она́ си́него цве́та.
1. — Вам наве́рно нра́вится э́тот цвет?
2. — Что зна́чит "наве́рно"? Я не зна́ю э́того сло́ва.
1. — Наве́рно зна́чит "surely."
2. — О да! Си́ний цвет мне о́чень нра́вится. Моя́ ко́мната то́же си́няя. Неда́вно я купи́л си́нюю ва́зу и си́нее кре́сло.
1. — Вы наве́рно лю́бите смотре́ть на мо́ре, потому́ что оно́ си́нее.
2. — Коне́чно. Я ча́сто сижу́ у окна́ и смотрю́ на си́нее мо́ре. Это ваш после́дний вопро́с?
1. — Да.
2. — Ну, сла́ва бо́гу!

89

Слова́рь (Vocabulary)

да́ча summer house
бе́рег (when governed by **в** or **на**, the *prep.* **берегу́** is used) shore
на берегу́ on the shore
мо́ре (*n.*) (*gen.* **мо́ря**) sea
на да́че (**на** is used instead of **в** with **да́ча**) at a summer house
весно́й (*adv.*) in the spring
ле́том (*adv.*) in the summer
о́сенью (*adv.*) in the fall
зимо́й (*adv.*) in the winter
нахо́дится (*pr.* **нахо́дица**) is situated
э́тот, э́та, э́то (*pron.*) this (see ¶ 14-1)
краси́вую *acc. of* **краси́вая** (see ¶ 14-2)
цвет color
како́й, кака́я, како́е what kind of
како́го (*pr.* **како́во**) **цве́та**? (of) what color?
си́ний, си́няя, си́нее blue
си́него цве́та (of) blue color
наве́рно surely, most likely
зна́чит means
сло́во word
ва́за vase
смотре́ть (II); **смотрю́, смо́тришь, смо́трят** to look
смотре́ть на (+ *acc.*) to look at
после́дний, после́дняя, после́днее last, final
вопро́с question
ну well!
сла́ва бо́гу! thank goodness! (*lit.* Glory to God!)

О́ЧЕНЬ ПРИЛЕ́ЖНЫЙ УЧЕНИ́К

1. **Учи́тель:** Почему́ вы сего́дня не зна́ете уро́ка?
2. **Учени́к:** Я не зна́ю уро́ка, потому́ что у меня́ нет кни́ги.
3. **Уч:** Почему́ у вас нет кни́ги?
4. **У:** У меня́ нет кни́ги, потому́ что у меня́ нет автомоби́ля.
5. **Уч:** Что э́то за ответ: "Не зна́ю уро́ка, потому́ что у меня́ нет автомоби́ля"? Что́бы знать уро́к вам не ну́жен автомоби́ль, вам нужна́ кни́га!
6. **У:** Коне́чно мне нужна́ кни́га. Но кни́га в автомоби́ле, а автомоби́ль тепе́рь в Нью-Йо́рке.
7. **Уч:** Ничего́ не понима́ю.
8. **У:** У меня́ но́вый автомоби́ль, и оте́ц ча́сто берёт его́.
9. **Уч:** Хорошо́! А где ва́ше сочине́ние?
10. **У:** Тетра́дь с сочине́нием то́же в автомоби́ле.
11. **Уч:** Како́й приле́жный учени́к!

Слова́рь (Vocabulary)

приле́жный, -ая, -ое diligent
отве́т answer
что э́то за отве́т? what kind of an answer is that?
что́бы in order to
ча́сто often
брать (II); беру́, берёшь, беру́т ; *past* брал, -ла́, -ло, -ли to take
сочине́ние (*n.*) (*instr.* сочине́нием) composition
тетра́дь (*f.*) notebook
како́й, -а́я, -о́е what a . . .

Грамма́тика (Grammar)

14-1. The Demonstrative Pronoun: э́тот, э́та, э́то

	m.	*f.*	*n.*
nom.	э́тот	э́та	э́то
gen.	э́того*	э́той	э́того*
acc.	э́тот *or* э́того*	э́ту	э́то

Note : In the masculine, pronouns and adjectives modifying *inanimate* objects are identical in the nominative and accusative; those modifying *animate* objects are identical in the genitive and accusative.

14-2. Declensions of Adjectives

a. Adjectival endings: *hard and soft.*

1. The last two letters of the adjective constitute its ending.
2. Compare the endings of the following two adjectives :

m.	*f.*	*n.*	*endings*
краси́вый	краси́вая	краси́вое	(-ый, -ая, -ое)
после́дний	после́дняя	после́днее	(-ий, -яя, -ее)

3. The last letter for each gender is the same in both adjectives (-й, -я, and -е), whereas the letter *next to the last* in the first adjective is a hard vowel (-ы-, -а-, and -о-), and in the second adjective a soft vowel (-и-, -я-, and -е-). These vowels determine the nature of the ending, which is accordingly *hard* or *soft.*

b. There are three declensions of adjectives, depending upon the nature of their endings:

* -ого is pronounced -ово.

1 *Hard* adjectives, having hard endings throughout.

но́в**ый**	но́в**ая**	но́в**ое**	(new)
молод**о́й**	молод**а́я**	молод**о́е**	(young)

2. *Soft* adjectives, having soft endings throughout.

си́н**ий**	си́н**яя**	си́н**ее**	(blue)

3. *Mixed* adjectives, having some soft and some hard endings.

ру́сск**ий**	ру́сск**ая**	ру́сск**ое**	(Russian)

Note: The masculine form is soft, whereas the feminine and neuter forms are hard.

c. Adjectives ending in **-о́й, -а́я, -о́е** (e.g., молод**о́й, -а́я, -о́е**) are always stressed on the ending; all others on the stem.

Never stressed on ending	*Always stressed on ending*
hard: **-ый, -ая, -ое**	*hard:* **-о́й, -а́я, -о́е**
soft: **-ий, -яя, -ее**	
mixed: **-ий, -ая, -ое**	

d. See page 93 for a table of case endings in the singular.

14-3. Direct Object of a Negative Verb

The direct object of a verb in the negative is usually in the genitive instead of in the accusative:

Я не зна́ю уро́к**а**.	I do not know the lesson.
Я не зна́ю **э́той** де́вушк**и**.	I do not know this girl.
Она́ не изуча́ла англи́йск**ого** язык**а́**.	She did not study English.

However, with verbs in the affirmative the direct object is in the accusative:

Я зна́ю уро́к.	I know the lesson.
Я зна́ю **э́ту** де́вушку.	I know this girl.

14-4. Мне нра́вится and я люблю́

a. **мне нра́вится** means *I like*, and refers to an object or a person producing a favorable impression, especially on first acquaintance:

Мне **нра́вится** Нью-Йо́рк.	I *like* New York. (I am favorably impressed — without knowing New York well.)
Мне **нра́вится** Ве́ра.	I *like* Vera.

CASE ENDINGS OF ADJECTIVES IN THE SINGULAR

Case	Hard		
	masculine	*feminine*	*neuter*
nom.	но́в**ый** журна́л но́в**ый** учени́к	но́в**ая** газе́та но́в**ая** учени́ца	но́в**ое** сло́во
gen.	но́в**ого** журна́ла но́в**ого** ученика́	но́в**ой** газе́ты но́в**ой** учени́цы	но́в**ого** сло́ва
acc.	но́в**ый** журна́л но́в**ого** ученика́	но́в**ую** газе́ту но́в**ую** учени́цу	но́в**ое** сло́во
	Soft		
nom.	после́дн**ий** журна́л после́дн**ий** учени́к	после́дн**яя** газе́та после́дн**яя** учени́ца	после́дн**ее** сло́во
gen.	после́дн**его** журна́ла после́дн**его** ученика́	после́дн**ей** газе́ты после́дн**ей** учени́цы	после́дн**его** сло́ва
acc.	после́дн**ий** журна́л после́дн**его** ученика́	после́дн**юю** газе́ту после́дн**юю** учени́цу	после́дн**ее** сло́во
	Mixed		
nom.	ру́сск**ий** журна́л ру́сск**ий** учсни́к	ру́сск**ая** газе́та ру́сск**ая** учени́ца	ру́сск**ое** сло́во
gen.	ру́сск**ого** журна́ла ру́сск**ого** ученика́	ру́сск**ой** газе́ты ру́сск**ой** учени́цы	ру́сск**ого** сло́ва
acc.	ру́сск**ий** журна́л ру́сск**ого** ученика́	ру́сск**ую** газе́ту ру́сск**ую** учени́цу	ру́сск**ое** сло́во

b. **я люблю́** means *I am fond of* or *I love*, and implies some attachment or emotion:

Я люблю́ Нью-Йо́рк.   I *am fond* of New York (as a result of knowledge or habit).

Я люблю́ Ве́ру.   I *love* Vera (with deep emotion, irrespective of knowledge).

c. When "liking" refers to a verb, it is rendered by **люби́ть**:

Я люблю́ смотре́ть на мо́ре.   I *like to look* at the sea.

Упражнéния (Exercises)

A. Decline the following phrases in the *nominative, genitive,* and *accusative.*

1. э́тот отвéт   2. э́та вáза   3. э́то слóво   4. э́тот дóктор
5. прилéжный учени́к   6. прилéжная учени́ца   7. у́мный человéк   8. си́няя бумáга   9. си́нее окнó   10. ру́сская дéвушка
11. си́ний цвет   12. ру́сский теáтр   13. какáя рабóта   14.
мáленький брат   15. плохáя кóмната

B. Translate the following phrases.

1. blue notebook   2. good answer   3. last word   4. diligent
student (*f*.)   5. blue sea   6. beautiful summer house   7. good
hostess   8. this girl   9. interesting lesson   10. What a clever
dog!   11. last big town   12. last small village   13. What a good
composition!   14. What kind of a question is this?   15. Thank
goodness!

C. Change the following affirmative sentences to negative ones.
For example:

Я пишу́ урóк. — Я **не** пишу́ урóк**а**.

У меня́ **есть** ру́ск**ая** кни́г**а**. — У меня́ **нет** ру́ск**ой** кни́г**и**.

1. Ты берёшь кни́гу.   2. У негó есть гарáж.   3. Мы
изучáем ру́сский язы́к (*gen.* **языкá**).   4. Онá купи́ла по-
слéднюю вáзу.   5. Я знáю э́ту стáрую учи́тельницу.   6. Они́
пóмнят секрéт.   7. У них есть дáча.   8. Вы понимáете вопрóс.
9. Вы пóмните э́того человéка.   10. У них есть си́ний дивáн.

Перевóд (Translation)

A. Omit words in parentheses and include words in brackets.

1. I do not know this town.   2. They did not know the last
lesson.   3. She did not remember this Russian word.   4. We do
not like her room.   5. She does not like blue [color].   6. They
do not like your family, but they like you.   7. You surely like to sit
at the window and look at the new summer house.

B. Omit words in parentheses and include words in brackets.

1. We shall live at the summer house in the spring.   2. In the
summer grandfather and grandmother will also live at our house.
3. They like the sea very (much).   4. They often go (by conveyance) to the summer house, even in the winter.   5. Our summer

house is situated on the sea shore [on the shore of the sea].   6. It
(the summer house) is far from town, and we need a car [in order to]
to go (drive) to the store.   7. I often take father's car [in order to]
to drive to town in the evening.   8. I like to drive (go by conveyance) in the evening or at night.

Вопро́сы (Questions)

1. Где вы живёте зимо́й?   2. Вы та́кже живёте там ле́том?
3. Что вы де́лаете в го́роде?   4. Что вы де́лаете на да́че?
5. Где нахо́дится ва́ша да́ча?   6. Мо́ре далеко́ от да́чи?
7. Вы лю́бите смотре́ть на мо́ре?   8. Како́го цве́та мо́ре?
9. Вам нра́вится э́тот цвет?   10. Вам нра́вится ва́ша да́ча?
11. Кто купи́л э́ту да́чу?   12. Что оте́ц ча́сто берёт у вас?
13. Где ва́ша тстра́дь с сочине́нием?   14. Вы ча́сто е́здите в
Нью-Йо́рк?   15. Вы приле́жный учени́к?   16. Вам нра́вится
э́тот вопро́с?

U N I T 15

I

МАКСИ́М ИВА́НОВИЧ БО́ЛЕН

Макси́м Ива́нович бо́лен. У него́ нет аппети́та. Он почти́ ничего́ не ест и о́чень ма́ло спит. У него́ боли́т голова́. Иногда́ он пьёт немно́го воды́ и́ли молока́ и ест немно́го су́па. Это всё, что он мо́жет пить и́ли есть.

Он уже́ це́лую неде́лю сиди́т до́ма и не хо́дит в конто́ру. Весь день он лежи́т на дива́не и ничего́ не де́лает. Почему́ он не идёт к до́ктору?

Слова́рь (Vocabulary)

Макси́м Maxim
Ива́нович Ivanovich (*lit.* son of Ivan) (see ¶ 15-1)
бо́лен (*adj.*, *m.*), **больна́** (*f.*) sick
аппети́т appetite
почти́ almost
ест eats
есть (*irr.*) to eat (see ¶ 15-2)
боли́т aches
голова́ (*gen.* **головы́**) head
у него́ боли́т голова́ his head aches
пить (**I**); **пью, пьёшь, пьют;** *past* **пил, -ла́, -ло, -ли;** *imper.* **пей, пе́йте** to drink
немно́го a little
вода́ water
молоко́ milk
суп soup
э́то всё that is all
це́лый, -ая, -ое whole
неде́ля (*f.*) week
це́лую неде́лю a whole week (see ¶ 15-3 & 15-4)
лежа́ть (**II**); **лежу́, лежи́шь, лежа́т** to lie
к (with *dat.*) to, towards (see ¶ 15-5)

II

ТЕБЕ́ НУ́ЖЕН СПЕЦИАЛИ́СТ

А́нна Никола́евна, жена́ Макси́ма Ива́новича, ду́мает, что её муж серьёзно бо́лен. Она́ зна́ет, что у него́ всегда́ мно́го эне́ргии, когда́ он здоро́в. Тепе́рь же он весь день лежи́т на дива́не и ничего́ не де́лает. Он да́же не слу́шает ра́дио и не смо́трит телеви́зор.

— Макси́м, — говори́т А́нна Никола́евна — вот хоро́ший суп. Ку́шай, пожа́луйста.

— Нет, спаси́бо — отвеча́ет Макси́м Ива́нович — ничего́ не могу́ есть.

— Почему́ же ты не идёшь к до́ктору? Ты уже́ це́лую неде́лю не рабо́таешь, ничего́ не ешь и почти́ не спишь.

— Я уже́ был у до́ктора две неде́ли тому́ наза́д, и мне тепе́рь ху́же, а не лу́чше.

— Тебе́ ну́жен специали́ст. Бори́с Никола́евич большо́й специали́ст. Пожа́луйста, Макси́м . . .

— Хорошо́! хорошо́! Я зна́ю, что мне ну́жен специали́ст. За́втра у́тром иду́ к Бори́су Никола́евичу. Он живёт о́коло университе́та, и э́то о́чень бли́зко.

— Ну, спаси́бо, Макси́м! Я о́чень ра́да, что ты за́втра бу́дешь у специали́ста.

Слова́рь (Vocabulary)

специали́ст specialist
Никола́евна Nikolaevna (see ¶ 15-1)
ду́мать (I); **ду́маю, -ешь, -ют** to think
серьёзно seriously
эне́ргия (*pr.* эне́ргия) energy
же however, but
слу́шать (I); **слу́шаю, -ешь, -ют** to listen to
ра́дио (*n.*) (*not decl.*) radio
телеви́зор television set
смотре́ть телеви́зор to watch television
ку́шать (I); **ку́шаю, -ешь, -ют** to eat (see ¶ 15-6)
две (*f.*) two
тому́ наза́д ago
ху́же (*adv.*) worse
мне ху́же I feel worse
мне лу́чше I feel better
хорошо́! O.K., all right
за́втра у́тром tomorrow morning
университе́т university
рад (*m.*), **ра́да** (*f.*) glad

Грамма́тика (Grammar)

Part I

15-1. Patronymics

a. *Patronymics* are names formed by the addition of a suffix to the father's first name.

b. The following are common suffixes:

m.	**-ович,**	**-евич**
f.	**-овна,**	**-евна**

c. Patronymics are formed thus:

Ива́н + **ович** = Ива́н**ович**	(*lit.* son of Ivan)
Никола́(й) + **евич** = Никола́**евич**	(*lit.* son of Nicholas)
Ива́н + **овна** = Ива́н**овна**	(*lit.* daughter of Ivan)
Никола́(й) + **евна** = Никола́**евна**	(*lit.* daughter of Nicholas)

d. The first name and the patronymic are used by Russians in addressing each other, unless they are relatives or close friends. For example: **Макси́м Ива́нович, Ве́ра Ива́новна.**

Note: **Господи́н** or **госпожа́** can never be used alone as a form of address. The surname must always accompany it.

15-2. Infinitive: есть (*irr.*) *to eat*

Note: Do not confuse **е́хать** with **есть.**

a. Present tense.

я ем	мы еди́м
ты ешь	вы еди́те
он ест	они́ едя́т

b. Past tense.

ел,   е́ла,   е́ло,   е́ли

c. Compound future.

я бу́ду есть, *etc.* (see ¶ **11-3**)

15-3. Expressions of Time with the Accusative

To express length of time or recurrence in time, the accusative without a preposition is used:

весь день	the whole day
це́лую неде́лю	a whole week
ка́ждое у́тро	every morning

15-4. Present Tense Used as English Present Perfect

To indicate an action which has been going on and is continued in the present, the present tense is used.   For example:

Я ужé в Москвé три дня.	I have been in Moscow three days (*i.e.*, have been and am *now* in Moscow).
Он ужé цéлую недéлю не рабóтает.	He has not been working for a whole week (*i.e.*, has not been and is not *now* working).

15-5. The Dative with Verbs of Motion

The preposition **к** + dative is used to indicate:

a. Motion toward an object (*up to it, but not inside it*).

Я идý к окнý.	I am going to the window (*up to it*).
Я идý к доскé.	I am going to the board.

b. A person as the destination.

Я идý к сестрé.	I am going to my sister's (*i.e.*, to her *place*, or to *see* her).
Я идý к дóктору.	I am going to the doctor.

Note: In the above examples, motion is not to the interior of the object; otherwise **в** (*into*) would have to be used.   Compare:

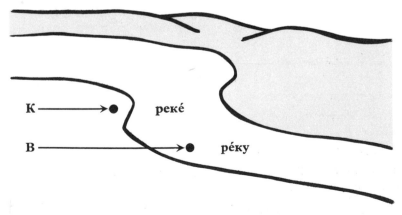

Я идý **к** рекé.	I am going *to* the river (*up to it*).
Я идý **в** рéку.	I am going *into* the river.

Part II

15-6. The Verbs "to eat": есть and кушать

a. **Есть** is the conversational form.   It should be used in the first person.

b. Politeness requires the use of **кушать** instead of **есть** in the second person, especially in the imperative.

15-7. Declension of Nouns

There are three declensions of nouns in Russian.   These are determined on the basis of gender.

a. First Declension — membership.

1. All feminine nouns ending in **-а**, **-я**, or **-ия** in the nominative singular belong to the First Declension.   For example:

ка́рта, неде́ля, а́рмия (army).

2. A few masculine nouns with feminine endings, such as де́душка, дя́дя, or Ва́ня, also belong to the First Declension. Although they are declined as feminine nouns, they are otherwise treated as masculine.   For example:

Мой де́душка хоро́ший учи́тель.
My grandfather is a good teacher.

b. The declensions are subdivided into two classes of nouns: *hard* and *soft*.

1. Nouns ending in **-а** are *hard*; those in **-я** or **-ия** are *soft*.

2. The inflection of soft nouns in **-я** differs from that of the hard vowels in **-а** only in the substitution of soft vowels for the corresponding hard ones.

c. First Declension in the singular.

	Hard	Soft		
	-а	**-я**		**-ия**
nom.	ка́рта	неде́ля	дя́дя	а́рмия
gen.	ка́рты	неде́ли	дя́ди	а́рмии
dat.	ка́рте	неде́ле	дя́де	а́рмии
acc.	ка́рту	неде́лю	дя́дю	а́рмию
instr.	ка́ртой (**-ою**)	неде́лей (**-ею**)	дя́дей (**-ею**)	а́рмией (**-ею**)
prep.	о ка́рте	о неде́ле	о дя́де	об а́рмии

1. The preposition **o**, meaning *about* or *concerning*, is used so frequently with the prepositional that it is usually included in declension tables.   Before a vowel, **об** is used instead of **o**.

2. In the singular, the accusative endings of animate and inanimate nouns are identical.   Compare : дя́дю with неде́лю.

Упражне́ния (Exercises)

A. Put the words in parentheses in the appropriate case, and fill in the blanks with appropriate words.

1. (Я) тепе́рь ху́же.   2. (Макси́м Ива́нович) ху́же, а не
_____.   3. Почему́ вы не идёте к (до́ктор), е́сли вам
_____?   4. Вы пьёте мно́го (во́да), но ничего́ не
_____.   5. Мы говори́м с (дя́дя) об (а́рмия).   6. Она́
ча́сто _____ к (ба́бушка).   7. Ба́бушка уже́ четы́ре
(неде́ля) живёт на (да́ча).   8. Да́ча нахо́дится на _____
мо́ря.   9. У отца́ боли́т _____.   10. Мы лю́бим смо-
тре́ть на (си́няя ва́за).   11. У них нет (аппети́т).   12. Она́ уже́
(це́лая неде́ля) сиди́т _____.

B. Decline the following in the singular.

1. ко́мната		5. эне́ргия
2. кни́га		6. ва́за
3. тётя		7. ко́нтора
4. де́душка		8. дя́дя

C. Conjugate the following verbs in the present, past, and compound future.

1. есть		6. смотре́ть
2. ку́шать		7. ду́мать
3. пить		8. ходи́ть
4. лежа́ть		9. е́здить
5. слу́шать		10. брать

Перево́д (Translation)

Include words in brackets.

1. Anna Nikolaevna is sick [**больна́**].   2. She always has a headache.   3. She eats almost nothing.   4. Yesterday she drank a little water, but ate nothing.   5. She has no energy, and she lies all day on the divan.   6. Her husband thinks that she needs a

doctor.   7. Every day he asks her [**её**] why she does not go to a
doctor.   8. Every day she answers that she is well, and that she does
not need a doctor.   9. But she stays home and does not go to the
office.   10. She likes very much to listen to the radio or to look at
television.   11. Now, however [**же**], she does nothing all day.
12. She likes very much to go to the theater, but now she does not
even want to talk about the theater.   13. Nothing pleases her now
[**Ничего́ ей тепе́рь не нра́вится**].   14. Her husband thinks
that she is seriously ill, but what can [**мо́жет**] he do?

Вопро́сы (Questions)

1. Кто бо́лен? 2. Почему́ у Макси́ма Ива́новича нет
аппети́та? 3. Его́ жена́, А́нна Никола́евна, то́же больна́?
4. У неё есть аппети́т? 5. Что боли́т у Макси́ма Ива́новича?
6. Что он мо́жет есть и пить? 7. Э́то всё что он мо́жет есть?
8. Как до́лго он уже́ сиди́т до́ма? 9. Что он де́лает весь день?
10. Он слу́шает ра́дио? 11. Он смо́трит телеви́зор? 12. Вы
ду́маете, что он серьёзно бо́лен? 13. Почему́ он не идёт к
до́ктору? 14. У кого́ он уже́ был две неде́ли тому́ наза́д?
15. Кто большо́й специали́ст? 16. Где живёт э́тот специа-
ли́ст? 17. Жена́ ра́да, что её муж за́втра идёт к специали́сту?

U N I T 16

I

ИЗ ДНЕВНИКА́ МОЛОДО́Й ДЕ́ВУШКИ—У́тром

Сего́дня о́чень плоха́я пого́да. Не́бо се́рое. Идёт дождь. Хо́лодно. В ко́мнате темно́. Мне ску́чно. Чита́ть нс хочу́. Игра́ть на роя́ле не хочу́. За́втра у меня́ экза́мен, но я ничего́ не де́лаю. То́лько сижу́ у окна́ и смотрю́ на се́рое не́бо, на дождь и на пусту́ю у́лицу.

Всё у́тро ду́маю об Аки́ме. Почему́ его́ ещё нет? Мо́жет быть он забы́л, что я его́ жду . . . Нет, не мо́жет быть! Он тако́й ми́лый и так меня́ лю́бит! . . . Он ча́сто говори́т мнс: "Кака́я ты краса́вица, Ма́ша!"

Слова́рь (Vocabulary)

из (*with gen.*) from, out of
дневни́к (*gen.* **дневника́**) diary
молодо́й, -а́я, -о́е young
пого́да weather
не́бо sky
се́рый, -ая, -ое gray
хо́лодно it is cold (see ¶ 16-1)
темно́ it is dark
мне ску́чно I am bored
роя́ль (*m.*) piano
игра́ть на роя́ле to play the piano (see ¶ 16-2)
экза́мен examination
пусто́й, -а́я, -о́е empty, deserted
у́лица street
Аки́м Joachim

103

егó ещё нет he is not here yet (see ¶ 16-3)
забы́л (*past of* **забы́ть**) forgot
ждать (I); **жду, ждёшь, ждут** to wait
не мóжет быть (it is) impossible
такóй, -áя, -óе such a . . .
ми́лый, -ая, -ое nice, dear, lovely
он такóй ми́лый he is such a dear
так (*adv.*) so

II

ИЗ ДНЕВНИКÁ МОЛОДÓЙ ДÉВУШКИ—Днём

Урá! Аки́м приéхал!

Он приéхал так пóздно, потомý что всё ýтро шёл дождь, и нýжно бы́ло éхать óчень мéдленно.   Нет, он не забы́л меня́! Он ничегó не говори́т, но я знáю, что он меня́ лю́бит.

Погóда тепéрь óчень хорóшая. Нéбо я́сное. Теплó и светлó. Я пишý óчень бы́стро, потомý что скóро мы éдем купáться, а потóм бýдем игрáть в тéннис.

Ах, как Аки́м мне нрáвится! Какóй он ýмный, ми́лый, интерéсный! . . . Мой млáдший брат, Бори́с, говори́т, что Аки́м мне так нрáвится, потомý что у негó нóвый автомоби́ль. Но э́то не прáвда! Бори́с глýпый мáльчик.

Словáрь (Vocabulary)

урá hurrah
приéхал (*past of* **приéхать**) arrived (by conveyance)
шёл дождь it rained
нýжно бы́ло it was necessary (see ¶ 16-5)
я́сный, -ая, -ое clear
теплó it is warm
светлó it is bright
скóро soon
купáться (*pr.* **купáца**) (I); **купáюсь, купáешься** (*pr.* **купáешса**), **купáются** (*pr.* **купáюца**) to bathe (oneself) (see ¶ 16-6)
тéннис tennis
игрáть в тéннис to play tennis (see ¶ 16-2)
какóй он ýмный how clever he is!
интерéсный, -ая, -ое attractive (of a person)
млáдший, -ая, -ее younger, junior
прáвда truth
э́то не прáвда this is not true
глýпый, -ая, -ое stupid
мáльчик boy

Грамма́тика (Grammar)

Part I

16-1. Impersonal Expressions in the Present Tense

a. Impersonal expressions like *it is cold*, *it is boring*, are rendered by one word: **хо́лодно, ску́чно.** The subject *it* and the verb *is* of the English sentence are understood. For example:

хо́лодно	*it is* cold
ску́чно	*it is* boring
лу́чше	*it is* better
ху́же	*it is* worse
ну́жно	*it is* necessary

b. When such impersonal expressions refer to persons, the latter must be in the dative in Russian. For example:

Мне хо́лодно.	*I* am cold (*lit. to me* it is cold).
Ученику́ ску́чно.	The *pupil* is bored (*lit. to the pupil* it is boring).
Сестре́ тепе́рь лу́чше.	*Sister* is now better (*lit. to sister* it is now better).
Ему́ ну́жно.	*He* has to (*lit.* it is necessary *to him*).

16-2. Idioms with игра́ть

a. **игра́ть** + **на** + *prep.* = to play an instrument.

Она́ игра́ет на роя́ле.	She plays (is playing) the piano.
Ты игра́ешь на гита́ре.	You play (are playing) the guitar.

b. **игра́ть** + **в** + *acc.* = to play a game.

Мы игра́ем в те́ннис.	We play tennis.
Они́ игра́ют в ка́рты.	They play cards.

16-3. Expressions of Absence or Lack

a. **Есть** means *there is, there are.* It asserts the existence or presence of an object. For example:

В го́роде **есть** теа́тр.	There is a theater in town.
На да́че **есть** вода́.	There is water at the summer house.

b. **Нет** is a contraction of **не** + **есть.** It means *there is not,*
there are not, or *there is no, there are no.* It expresses *absence, lack,*
or the *non-existence* of an object—in effect, the opposite of **есть.**

Ива́на **нет** в кла́ссе.	Ivan *is not* in class. (*Absence*)
Его́ ещё **нет.**	He *is not* here yet. (*Absence*)
В го́роде **нет** теа́тра.	There *is no* theater in town. (*Non-existence*)
На да́че **нет** воды́.	There *is no* water at the summer house. (*Non-existence or temporary lack*)

Note: The subject of such negative sentences must be in the
genitive.

c. Do not confuse possessive phrases in the negative (see **¶ 13-1**)
with expressions of absence or lack.

Compare:

У нас **нет автомоби́ля.**	We have no car.
Автомоби́ля **нет.**	The car is not here. (It is gone, or has not arrived; it is absent from a certain place.)

Note: In the first sentence, *car* is rendered in English as the
direct object; in the second sentence, it is the *subject.*

16-4. Direct Object with **ждать**

a. **Ждать** means *to wait.*

b. *To wait for* is rendered thus:

1. **ждать** + *gen.* of a thing. For example:

Она́ ждёт **журна́ла.**	She is waiting *for* a magazine.
Они́ ждут **отве́та.**	They are waiting *for* an answer.

2. **ждать** + *acc.* of a person, when definite. For example:

Я жду **сестру́.**	I am waiting *for* my sister.
Ты **его́** ждёшь.	You are waiting *for* him.

Part II

16-5. Impersonal Expressions—Present, Past, and Future

a. The present tense consists of the adverb alone (see **¶ 16-1**).
The past is formed by adding **бы́ло,** and the future by adding
бу́дет.

b. Examples. (*Note* position of **не** for the negative, and the stress on **нé** in the past tense.)

PRESENT TENSE

Affirmative	хóлодно it *is* cold	мне тебé емý ей	} хóлодно	I am you are he is she is	} cold		
		нам вам им	} хóлодно	we are you are they are	} cold		
Negative	**не** хóлодно it *is not* cold	мне **не** хóлодно I am not cold, *etc.*					

PAST TENSE

Affirmative	бы́ло хóлодно it *was* cold	мне тебé емý ей	} бы́ло хóлодно	I was you were he was she was	} cold
		нам вам им	} бы́ло хóлодно	we were you were they were	} cold

Negative	**нé** было хóлодно
	    it *was not* cold
		мне **нé** было
		    хóлодно
			I was not cold, *etc.*		

FUTURE TENSE

Affirmative	бýдет хóлодно it *will be* cold	мне тебé емý ей	} бýдет хóлодно	I shall be you will be he will be she will be	} cold
		нам вам им	} бýдет хóлодно	we shall be you will be they will be	} cold

Negative	**не** бýдет хóлодно
	    it *will not* be cold
		мне **не** бýдет
		    хóлодно
			I shall not be cold, *etc.*		

16-6. Reflexive Verbs

a. A *reflexive verb* denotes action which the subject is performing upon himself.   Compare:

купа́ть   to bathe (*someone else*)
купа́ть**ся**   to bathe (*oneself*)

b. Reflexive verbs are formed by adding **-ся** or **-сь** to regular verb endings.

1. **-ся** is added after a *consonant*, **ь**, or **й**.
2. **-сь** is added after a *vowel*.

c. Infinitive: **купа́ться** (**I**) *to bathe (oneself)*

PRESENT TENSE

я купа́ю**сь**
ты купа́ешь**ся**   (*pr.* купа́ешь**са**)
он, она́, оно́ купа́ет**ся**   (*pr.* купа́е**ца**)
мы купа́ем**ся**   (*pr.* купа́ем**са**)
вы купа́ете**сь**
они́ купа́ют**ся**   (*pr.* купа́ю**ца**)

PAST TENSE

я, ты, он купа́л**ся**   мы ⎫
я, ты, она́ купа́ла**сь**   вы ⎬ купа́ли**сь**
оно́ купа́ло**сь**   они́ ⎭

FUTURE TENSE

я бу́ду купа́ть**ся**, *etc.*

IMPERATIVE

купа́й**ся** (*fam. sing.*)   купа́йте**сь** (*pl.*, or *pol. sing.*)

Упражне́ния (Exercises)

A. Translate.   (Review ¶ 5-2.)

1. Се́рое не́бо; не́бо се́рое.   2. Пуста́я у́лица; у́лица пуста́я. 3. Ми́лая де́вушка; де́вушка ми́лая.   4. Плоха́я пого́да; пого́да плоха́я.   5. Ма́ленький ма́льчик; ма́льчик ма́ленький. 6. Глу́пая жена́; жена́ глу́пая.   7. Приле́жная учени́ца; учени́ца приле́жная.   8. У́мная соба́ка; соба́ка у́мная.   9. Хоро́ший телеви́зор; телеви́зор хоро́ший.   10. Си́нее мо́ре; мо́ре си́нее.

B. Conjugate the following in the *present*, *past*, and *future*, using ⊄ 16-5 as a sample.

1. ску́чно; мне ску́чно.
2. тепло́; мне тепло́.
3. ну́жно; мне ну́жно.
4. лу́чше; мне лу́чше.
5. ху́же; мне ху́же.

C. Supply the proper forms of **купа́ться** and translate.

1. Я не люблю́ _____, когда́ идёт дождь.
2. Ты о́чень ча́сто _____ в мо́ре.
3. Заче́м вы живёте на берегу́ мо́ря, е́сли вы никогда́ не _____?
4. Вчера́ А́нна до́лго _____ с бра́том и с сестро́й.
5. Мы ещё никогда́ не _____ в мо́ре.
6. Ле́том она́ бу́дет _____ ка́ждый день.
7. Ско́ро мы то́же бу́дем _____.

D. Supply the proper equivalents for words in parentheses.

1. Аки́м забы́л (her) и она́ забы́ла (Joachim).
2. Она́ не зна́ет (this Russian word).
3. Вы всё у́тро ду́маете (about the book).
4. Кого́ вы ждёте? Я жду (for sister).
5. Они́ ждут (for an answer) от учи́тельницы.
6. Они́ до́лго смотре́ли (at this picture).
7. (I was not cold) на берегу́ мо́ря.
8. (You will be bored) в дере́вне.
9. За́втра в го́роде (it will be very warm).
10. (Do not bathe) так ча́сто.

Перево́д (Translation)

A. Omit words in parentheses and include words in brackets.

1. Joachim was at Masha's (home) two weeks ago.   2. He did not come [arrive by conveyance] today, because he is sick.   3. Masha has been waiting for him all morning.   4. She thinks [that] he has forgotten her.   5. Masha lives in the country, and is very bored when the weather is bad.   6. She likes to play the piano when it rains.   7. When the weather is good, she prefers to play tennis.

B. Omit words in parentheses and include those in brackets.

1. I am cold because it is so cold today.   2. It was very dark, and it was necessary [**ну́жно бы́ло**] to go (by vehicle) very slowly. 3. It was very late when we got [arrived] home.   4. Is there a school in the village? (See ¶ **16-3**.)   5. No, there is no school in the village.   6. There is no water in the house.   7. Is Boris in school?   No, Boris is not in school (absent).   8. The teacher (*f.*) is not here yet.   Why is she not here (absent)?   9. We are not waiting for a car.   We have one [a car].   We are waiting for Vera. 10. The car is not here (missing).   Who has [**у кого́**] it?

C. Translate.

1. Yesterday the weather was very good.   2. The sky was clear, and it was bright and warm.   3. Yesterday Masha had no examination, and today she also has no examination.   4. Yesterday she bathed in the sea, and today she will play tennis with Joachim. 5. She is very fond of Joachim, because he plays tennis so well, plays the piano well, and has a new car.

Вопро́сы (Questions)

1. Кака́я сего́дня пого́да?   2. Како́го цве́та не́бо сего́дня? 3. Како́го цве́та оно́ бы́ло вчера́?   4. Како́го цве́та оно́ бу́дет за́втра?   5. Что вы предпочита́ете де́лать, когда́ идёт дождь? 6. Тепе́рь темно́ и́ли светло́?   7. О́сенью хо́лодно и́ли тепло́? 8. О ком (of whom) ду́мает Ма́ша?   9. Кого́ она́ ждёт всё у́тро?   10. Почему́ Аки́ма ещё нет?   11. Как вы ду́маете, (What do you think) Аки́м забы́л молоду́ю де́вушку?   12. Почему́ Аки́м так нра́вится Ма́ше?   13. Что он ей ча́сто говори́т? 14. Почему́ Аки́м прие́хал так по́здно?   15. Что говори́т Бори́с, мла́дший брат Ма́ши?   16. Э́то пра́вда и́ли не пра́вда? 17. Как вы ду́маете, Бори́с у́мный и́ли глу́пый ма́льчик? 18. Как вам нра́вится дневни́к Ма́ши?   Почему́?

REVIEW LESSON

Vocabulary and Grammar Review

A. Place the nouns in parentheses in the appropriate case, supply required case endings for adjectives and pronouns, and translate at sight. For example:

Я не зна́ю э́т_____ (де́вушка).
Я не зна́ю э́той де́вушки.

1. Далеко́ от (го́род). 2. У (оте́ц) нет (автомоби́ль). 3. Мы бу́дем рабо́тать в (конто́ра). 4. У меня́ нет ру́сск_____ (учи́тельница). 5. Они́ нам да́ли (телеви́зор) на четы́ре (день). 6. Оте́ц купи́л краси́в_____ (да́ча). 7. Наш_____ семья́ живёт на (да́ча) весно́й и ле́том. 8. Моё кре́сло син_____ (цвет). 9. Вы лю́бите смотре́ть на син_____ (мо́ре)? 10. Э́то мой после́дн_____ вопро́с. 11. Ты не зна́ешь эт_____ (сло́во). 12. Они́ живу́т на (бе́рег) (мо́ре). 13. Мы купи́ли после́дн_____ (ва́за). 14 Они́ уже́ це́л_____ (неде́ля) сидя́т до́ма. 15. Почему́ вы не идёте к (специали́ст)? 16. У (Макси́м Ива́нович) боли́т голова́. 17. Ма́ша смо́трит на пуст_____ (у́лица). 18. Вы не чита́ли (дневни́к) молод_____ (де́вушка). 19. Сего́дня о́чень хоро́ш_____ (пого́да). 20. У (Ма́ша) за́втра нет (экза́мен).

B. Here is a list of verbs given in Lessons XIII–XVI. Supply their English meanings, and conjugate them orally in the *present*, *past*, and *compound future*. When in doubt, refer to the vocabulary section or to the individual lessons.

111

1. ходи́ть	6. есть
2. е́здить	7. пить
3. смотре́ть	8. лежа́ть
4. брать	9. ждать
5. слу́шать	10. купа́ться

C. Supply the imperatives for the above verbs, except for **е́здить** and **есть** which will be studied later.

Reading and Comprehension Drill

A. Read the following affirmative sentences aloud and translate them; then change them to the negative in Russian.

1. У вас есть ру́сская газе́та.
2. Мы купи́ли после́днюю ва́зу.
3. Они́ изуча́ли англи́йский язы́к.
4. Мне нра́вится Нью-Йо́рк.
5. Вчера́ мне бы́ло ску́чно на да́че.
6. За́втра мы бу́дем купа́ться.

B. Translate the following sentences into idiomatic English.

1. У него́ боли́т голова́. 2. У них нет да́чи. 3. Она́ должна́ ходи́ть в шко́лу пешко́м. 4. Ты игра́ешь на роя́ле ка́ждый день. 5. Ба́бушка живёт у нас. 6. Вчера́ шёл дождь. 7. Мы тепе́рь идём к сестре́. 8. Мне ну́жно перо́. 9. Вы хорошо́ игра́ете в те́ннис. 10. Ты дал ей кни́гу то́лько на две неде́ли. 11. Их да́ча нахо́дится на берегу́ мо́ря. 12. Что э́то за отве́т? 13. У меня́ нет эне́ргии. 14. Как жаль, что до́ктора нет. 15. В го́роде нет теа́тра. 16. Моя́ ко́мната си́него цве́та. 17. Заче́м вы купи́ли дом в го́роде? 18. Они́ ча́сто е́здят в дере́вню? 19. Бори́с глу́пый ма́льчик и ничего́ не понима́ет. 20. Мы ждём сестру́ и бра́та.

C. Supply the words in parentheses; read and translate at sight.

Бори́с и Ма́ша

1. Бори́с (diligent) ма́льчик. 2. Он о́чень лю́бит (school). 3. Ча́сто он (is obliged) (to walk) в шко́лу пешко́м, но (he likes it). 4. Он (every day) зна́ет уро́к и о́чень хорошо́ (answers) в кла́ссе.

5. Ма́ша, (the younger) сестра́ Бори́са, (likes) сиде́ть до́ма. 6. Ча́сто её нет в кла́ссе. 7. Она́ (does not go on foot) в шко́лу,

когда́ (it is cold) и́ли когда́ (it rains).   8. (She is very bored) в шко́ле.   9. До́ма же (she is never bored).   10. Она́ игра́ет (the piano), (listens to the) ра́дио, и́ли (watches) телеви́зор.

11. В кла́ссе у Ма́ши никогда́ нет (paper) и о́чень ча́сто нет (a pen).   12. Е́сли учи́тель (her) спра́шивает:—Почему́ вы (are looking at the street) и не пи́шете?   13. Она́ отвеча́ет — Я ду́маю.   14. — О чём [about what] вы ду́маете?   15. — Э́то (a secret).   16. — (Please write) — говори́т учи́тель. '17. — (I have no paper and no pen) — отвеча́ет Ма́ша.   18. — Вот перо́ и бума́га.   19. — Спаси́бо — говори́т Ма́ша, но ничего́ не пи́шет.   20. — Почему́ же вы ничего́ не де́лаете? — ещё раз спра́шивает учи́тель.   21. — Я о́чень (want to sleep).

D. Rewrite the text of Exercise C above, substituting **Ма́ша** for **Бори́с**, **де́вушка** for **ма́льчик**, **учени́к** for **учени́ца**, and vice versa.   For example: Ма́ша приле́жная де́вушка.

Перево́д (**Translation**)

Include the words in brackets.

1. Such a nice boy!   2. What a beautiful street!   3. We have no energy.   4. Sister has no work.   5. They have no appetite. 6. We have a picture.   7. The picture is now at our house.   8. I need a map.   9. I am taking your map.   10. They need a piano. 11. This is all [that] I know.   12. I do not remember this person. 13. She likes to play tennis.   14. We like your dog.   15. Drink [**пе́йте**] a little milk.   16. Thank goodness, this is my last examination.   17. Do you know this pupil?

Вопро́сы (**Questions**)

1. Где вы живёте, в го́роде и́ли в дере́вне?   2. Вы хо́дите и́ли е́здите в го́род?   В дере́вню?   3. У вас есть автомоби́ль? 4. Вам нра́вится ваш автомоби́ль?   5. Како́го он цве́та? 6. Вам ну́жен автомоби́ль ка́ждый день?   7. Когда́ вы живёте на да́че?   8. Где нахо́дится ва́ша да́ча?   9. Почему́ Макси́м Ива́нович сиди́т до́ма?   10. Почему́ у него́ так ма́ло эне́ргии тепе́рь?   11. Кого́ ждёт Ма́ша?   12. Почему́ Аки́м прие́хал так по́здно?   13. Почему́ Ма́ша так ра́да, что он прие́хал? 14. Почему́ Ма́ша так нра́вится Аки́му?   15. Когда́ Аки́м и Ма́ша е́дут купа́ться?

U N I T 18*

I

ПИСЬМО́

Дорого́й Ва́ся,

Вчера́ я пое́хал в дере́вню к Ма́ше. Всё у́тро шёл дождь, и я до́лжен был е́хать о́чень ме́дленно. Оте́ц купи́л мне но́вый автомоби́ль, и Ма́ша о́чень хоте́ла его́ ви́деть. Она́, коне́чно, хоте́ла ви́деть не то́лько автомоби́ль, но и меня́. Ты наве́рно хорошо́ её по́мнишь. Она́ о́чень у́мная, краси́вая и ми́лая де́вушка. Она́ мне о́чень нра́вится, и я зна́ю, что я ей то́же нра́влюсь.

Ле́том семья́ Ма́ши живёт на да́че, кото́рая нахо́дится на берегу́ большо́го о́зера. Ма́ша купа́ется в о́зере ка́ждый день, и вчера́ мы то́же пое́хали купа́ться. По́сле дождя́ вода́ была́ дово́льно холо́дная, но я о́чень люблю́ пла́вать в холо́дной воде́. Мы бы́ли на о́зере це́лый час, а пото́м пое́хали в парк игра́ть в те́ннис. Ма́ша о́чень лю́бит спорт и прекра́сно игра́ет в те́ннис, в волейбо́л, и да́же в бейзбо́л.

Уже́ о́чень по́здно, а за́втра, ра́но у́тром, я до́лжен быть в го́роде. У меня́ не бу́дет автомоби́ля и ну́жно бу́дет е́хать на трамва́е. Ита́к, споко́йной но́чи!

Слова́рь (Vocabulary)

письмо́ letter
дорого́й, -а́я, -о́е dear
Ва́ся (*m.*) Basil
пое́хал (*past of* **пое́хать**) went (by conveyance)
я до́лжен был I had to

* This unit is intended as a *double* unit, requiring approximately twice as much time as the average unit.

114

ви́деть (II); **ви́жу, ви́дишь, ви́дят;** (*no imperative*) to see
её (*acc. of* **она́**) her
нра́виться (II); **нра́влюсь, нра́вишься, нра́вятся** to like, to please (see
¶ 18-1)
кото́рый, -ая, -ое (*rel. & interr. pron.*) which, who (see ¶ 18-2)
о́зеро lake
дово́льно (*adv.*) quite, rather
холо́дный, -ая, -ое cold
пла́вать (I) *hab.*; **пла́ваю, -ешь, -ют** to swim
на о́зере at the lake
час hour
спорт sport
прекра́сно very well, excellently
волейбо́л volleyball
бейзбо́л baseball
трамва́й (*m.*) streetcar
е́хать на трамва́е to go by streetcar
ита́к well then
споко́йной но́чи! (*idiom*) good night!

II

ПИСЬМО́ (Continued)

Дорого́й Ва́ся,

Я весь день был в го́роде и прие́хал домо́й дово́льно по́здно,
но продолжа́ю письмо́.

Мать Ма́ши пригото́вила прекра́сный обе́д: борщ, котле́ты,
и сала́т, а на десе́рт — компо́т.   Аппети́т у меня́, сла́ва бо́гу,
всегда́ о́чень хоро́ший, и я мно́го ел и пил.   Бы́ло о́чень
ве́село.   Все гро́мко разгова́ривали и смея́лись.

На столе́ стоя́л большо́й самова́р и все пи́ли чай.   Оте́ц
Ма́ши ру́сский и всегда́ пьёт чай из стака́на.   Но мне да́ли
ча́шку, потому́ что я америка́нец.

Я пло́хо рису́ю, но зна́ю, что
ты никогда́ не́ был в ру́сском
до́ме и никогда́ не ви́дел самова́ра.

Вот самова́р!

По́сле обе́да я пое́хал домо́й.
Ну, э́то всё.   А ты, как живёшь
и что де́лаешь?   Жду отве́та.

Твой друг Аки́м

Слова́рь (Vocabulary)

продолжа́ть (I); **продолжа́ю, -ешь, -ют** to continue
приготóвила (*past of* **приготóвить**) she prepared
прекрáсный, -ая, -ое excellent
обéд dinner
борщ (*gen.* **борщá**) borshch, beet soup
котлéты (*pl. of* **котлéта**) Russian hamburgers
салáт salad
десéрт dessert
на десéрт for dessert
компóт stewed fruit
вéсело it is cheerful, gay
разговáривать (I); **разговáриваю, -ешь, -ют** to converse
смея́ться (I); **смею́сь, смеёшься, смею́тся** to laugh (see ¶ 18-1)
самовáр samovar (a Russian urn for making tea)
чай (*m.*) tea
стакáн glass
ча́шка cup
америкáнец *Л* (*noun, m.*) (*gen.* **америкáнца**) American (see ¶ 18-5)
рисовáть (I); **рису́ю, рису́ешь, рису́ют** to draw
твой, твоя́, твоё (*adj. & pron.*) your, yours (*fam. sing.*)
друг (*m.*) friend (*used for man or woman*)

Граммáтика (Grammar)

Part I

18-1. Intransitive Verbs in -ся

a. Intransitive verbs do not take a direct object.

b. Many intransitive verbs have the ending **-ся** in the infinitive and are conjugated as reflexives even though they do not have a reflexive meaning. For example: **нрáвиться, смея́ться**.

c. Note the conjugation of **смея́ться**:

PRESENT	PAST
я сме**ю́сь**	я, ты, он сме**я́лся**
ты сме**ёшься**	я, ты, онá сме**я́лась**
он сме**ётся**	онó сме**я́лось**
мы сме**ёмся**	мы, вы, они́ сме**я́лись**
вы сме**ётесь**	
они́ сме**ю́тся**	

FUTURE

я бу́ду смея́ться, *etc.*

IMPERATIVE

сме́**йся**   сме́**йтесь**

d. The use of **нра́виться** requires the normal English subject in the *dative*, and the normal English object in the *nominative*. (See ¶ 13-5 and 14-4.)

PRESENT

я нра́**влюсь** учи́тельнице
{ The teacher likes me (*lit.* I am
  pleasing to the teacher).

ты нра́ви**шься** учи́тельнице
{ The teacher likes you (*lit.* you
  are pleasing to the teacher).

он нра́в**ится** учи́тельнице
etc.

мы нра́в**имся** учи́тельнице
вы нра́ви**тесь** учи́тельнице
они́ нра́в**ятся** учи́тельнице

18-2. The Relative Pronoun: кото́рый

a. The relative pronoun **кото́рый** introduces a subordinate clause. For example:

Я зна́ю де́вушку, **кото́рая** пи́шет кни́гу.

I know the girl *who* is writing a book.

b. **Кото́рый** agrees in *number* and *gender* with the noun in the main clause to which it refers. The *case* of **кото́рый**, however, is determined by its own function in the relative clause. For example:

Мы живём на **да́че** (*sing., fem., prep.*), **кото́рая** (*sing., fem., nom.*) нахо́дится на бе́регу о́зера.

Note: In both examples above, **кото́рая** is the *subject* of the subordinate clause and is therefore in the *nominative* case, although **де́вушку** is in the *accusative* in the first example, and **да́че** is in the *prepositional* in the second.

18-3. Prepositional Case of Adjectives in the Singular

Declension	Case	Masculine	Feminine	Neuter
Hard	*nom.* *prep.*	но́в**ый** о но́в**ом**	но́в**ая** о но́в**ой**	но́в**ое** о но́в**ом**
Soft	*nom.* *prep.*	после́дн**ий** о после́дн**ем**	после́дн**яя** о после́дн**ей**	после́дн**ее** о после́дн**ем**
Mixed	*nom.* *prep.*	ру́сск**ий** о ру́сск**ом**	ру́сск**ая** о ру́сск**ой**	ру́сск**ое** о ру́сск**ом**

Part II

18-4. Second Declension of Nouns in the Singular*

a. Membership consists of:

1. Masculine nouns ending in a *consonant*, **-ь**, or **-й** in the nominative singular. For example:

inanimate: журна́л	автомоби́ль	трамва́й
animate: студе́нт	учи́тель	геро́й (hero)

2. Neuter nouns ending in **-о**, **-е**, or **-ие**. For example:

сло́во, мо́ре, сочине́ние.

b. Classes: *hard* and *soft*.

1. Nouns ending in a *consonant* or in **-о** are *hard*.

2. Those ending in **-ь, -й**, or **-е** are *soft*.

Note: In the case of adjectives, the designations *hard, soft,* and *mixed* refer to the declensions themselves, whereas in the case of nouns, *hard* and *soft* refer to classes which are subdivisions within the declensions of nouns.

c. Stress.

1. All the cases, except the nominative, are called *oblique*.

2. In the singular, the stress in the *genitive* determines the pattern for the other oblique cases. It is therefore necessary to know the *genitive* as well as the *nominative* of every noun. Compare:

nom.	стул	стол	учени́к	челове́к	сло́во	перо́
gen.	сту́ла	стола́	ученика́	челове́ка	сло́ва	пера́
dat.	сту́лу	столу́	ученику́	челове́ку	сло́ву	перу́
	etc.	*etc.*	*etc.*	*etc.*	*etc.*	*etc.*

3. Henceforth, the *genitive* of a noun will be given in the vocabulary if it is not stressed on the same syllable as the nominative. The same applies to the Russian-English vocabulary at the end of the book.

d. Masculine nouns.

1. Masculine *inanimate* nouns are identical in the *nominative* and *accusative*. Note also that, when stressed, the ending **-ем** becomes **-ём**.

---

* See ¶ **15-7** for the First Declension of nouns in the singular.

	Hard	Soft		
	Consonant	**-ь**		**-й**
		Stress on stem	Stress on ending	
nom.	журна́л	автомоби́ль	дождь	трамва́й
gen.	журна́ла	автомоби́ля	дождя́	трамва́я
dat.	журна́лу	автомоби́лю	дождю́	трамва́ю
acc.	журна́л	автомоби́ль	дождь	трамва́й
instr.	журна́лом	автомоби́лем	дождём	трамва́ем
prep.	о журна́ле	об автомоби́ле	о дожде́	о трамва́е

2. Masculine *animate* nouns are identical in the *genitive* and *accusative*; otherwise, they arc declined as above.

nom.	студе́нт	учи́тель	царь (tsar)	геро́й (hero)
acc.	студе́нта	учи́теля	царя́	геро́я

e. Neuter nouns are identical in the *nominative* and the *accusative*.

	Hard	Soft	
	-о	**-е**	**-ие**
nom.	сло́во	мо́ре	сочине́ние
gen.	сло́ва	мо́ря	сочине́ния
dat.	сло́ву	мо́рю	сочине́нию
acc.	сло́во	мо́ре	сочине́ние
instr.	сло́вом	мо́рем	сочине́нием
prep.	о сло́ве	о мо́ре	о сочине́нии

18-5. Capitalization of Terms of Nationality

Nouns and adjectives that designate nationality are not capitalized except at the beginning of a sentence.   For example:

nouns:	америка́нец (*m.*)	American
	ру́сская (*f.*)	Russian
adjectives:	америка́нский, -ая, -ое	American
	ру́сский, -ая, -ое	Russian

Упражнёния (Exercises)

A. Translate the following nouns and adjectives, and decline them in the *genitive*, *accusative*, and *prepositional* cases (review ¶ 14-2).   For example:

nom.	стáрый дом	old house
gen.	стáрого дóма	
acc.	стáрый дом	
prep.	о стáром дóме	

1. молодóй человéк.   2. дорогáя тётя.   3. холóдный дождь.   4. ясное нéбо.   5. пустóй гóрод.   6. глýпый мáльчик. 7. прекрáсный обéд.   8. рýсский чай.   9. большóе óзеро. 10. послéднее письмó.   11. мúлый учúтель.   12. сúнее мóре. 13. интерéсное сочинéние.   14. послéдний трамвáй.   15. плохóй хозяин.

B. Decline the following nouns in the singular, and indicate the stress.

Group I (oblique cases stressed like the nominative):

1. друг   2. суп   3. дóктор   4. студéнт   5. чай   6. учúтель 7. крéсло   8. мóре   9. самовáр   10. Ивáн   11. стакáн   12. рояль

Group II (oblique cases stressed on endings):

1. язык   2. стол   3. борщ   4. карандáш   5. гарáж   6. дождь 7. ученúк   8. окнó   9. потолóк   10. отéц   11. дневнúк 12. письмó

C. Conjugate the following verbs in all the forms studied thus far (i.e., *present, past, compound future, imperative*).

1. плáвать	5. разговáривать
2. рисовáть	6. смеяться
3. вúдеть (no imperative)	7. лежáть
4. продолжáть	8. смотрéть

D. Supply the proper cases of the Russian words in parentheses and replace the English words with Russian equivalents.   For example: Я *lived* в (большóй гóрод). **Я жил в большóм гóроде**.

1. Вчерá *there was no* (дождь).   2. Зáвтра *it will not be* хóлодно.   3. Мáша *wanted* вúдеть (учúтель).   4. В (гóрод) нет (трамвáй).   5. *We do not like* éздить на (трамвáй).   6. Онá не *bathed* вчерá в (óзеро).   7. Онú тепéрь *are walking* к (мóре). 8. Мы весь вéчер *talked* о (сочинéние).   9. Я дóлго *conversed* с (учúтель).   10. Все грóмко *laughed*, тóлько мой друг не

laughed.   11. Дéвушка, (котóрая) вы *saw* недéлю тому́ назáд, моя́ сестрá.   12. Онá никогдá не *drank* (чай) из (стакáн). 13. Акúму *they gave* (чáшка), потому́ что он америкáнец. 14. Он *does not see* (нéбо), потому́ что темнó.   15. Николáй *eats* с (аппетúт), когдá он у (тётя).   16. Вы *are not conversing* и *are not laughing*, потому́ что (вы) скýчно.   17. Онú чáсто *swim* в (холóдная водá).   18. Вы прекрáсно *played* на (роя́ль).   19. Ты хорошó *draw* (дерéвня).   20. Пóсле (обéд) мы поéхали к (отéц), но егó нé было в (гóрод).

Перевóд (Translation)

Omit the words in parentheses and include the words in brackets.

1. It rained yesterday and it is also raining today.   2. I have to continue the letter which I have been writing [**ужé пишý**] (for) two days.   3. It is quite late now, but I do not want to sleep. 4. He knows that Masha likes him [that he is pleasing to Masha], and that she wants to see him.   5. Do not bathe and do not swim in cold water.   6. Basil went [**поéхал**] to town by streetcar and arrived at the office very late.   7. They conversed about volleyball and baseball (for) a whole hour.   8. My mother prepared an excellent dinner.   9. I do not like to drink tea out of a glass. 10. Tanya never listens (to the) teacher, and only laughs and talks [converses] in class.   11. They had no borshch, but they gave us tea and stewed fruit.   12. Here is paper.   Draw a summer home on the shore of a big lake.   13. They gave the American a small cup.   14. You have never been in a Russian home [house], 15. That is all.   Good night.

Вопрóсы (Questions)

1. Кто пúшет письмó?   2. Комý он пúшет э́то письмó? 3. Где был Акúм и когó он вúдел?   4. Почемý Акúм дóлжен был éхать мéдленно?   5. Что отéц купúл Акúму?   6. Где живёт семья́ Мáши?   7. Где нахóдится э́та дáча?   8. Óзеро большóе úли мáленькое?   9. Мáша чáсто купáется в óзере? 10. Как дóлго Акúм и Мáша бы́ли на óзере?   11. Где онú потóм игрáли в тéннис?   12. Почемý Акúм дóлжен éхать в гóрод на трамвáе?   13. Акúму нрáвился обéд, котóрый приготóвила мать Мáши?   14. Вы лю́бите борщ?   15. Что вы кýшаете на десéрт?   16. Вы ужé вúдели самовáр?   17. Кудá Акúм поéхал пóсле обéда у Мáши?

ОТВЕ́Т ВА́СИ

Дорого́й Аки́м,

Большо́е спаси́бо за дли́нное письмо́, в кото́ром ты так мно́го пи́шешь о Ма́ше и так ма́ло о себе́.

Вот замеча́тельная де́вушка! — прекра́сно игра́ет в те́ннис, в волейбо́л и да́же в бейзбо́л, прекра́сно игра́ет на роя́ле, пла́вает как ры́ба и поёт как пти́ца. А оте́ц Ма́ши ру́сский и пьёт чай из стака́на. А мать её уме́ет приготовля́ть борщ, котле́ты и компо́т! И кака́я у Ма́ши ми́лая семья́! — все сидя́т вокру́г самова́ра, пьют чай, гро́мко разгова́ривают и смею́тся. Ну, почему́ ты ду́маешь, что всё э́то интере́сно? Ты прекра́сно зна́ешь, что де́вушки меня́ не интересу́ют.

У тебя́ тепе́рь но́вый автомоби́ль — вот э́то интере́сно! Тепе́рь ты мо́жешь е́здить к нам ча́ще. У нас, коне́чно, нет да́чи на берегу́ большо́го о́зера, но у нас есть прекра́сная фе́рма.

Ты по́мнишь на́шу се́рую ло́шадь? Ты ча́сто дава́л ей са́хар и она́ тебя́ за э́то о́чень люби́ла. Когда́ бу́дешь на фе́рме, бу́дем вме́сте е́здить верхо́м, ты на се́рой ло́шади, а я на бе́лой.

Мы все тебя́ ждём: и я, и моя́ сестра́ Ири́на, и на́ша се́рая ло́шадь.

Ита́к, до свида́ния.

Твой друг Ва́ся

Слова́рь (Vocabulary)

большо́е спаси́бо many thanks
за (*with acc.*) for

дли́нный, -ая, -ое long
себя́ (*reflex. pron.*) self, oneself (see ¶ 19-1)
замеча́тельный, -ая, -ое remarkable
ры́ба fish
петь (II); пою́, поёшь, пою́т to sing
пти́ца bird
уме́ть (I); уме́ю, уме́ешь, уме́ют to know how (see ¶ 19-3)
приготовля́ть (I); приготовля́ю, -ешь, -ют to prepare
вокру́г (*with gen.*) around
интере́сно it is interesting
де́вушки (*pl. of* де́вушка) girls
интересова́ть (I); интересу́ю, интересу́ешь, -ют to interest
ча́ще (*comp. of* ча́сто) more frequently
фе́рма farm
ло́шадь (*f., third decl.*) horse (see ¶ 19-2)
са́хар sugar
вме́сте (*adv.*) together
верхо́м (*adv.*) astride
е́здить верхо́м
е́здить на ло́шади   } to ride horseback
е́здить верхо́м на ло́шади
бе́лый, -ая, -ое white
Ири́на Irene

АКИ́М НА ФЕ́РМЕ

Ве́чер. Ва́ся у себя́ в ко́мнате. Он чита́ет рома́н "Война́ и Мир." Рома́н о́чень интере́сный, и Ва́ся ничего́ не слы́шит. Вдруг в ко́мнату вхо́дит Аки́м, но Ва́ся продолжа́ет чита́ть. Аки́м стои́т в ко́мнате це́лую мину́ту, смо́трит на Ва́сю и ждёт. Но Ва́ся ничего́ не ви́дит и не слы́шит. Наконе́ц Аки́м говори́т:

— Слу́шай, Ва́ся! Это я . . .

— Ах, Аки́м! Како́й прия́тный сюрпри́з! Когда́ ты прие́хал?

— То́лько что.

— Как до́лго ты бу́дешь у нас на фе́рме?

— Неде́лю.

— То́лько одну́ неде́лю! Почему́ не две и́ли три?

— Че́рез неде́лю я е́ду в дере́вню к Ма́ше.

— Как жаль, что ты до́лжен е́хать к Ма́ше . . . Но об э́том бу́дем говори́ть пото́м. А тепе́рь идём у́жинать. Моя́ сестра́, Ири́на, приготовила прекра́сный у́жин. Она́ не игра́ет в бейзбо́л, но она́ о́чень хоро́шая хозя́йка.

Слова́рь (Vocabulary)

на фе́рме at the farm
Ва́ся у себя́ в ко́мнате Vasya is in his (own) room
рома́н novel
война́ war
мир peace
слы́шать (II); слы́шу, слы́шишь, слы́шат to hear
вдруг suddenly
входи́ть (II); вхожу́, вхо́дишь, вхо́дят to go in; to enter
мину́та minute
наконе́ц at last
прия́тный, -ая, -ое pleasant
сюрпри́з surprise
то́лько что just now
одну́ (*acc. of* **одна́**) **неде́лю** one week
че́рез (*with acc.*) in (*lit.* after the lapse of)
че́рез неде́лю in a week
идём let's go
у́жинать (I); у́жинаю, -ешь, -ют to have supper
у́жин supper
хозя́йка *here:* housekeeper

Грамма́тика (Grammar)

19-1. The Reflexive Pronoun: себя́

a. **Себя́** (*self*) can be used with all genders, persons, and numbers, but must always refer to the subject of the sentence. It has no *nominative* form and cannot itself be the subject.

b. **Себя́** is declined as follows:

DECLENSION		EXAMPLES	
nom.	none		
gen.	себя́	Он у **себя́** в ко́мнате.	He is in his (own) room.
dat.	себе́	Она́ купи́ла **себе́** кни́гу.	She bought (for) herself a book.
acc.	себя́	Я ви́жу **себя́**.	I see myself.
instr.	собо́й (-о́ю)	Мы берём сестру́ с **собо́й**.	We are taking sister along (with ourselves).
prep.	о себе́	Ты ма́ло пи́шешь о **себе́**.	You are writing little about yourself.

19-2. Third Declension in the Singular

a. Soft feminine nouns in **-ь** belong to the Third Declension.

nom.	ло́шадь	*acc.*	ло́шадь
gen.	ло́шади	*instr.*	ло́шадью
dat.	ло́шади	*prep.*	о ло́шади

b. Animate and inanimate nouns of this declension are identical in the nominative and accusative singular.

Note: The *genitive, dative,* and *prepositional* are alike.

19-3. Мочь and уме́ть

Note the difference in the meaning of these verbs.

a. **Мочь** means *to be able physically, to be in a position to.* For example:

Я не **могу́** писа́ть, потому́ что темно́. *I cannot* write because it is dark (*i.e.,* I know how, but *am physically unable* to do it now).

b. **Уме́ть** means *to know how* as a result of acquired knowledge, skill, or training. For example:

Он не **уме́ет** писа́ть по-ру́сски, потому́ что никогда́ не изуча́л ру́сского языка́. He *cannot* (*does not know how to*) write Russian because he has never studied Russian (*i.e., has never acquired such knowledge, has never had such training*).

c. Conjugation of **мочь** in the

> *Present Tense:* see ¶ **9-6**.
> *Past Tense:* **мог, могла́, могло́, могли́**
> *Compound Future:* none.
> *Imperative:* none.

Упражне́ния (Exercises)

A. Replace the English words with the required case of **себя́**, and supply the proper case endings for the Russian words in parentheses.   Refer to the examples in ¶ **19-1b**.

1. Они́ купи́ли *themselves* (фе́рма). 2. В э́том (дли́нное письмо́) они́ ничего́ не пи́шут *about themselves*. 3. Она́ всегда́ сиди́т у *her* (*own*) в (ко́мната). 4. Он ду́мает то́лько *about himself*. 5. Почему́ вы никогда́ не берёте (соба́ка) *with you*? 6. Она́ *herself* не зна́ет.   7. Челове́к никогда́ *himself* не зна́ет.

8. Они́ хорошо́ *themselves* ви́дят в (вода́).   9. Бери́те меня́ *along* (*with you*) когда́ вы е́здите на (да́ча).   10. Она́ приготовля́ет (*for*) *herself* у́жин.

B. Supply the proper forms of **мочь** or **уме́ть** as required, according to ¶ **19-3**.

1. Она́ тепе́рь больна́ и не _____ рабо́тать.   2. Она́ _____ рабо́тать, когда́ она́ была́ здоро́ва.   3. Вчера́ шёл дождь и мы не _____ е́хать о́чень бы́стро.   4. Мой друг Ва́ся не лю́бит спо́рта и не _____ игра́ть в те́ннис. 5. У меня́ никогда́ не́ было ло́шади и я не _____ е́здить верхо́м.   6. Четы́ре го́да тому́ наза́д он _____ говори́ть по-ру́сски, но тепе́рь он всё забы́л.   7. Мы не _____ чита́ть, когда́ все говоря́т так гро́мко.   8. Вы не _____ пла́вать, потому́ что никогда́ не жи́ли о́коло мо́ря и́ли о́зера.

C. Supply the proper case ending for the words in parentheses. (Memorize ¶ **19-2** before doing this exercise.)

1. У меня́ нет (ло́шадь).   2. Она́ купи́ла себе́ но́вую (тетра́дь).   3. Пиши́те сочине́ние в (тетра́дь).   4. Сего́дня он прие́хал в шко́лу с (кни́га), с (тетра́дь) и с (перо́).   5. Но он ча́сто е́здит в шко́лу без (кни́га), без (тетра́дь), и без (перо́). 6. Ты лю́бишь е́здить на (ло́шадь).   7. Ты всегда́ даёшь са́хар (ло́шадь), но (соба́ка) ты ничего́ не даёшь.   8. Кого́ вы ждёте? Я жду (мать).   9. Я ви́дел (америка́нец) верхом на (ло́шадь).   10. Че́рез (неде́ля) Аки́м е́дет в (дере́вня) к (Ма́ша).

D. Conjugate the following verbs in the present, past, and compound future.

1. уме́ть   4. интересова́ть
2. петь   5. входи́ть
3. приготовля́ть   6. у́жинать

E. Translate the following sentences, and *memorize* the forms of the imperative.

1. **По́йте,** пожа́луйста, вме́сте.
2. **Живи́те** на фе́рме.
3. **Слу́шайте** ра́дио.
4. **У́жинай** ра́но.
5. **Входи́те** в ко́мнату ти́хо, когда́ все спят.

6. Она́ тепе́рь поёт.   Пожа́луйста, **слу́шайте**.

7. **Уме́йте** нра́виться учи́телю.

8. **Жди** меня́.

9. **Приготовля́йте** тако́й обе́д ча́ще.

Перево́д (Translation)

Translate, omitting the words in parentheses and including the words in brackets.   Note that a girl is writing this letter to her friend.   Therefore, use *feminine* and *familiar* forms where necessary.

1. Dear Irene,

2. Today I was all day at the office, and did not know that your letter (was) [is] lying on my [**у меня́ на**] table.   3. What a pleasant surprise!   4. At last I know where you arc and what you are doing.   5. Many thanks for such a long and interesting letter. 6. I have been waiting for this letter (for) four weeks.   7. Thank goodness [that] you are well!

8. You write too little about Boris, but he interests me very (much).   9. Who is he, where does he live, and what is hc doing? 10. You write that girls are fond of him [**его́ лю́бят**], but you do not say [**говори́шь**] why.

11. We just bought an excellent farm, which is situated on the shore of a beautiful lake.   12. In a week we shall have on (our) farm a white horse.   13. I know that you like to ride horseback. 14. When you (are) [will be] here, we shall do everything together— we shall swim in the lake, ride horseback, and play tennis.   15. In the evening we shall play the piano and sing.

16. How glad I am (to have) [that I have] a friend who can [knows how to] do everything so well.   17. Please write more frequently.

18. Your friend Vera.

Вопро́сы (Questions)

1. Кому́ Ва́ся пи́шет письмо́?   2. Аки́м мно́го пи́шет о себе́?   3. О ком он мно́го пи́шет?   4. Ва́ся ду́мает, что Ма́ша замеча́тельная де́вушка?   5. Кто пла́вает как ры́ба?   6. Кто поёт как пти́ца?   7. Вы уме́ете пла́вать?   8. А купа́ться вы уме́ете?   9. Что мать Ма́ши уме́ет приготовля́ть?   10. Что

семья́ Ма́ши де́лает вокру́г самова́ра?   11. Кто ждёт Аки́ма?
12. Что Ва́ся чита́ет у себя́ в ко́мнате?   13. Кто вдруг вхо́дит
в ко́мнату Ва́си?   14. Почему́ Ва́ся ничего́ не ви́дит и не
слы́шит?   15. Что де́лает Аки́м, когда́ Ва́ся продолжа́ет
чита́ть?   16. Ва́ся рад, что Аки́м прие́хал?   17. Как до́лго
Аки́м бу́дет на фе́рме?   18. Куда́ он е́дет че́рез неде́лю?
19. Кто приго́то́вил прекра́сный у́жин?   20. Ири́на хоро́шая
хозя́йка?   Почему́ вы так ду́маете?

U N I T 20

ПИСЬМО́ АКИ́МА К МА́ШЕ

Ми́лая Ма́ша,

Я тепе́рь у Ва́си на фе́рме. Ты зна́ешь, что мы хоро́шие
това́рищи и о́чень лю́бим друг дру́га. Ва́ся о́чень у́мный,
до́брый и весёлый ю́ноша, но немно́го стра́нный. Де́вушки
его́ не интересу́ют. Он ре́дко хо́дит в кино́, и ре́дко смо́трит
телеви́зор. Он чита́ет дли́нные и серьёзные рома́ны, как
наприме́р: "Отцы́ и де́ти," "Война́ и мир" и́ли "Америка́нская
траге́дия."

Ва́ся о́чень лю́бит иностра́нные языки́. Он чита́ет по-
францу́зски, по-неме́цки и по-ру́сски и тепе́рь та́кже изуча́ет
испа́нский язы́к. На столе́ у него́ лежа́т: испа́нские словари́,
неме́цкие журна́лы, ру́сские рома́ны и францу́зские газе́ты.
Он уже́ хорошо́ зна́ет испа́нскую грамма́тику, по́мнит са́мые
тру́дные слова́ и да́же пи́шет дли́нные сочине́ния по-испа́нски.
Но Ва́ся та́кже хоро́ший спортсме́н. Он прекра́сно игра́ет в
футбо́л и в баскетбо́л и о́чень хорошо́ е́здит верхо́м.

Сестра́ Ва́си, Ири́на, то́же прекра́сная спортсме́нка и ча́сто
е́здит с на́ми купа́ться, игра́ет с на́ми в те́ннис и е́здит верхо́м.

Слова́рь (Vocabulary)

това́рищ comrade, friend
друг дру́га each other
весёлый, -ая, -ое cheerful, gay
ю́ноша (*m.*) youth, young man
стра́нный, -ая, -ое strange, odd

129

ре́дко (*adv.*) rarely, seldom
кино́ (*n.*) (*not decl.*) movies, movie theater
серьёзный, -ая, -ое serious
наприме́р for instance
как наприме́р as for instance
де́ти (*pl. of* **дитя́**) children
америка́нский, -ая, -ое American
траге́дия tragedy
иностра́нный, -ая, -ое foreign
по-францу́зски (*adv.*) French (in French)
по-неме́цки (*adv.*) German (in German)
испа́нский, -ая, -ое Spanish
слова́рь (*m.*) (*gen.* **словаря́**) dictionary
неме́цкий, -ая, -ое German
францу́зский, -ая, -ое French
грамма́тика grammar
са́мый, -ая, -ое (*used with adj. to form superlative*) the most
тру́дный, -ая, -ое difficult
по-испа́нски (*adv.*) Spanish (in Spanish)
спортсме́н (*m.*) sportsman
футбо́л football
баскетбо́л basketball
спортсме́нка (*f.*) sportswoman
с на́ми (*instr. of* **мы**) with us

II

ПИСЬМО́ АКИ́МА К МА́ШЕ (Continued)

Ах, как хорошо́ жить на фе́рме! Всё мне здесь нра́вится: и
роди́тели Ва́си, и его́ сестра́ Ири́на, и коро́вы, и ло́шади, и
чёрная соба́ка, и бе́лая ко́шка, и пти́цы, кото́рые ве́село пою́т в
саду́.

Все здесь встаю́т о́чень ра́но. Роди́тели Ва́си встаю́т в пять
часо́в утра́, Ва́ся и Ири́на встаю́т в шесть, а я встаю́ в семь
часо́в. Я умыва́юсь, одева́юсь и иду́ в столо́вую. Ва́ся уже́
ждёт меня́ в столо́вой, и мы за́втракаем вме́сте.

Ири́на всегда́ приготовля́ет за́втрак. Она́ не то́лько хоро́-
шая спортсме́нка, но и прекра́сная хозя́йка . . .

Вдруг Ма́ша начина́ет пла́кать и не мо́жет чита́ть да́льше.

Слова́рь (Vocabulary)

здесь here
роди́тели (*m. pl.*) parents, father and mother
коро́ва cow
чёрный, -ая, -ое black

ко́шка cat
ве́село (*adv.*) cheerfully, gaily
сад garden
в саду́ in the garden (see ¶ **20-6**)
встава́ть (I); **встаю́, встаёшь, встаю́т** to get up, to rise
пять five
часы́ (*gen. pl.* **часо́в**) hours
в пять часо́в утра́ at five o'clock in the morning
шесть six
семь seven
умыва́ться (I); **умыва́юсь, -ешься, -ются** to wash oneself
одева́ться (I); **одева́юсь, -ешься, -ются** to dress oneself
столо́вая (*noun, f.*) dining room
за́втракать (I); **за́втракаю, -ешь, -ют** to have breakfast
за́втрак breakfast
начина́ть (I); **начина́ю, -ешь, -ют** to begin
пла́кать (I); **пла́чу, пла́чешь, пла́чут;** *imper.* **плачь, пла́чьте** to weep
   (see ¶ **20-10**)
да́льше (*adv.*) further

Грамма́тика (Grammar)

Part I

20-1. Position of Adverbs

a. Adverbs modifying adjectives or other adverbs precede the word they modify, as in English.   For example:

Он **о́чень** хоро́ший учени́к.	He is a *very* good pupil.
Он **о́чень** хорошо́ чита́ет.	He reads *very* well.
Он **сли́шком** мно́го говори́т.	He talks *too* much.
Не встава́йте **так** поздно.	Do not get up *so* late.

b. The position of adverbs modifying verbs is not rigidly fixed.

1. Usually such adverbs precede the verb.   They may, however, follow the verb for the sake of emphasis.   For example:

Он хорошо́ чита́ет.	He reads well.
Он чита́ет **хорошо́**.	He reads *well*.

2. The adverbs **по-ру́сски, по-англи́йски**, and the like generally follow the verb.   When emphasis is desired, they are placed before the verb.   For example:

Я хорошо́ говорю́ по-испа́нски.	I speak Spanish well.
По-испа́нски я говорю́ хорошо́.	*Spanish* I speak well.

3. Often, the position of the adverb in the sentence does not affect the meaning, any more than in English.

Я сегодня иду в город. } Today I am going to town.
Сегодня я иду в город.

Я иду в город сегодня.   I am going to town today.

20-2. Nominative Plural of Nouns*

a. Hard feminine and masculine nouns of the First and Second Declensions take **-ы**.

sing.	*pl.*
ка́рт**а**	ка́рт**ы**
журна́**л**	журна́**лы**

1. After **г**, **к**, or **х**, they take **-и**.

кни́**га**	кни́**ги**
учени́**к**	учени**ки́**

2. After **ж**, **ч**, **ш**, or **щ**, they take **-и**.

да́**ча**	да́**чи**
това́ри**щ**	това́ри**щи**

b. Soft feminine and masculine nouns of the First, Second, and Third Declensions take **-и**.

неде́л**я**	неде́л**и**
а́рми**я**	а́рми**и**
автомоби́л**ь**	автомоби́л**и**
дожд**ь**	дожд**и́**
трамва́**й**	трамва́**и**
тетра́д**ь**	тетра́д**и**
ло́шад**ь**	ло́шад**и**

c. Neuter nouns in **-о** take **-а** in the nominative plural, and usually shift the accent.

сло́в**о**	слов**а́**
письм**о́**	пи́сьм**а**

d. Neuter nouns in **-е** or **-ие** take **-я** or **-ия** in the nominative plural.

мо́р**е**	мор**я́**
сочине́н**ие**	сочине́н**ия**

* Nouns whose stress shifts in the plural are given in the Vocabulary at the end of the book.

20-3. Accusative Plural of Inanimate Nouns

The accusative plural of inanimate nouns, regardless of gender, is the same as the nominative plural:

	f.	*m.*	*f.*	*m.*	*n.*
nom.	ка́рт**ы**	журна́л**ы**	неде́л**и**	словар**и́**	мор**я́**
acc.	ка́рт**ы**	журна́л**ы**	неде́л**и**	словар**и́**	мор**я́**

20-4. Nominative Plural of Adjectives

The plural endings are the same for all three genders.

a. Hard adjectives take **-ые**:

SINGULAR	PLURAL (*m., f., n.*)
но́в**ый**, но́в**ая**, но́в**ое**	но́в**ые**
молод**о́й**, молод**а́я**, молод**о́е**	молод**ы́е**

b. Soft adjectives take **-ие**:

после́дн**ий**, после́дн**яя**, после́дн**ее**	после́дн**ие**

c. Mixed adjectives whose stems end in **г, к, х**, or **ж, ч, ш, щ** take **-ие**:

ру́сск**ий**, ру́сск**ая**, ру́сск**ое**	ру́сск**ие**
хоро́ш**ий**, хоро́ш**ая**, хоро́ш**ее**	хоро́ш**ие**

20-5. Accusative Plural of Adjectives with Inanimate Nouns

Adjectives of all three genders modifying inanimate nouns are identical in the nominative and accusative plural.

nom. & *acc.* но́в**ые** карти́н**ы**
nom. & *acc.* ру́сск**ие** журна́л**ы**
nom. & *acc.* си́н**ие** кре́сл**а**

Part II

20-6. Nouns with Prepositional in -ý

Some masculine nouns ending in a consonant in the *nominative* take the stressed **-ý** in the *prepositional* when governed by the prepositions **в** or **на**.

nom.	*prep.*	
пол	на пол**у́**	*on* the floor
бе́рег	на берег**у́**	*on* the shore
сад	в сад**у́**	*in* the garden
лес	в лес**у́**	*in* the forest

20-7. Genitive Plural of Nouns Ending in a Consonant

Masculine nouns ending in a *consonant* in the nominative singular take **-ов** in the genitive plural.

nom. sing.	nom. plural	gen. plural
журна́л	журна́лы	журна́л**ов**
ча**с**	часы́	час**о́в**
учени́**к**	ученики́	учени**ко́в**

Exceptions: Nouns ending in **-ж, -ч, -ш,** or **-щ** take **-ей** instead of **-ов** in the genitive plural.

гара́**ж**	гаражи́	гараж**е́й**
каранда́**ш**	карандаши́	карандаш**е́й**
това́ри**щ**	това́рищи	това́рищ**ей**

20-8. Genitive Plural with the Numbers 5 through 20

The cardinal numerals 5 through 20 govern the genitive plural.* (For the numerals 2, 3, and 4, which govern the genitive singular, see ¶9-3.)

пять журна́л**ов**	five magazines
шесть час**о́в**	six hours; six o'clock
семь това́рищ**ей**	seven friends

20-9. Adjectives Used as Nouns

Some adjectives are also used as nouns, but they are always declined as adjectives. For example:

nom. sing.	столо́в**ая**	dining room
gen. sing.	столо́в**ой**	of a dining room
nom. pl.	столо́в**ые**	dining rooms

20-10. The Imperative in -ь and -ьте

The imperative endings are **-ь** and **-ьте** instead of **-и** and **-ите** when (1) the first person singular in the present is stressed on the stem, *and* (2) the present stem ends in a consonant. For example:

INFINITIVE	PRESENT	IMPERATIVE
пла́кать	я пла́чу	
(to weep)	(*stressed on stem*)	
	ты пла́**ч** - ешь	{ пла́ч**ь** { пла́ч**ьте**

* The words for the numerals 8 through 20 will be given in ¶27-5.

INFINITIVE	PRESENT	IMPERATIVE
ста́вить (to put, place)	я ста́влю (*stressed on stem*)	
	ты ста́в - ишь	{ ставь { ста́вьте

Note: The imperative of **идти́** is **иди́, иди́те,** and the imperative of **люби́ть** is **люби́, люби́те** (see ¶ 11-5), because they do not meet both requirements of the rule above. Their present stems end in consonants, but the first person present is stressed on the ending, and not on the stem.

Упражне́ния (Exercises)

A. Give the plural of the following phrases and translate.

1. хоро́ший това́рищ. 2. чёрная коро́ва. 3. весёлый ю́ноша. 4. францу́зская траге́дия. 5. неме́цкий слова́рь. 6. тру́дный язы́к. 7. англи́йский трамва́й. 8. больша́я столо́вая. 9. прекра́сный за́втрак. 10. плохо́й у́жин. 11. прия́тный сюрпри́з. 12. молода́я де́вушка. 13. си́няя тетра́дь. 14. дли́нное письмо́. 15. после́днее сло́во.

B. Supply Russian equivalents for the English words in italics; then translate the sentences.

1. Ма́льчик лежи́т *on the floor.* 2. Де́ти сидя́т *in the garden.* 3. Ло́шади стоя́т *on the shore* о́зера. 4. Тепе́рь уже́ пять *o'clock.* 5. Он ка́ждый день рабо́тает семь *hours.* 6. В кла́ссе сего́дня то́лько шесть *pupils.* 7. Пять *friends* ждут Ва́сю. 8. *Do not cry,* Ма́ша. *Cry* то́лько ма́ленькие де́ти. 9. Роди́тели Аки́ма иду́т в *dining room.* 10. Ва́ся лю́бит *foreign languages.*

C. Count from 1 through 7 with each of the following masculine nouns, and indicate stress on the nouns throughout. (Refer to ¶ 20-7 and ¶ 20-8.) For example:

оди́н стол, два стола́, *etc.* . . . пять столо́в, *etc.* . . .

1. журна́л. 2. час. 3. учени́к. 4. гара́ж. 5. каранда́ш. 6. това́рищ. 7. рома́н. 8. стака́н (*pl.* стака́ны). 9. ма́льчик 10. оте́ц.

D. Memorize the nominative plural of the following nouns and adjectives, noting the stress. Then translate these phrases, and write them in the nominative singular. For example:

бе́лые да́чи: white summer homes; **бе́лая да́ча**

1. це́лые дни.   2. америка́нские чаи́.   3. ру́сские борщи́.
4. хоро́шие словари́.   5. холо́дные дожди́.   6. стра́нные
пи́сьма.   7. испа́нские траге́дии.   8. после́дние пти́цы.   9.
францу́зские супы́.   10. ми́лые ю́ноши.   11. замеча́тельные
ло́шади.   12. интере́сные дневники́.   13. прекра́сные потолки́.
14. плохи́е кре́сла.   15. больши́е о́кна.   16. пусты́е стака́ны.
17. краси́вые полы́.   18. прия́тные часы́.   19. весёлые ма́ль-
чики.   20. дли́нные во́йны.   21. чёрные до́ски.   22. се́рые
ко́шки.   23. бе́лые сте́ны.   24. неме́цкие дере́вни.   25. си́ние
моря́.

E. *Check yourself*!   Close the book and rewrite Exercise D from
your paper, changing the singular back to the plural.   Then compare the results with the text.

Перево́д (**Translation**)

A. Omit the words in parentheses and include the words in
brackets.

1. Please read on [further].   2. You cried yesterday and are
crying today.   Please, do not cry.   3. We have on our farm [**У нас
на фе́рме есть**] horses, cows, cats, and dogs.   4. The birds are
singing gaily in the garden.   5. You dress (yourself) too late.
6. You wash (yourselves) too rarely.   Please wash (yourselves)
more frequently.   7. Go to [into] the dining room.   Everybody
[all] is waiting (for) you.   8. Vasya bought a new German grammar.
9. The new lessons are very difficult (ones).   10. The students of
this university are good sportsmen.   11. The girls of this school
are good sportswomen.   12. Do you want to play basketball with
us in the garden?   13. Children like to watch television.   14.
Masha's parents often go to the movies.   15. Vasya and Akim have
breakfast together.

B. Translate at sight.

1. Here is our dining room.   2. Here we have breakfast and
supper.   3. In the morning I prepare breakfast, and in the evening
mother prepares supper.   4. We get up at six o'clock, and wash
and dress quickly.   5. At seven o'clock we begin to work.   6. I
like to work in the garden when the weather is good.   7. It is
pleasant [**прия́тно**] to work when the birds are singing gaily in the
garden.

C. Omit the words in parentheses and include the words in brackets.

1. I like [**люблю**] foreign languages very (much).   2. I am now studying French.   3. Two years ago I studied German, and in a year [**через год**] I shall be studying Spanish.   4. I want to speak Russian, French, Spanish, and German well.   5. My parents are Russians, but we rarely speak Russian at home.   6. My sister prefers to speak French, and my younger brother wants to speak only English.   7. But my friend Paul speaks Russian quite well, and we often converse in Russian (for) a whole hour.   8. We are very good friends and are very fond of each other.   9. Sometimes I think that he is too serious, and he thinks that I am too gay.   10. My parents think that I need such a friend.

Вопро́сы (Questions)

1. Кому́ Аки́м пи́шет э́то письмо́?   2. Где он тепе́рь? 3. Аки́м и Ва́ся лю́бят друг дру́га?   4. Почему́ Аки́м ду́мает, что Ва́ся немно́го стра́нный?   5. Каки́е рома́ны чита́ет Ва́ся? 6. Какой иностра́нный язы́к Ва́ся тепе́рь изуча́ет?.   7. Каки́е иностра́нные языки́ вы тепе́рь изуча́ете?   8. Что лежи́т у Ва́си на столе́?   9. Каки́е сочине́ния он пи́шет?   10. Как Ва́ся игра́ет в футбо́л?   11. Сестра́ Ва́си хоро́шая спортсме́нка? 12. Ири́на, сестра́ Ва́си, уме́ет е́здить верхо́м?   13. Когда́ роди́тели Ва́си встаю́т у́тром?   14. Когда́ Аки́м встаёт? 15. Куда́ он идёт за́втракать?   16. С кем он за́втракает в столо́вой?   17. Кто всегда́ приготовля́ет за́втрак?   18. Почему́ Ма́ша начина́ет пла́кать, когда́ она́ чита́ет, что Ири́на прекра́сная хозя́йка?

U N I T 21

МА́ЛЕНЬКАЯ ТРАГЕ́ДИЯ

Вдруг в ко́мнату вхо́дит А́нна Па́вловна, мать Ма́ши. Она́ ви́дит, что письмо́ Аки́ма лежи́т на полу́, и что Ма́ша сиди́т у стола́ и ти́хо пла́чет.

— Что с тобо́й? — спра́шивает А́нна Па́вловна. — Де́сять мину́т тому́ наза́д ты была́ так ра́да, когда́ я тебе́ дала́ письмо́ Аки́ма, а тепе́рь оно́ лежи́т на полу́, и ты пла́чешь.

Но Ма́ша ничего́ не отвеча́ет, кладёт го́лову на стол и продолжа́ет пла́кать. А́нна Па́вловна берёт письмо́ и чита́ет его́ о́чень внима́тельно. Вдруг она́ начина́ет смея́ться.

— Почему́ ты смеёшься, ма́ма? — кричи́т Ма́ша.—Аки́м лю́бит другу́ю де́вушку, Ири́ну, а меня́ он совсе́м забы́л! Он говори́т то́лько о ней: — Ири́на прекра́сная спортсме́нка, Ири́на замеча́тельная хозя́йка, Ири́на всегда́ приготовля́ет за́втрак . . . Э́то совсе́м не смешно́! А я ду́мала, что Аки́м меня́ лю́бит . . . — и Ма́ша опя́ть начина́ет пла́кать.

— Глу́пая де́вушка! — говори́т А́нна Па́вловна — ты не прочита́ла письма́ до конца́. Вот оно́. Чита́й!

— Не хочу́ чита́ть! — кричи́т Ма́ша — Аки́м меня́ не интересу́ет. Не хочу́ да́же ду́мать о нём.

А́нна Па́вловна ничего́ не отвеча́ет. Она́ берёт письмо́ Аки́ма и чита́ет его́ ме́дленно и гро́мко, а Ма́ша слу́шает о́чень внима́тельно.

Слова́рь (Vocabulary)

Па́вловна Pavlovna (*lit.* Paul's daughter)
ти́хо quietly
что с тобо́й? (*instr. of* **ты**) what is the matter with you?
де́сять ten

138

де́сять мину́т (*gen. pl. of* **мину́та**) ten minutes
дала́ (*f., past of* **дать**) gave
класть (**I**); **кладу́, кладёшь, кладу́т** to put
кладёт го́лову на стол (*acc. of* **стол** *indicates direction of motion*) puts her
    head on (*lit.* on to) the table
внима́тельно carefully, attentively
ма́ма mama
крича́ть (**II**); **кричу́, кричи́шь, крича́т** to shout, to scream
друго́й, -а́я, -о́е (*adj. & pron.*) other, another
совсе́м (*adv.*) entirely
о ней (*prep. of* **она́**) about her
совсе́м не not at all, not in the least
смешно́ it is funny
э́то совсе́м не смешно́! this is not at all funny!
опя́ть again
прочита́ла (*past of* **прочита́ть**) she read through
до (*with gen.*) to, up to, until
коне́цᶠˡ (*gen.* **конца́**) end
о нём (*prep. of* **он**) about him

ВСЁ ХОРОШО́, ЧТО ХОРОШО́ КОНЧА́ЕТСЯ

. . . Мы обыкнове́нно еди́м компо́т, пото́м я́йца и хлеб с
ма́слом и пьём ко́фе.*

Мы начина́ем рабо́тать в во́семь и́ли в де́вять часо́в. Иногда́
мы рабо́таем в саду́, а иногда́ в лесу́, кото́рый нахо́дится
недалеко́ от фе́рмы. Мы берём с собо́й са́ндвичи и за́втракаем
в оди́ннадцать и́ли в двена́дцать часо́в.

Мы обыкнове́нно конча́ем рабо́ту в пять часо́в дня, и в
шесть вся семья́ обе́дает в большо́й столо́вой. Мы еди́м
сли́шком бы́стро и ма́ло разгова́риваем. Э́то мне совсе́м не
нра́вится. По́мнишь как до́лго мы разгова́ривали по́сле
обе́да, когда́ я был у вас? Я тогда́ не знал как прия́тно сиде́ть
вокру́г самова́ра, пить чай и разгова́ривать.

Ве́чером мы ча́сто е́здим в го́род. Ва́ся обыкнове́нно
хо́дит в библиоте́ку, а мы с Ири́ной хо́дим в кино́ и́ли гуля́ем в
па́рке.

Ири́на о́чень ми́лая де́вушка. У неё краси́вое лицо́, больши́е
си́ние глаза́ и прия́тный го́лос, — но мне с ней ску́чно. Она́
ма́ло чита́ла, нигде́ не была́, и ма́ло зна́ет. То́лько с тобо́й,
Ма́ша, мне никогда́ не ску́чно. Ско́ро мы бу́дем вме́сте.

Твой друг Аки́м

Ма́ша, счастли́вая, весёлая, целу́ет ма́му. Всё хорошо́, что
хорошо́ конча́ется!

* For the beginning of this paragraph, see p. 130.

Слова́рь (Vocabulary)

что (*rel. pron.*) that
конча́ться (**I**) (*intrans., used mostly in third person*); **конча́ется, конча́ются**
    to end, to come to an end
всё хорошо́, что хорошо́ конча́ется all is well that ends well
обыкнове́нно usually
яйцо́ (*pl.* **я́йца**) egg
хлеб bread
ма́сло butter
ко́фе (*m.; not decl.*) coffee
во́семь eight
де́вять nine
лес (*prep. with* **в = лесу́**) forest
недалеко́ not far
са́ндвич sandwich
за́втракать (*when referring to noon meal*) to eat lunch
оди́ннадцать eleven
двена́дцать twelve
конча́ть (**I**); **конча́ю, -ешь, -ют** to finish
в пять часо́в дня at five o'clock in the afternoon
обе́дать (**I**); **обе́даю, -ешь, -ют** to dine, to have dinner
тогда́ then, at that time (see ¶ 21-5)
прия́тно it is pleasant
библиоте́ка library
мы с Ири́ной Irene and I (see ¶ 21-6)
лицо́ (*pl.* **ли́ца**) face
глаз (*pl.* **глаза́**) eye
го́лос (*pl.* **голоса́**) voice
счастли́вый, -ая, -ое (*pr.* **щастли́вый**) happy
целова́ть (**I**); **целу́ю, целу́ешь, целу́ют** to kiss

Грамма́тика (Grammar)

Part I

21-1. The Pronoun: что*

    a. Interrogative.

	DECLENSION	EXAMPLES
nom.	**что?** what?	**Что** лежи́т на столе́? **Газе́та** лежи́т на столе́.
gen.	**чего́?** of what?	**Чего́** вы не зна́ете? Я не зна́ю уро́ка.

* See ¶ 12-2.

dat.	**чему́?** to what? (often used idiomatically)	К **чему́** подхо́дит по́езд? По́езд подхо́дит к **ста́нции**. (То) what is the train approaching? The train is approaching the station.
acc.	**что?** what?	**Что** вы чита́ете? Я чита́ю **газе́ту**.
instr.	**чем?** with what?	**Чем** вы пи́шете? Я пишу́ **перо́м**.
prep.	**о чём?** about what?	**О чём** вы говори́те? Мы гово́рим **о пого́де**.

b. Relative.

1. The relative pronoun **что** (*what, that, which*) is declined like the interrogative but is used without the question mark. For example:

Я зна́ю, **что** он чита́л.	I know *what* he was reading.
Всё хорошо́, **что** хорошо́ конча́ется.	All is well *that* ends well.
Мы де́лаем всё, **что** мо́жем.	We do all (*that*) we can.

2. Do not confuse the subordinating conjunction **что** (see ¶ **7-4**) with the relative pronoun **что**. Compare:

Я зна́ю, **что** он чита́л.	I know *what* he was reading.
Я зна́ю, **что** он чита́л э́ту кни́гу.	I know *that* he was reading this book.

21-2. The Declension of Personal Pronouns in the Singular

The nominative, genitive, dative, and accusative forms of the personal pronouns in the singular were given in ¶ **3-4**, **9-1**, and **13-4**. The following tables summarize the singular declension of personal pronouns in *all* cases.

	FIRST PERSON (*m., f.,* & *n.*)	SECOND PERSON (*m., f.,* & *n.*)
nom.	я	ты
gen.	меня́	тебя́
dat.	мне	тебе́
acc.	меня́	тебя́
instr.	мной (мно́ю)	тобо́й (тобо́ю)
prep.	обо мне́	о тебе́

	THIRD PERSON (m. & n.)		THIRD PERSON (f.)	
		With governing prepositions		With governing prepositions
nom.	он онó		онá	
gen.	егó	у негó	её	у неё
dat.	емý	к немý	ей	к ней
acc.	егó	на негó	её	на неё
instr.	им	с ним	ей, éю	с ней, с нéю
prep.	о нём	о нём	о ней	о ней

Note: Pronouns of the third person take the prefix **н-** when they are governed by a preposition.

21-3. Possessives for the Third Person

a. The possessive adjective for the *first person* is **мой, моя́,** and **моё** in the singular, and **мои́** in the plural.

b. The possessive adjective for the *second person* is **твой, твоя́,** and **твоё** in the singular, and **твои́** in the plural.

c. There is no possessive adjective for the *third person.* To express such possession, the genitive forms of the corresponding personal pronouns are used.

SINGULAR

m.	(*nom.* он)	**егó**	his	(*lit.* of him)
f.	(*nom.* онá)	**её**	her	(*lit.* of her)
n.	(*nom.* онó)	**егó**	its	(*lit.* of its)

PLURAL

m. *f.* *n.*	(*nom.* они́)	**их**	their	(*lit.* of them)

Note: When the above forms are used as possessive adjectives (that is, when they are used to answer the question *whose?*), they are *not* declined and they are *never* prefixed by **н-**. (The prefix **н-** thus indicates that **егó, её, егó,** and **их** are personal pronouns, not adjectives.)   Compare:

PRONOUNS	ADJECTIVES
Я иду́ к **нему́**.	Я иду́ к **его́** бра́ту.
I am going to *him* (his home).	I am going to *his* brother.
Я иду́ к **ней**.	Я иду́ к **её** бра́ту.
I am going to *her* (her home).	I am going to *her* brother.
Э́то письмо́ от **него́**.	Э́то письмо́ от **его́** отца́.
This letter is from *him*.	This letter is from *his* father.
Мы бы́ли у **них**.	Мы бы́ли у **их** сестры́.
We were at *their* house.	We were at *their* sister's.

Part II

21-4. Time of Day—On the Hour

Memorize this paragraph, which is largely a matter of review. The table will greatly help your memory.

CARDINAL NUMERALS (1 to 12)	TIME OF DAY	
	P.M.	A.M.
1. оди́н, одна́, одно́	1:00 час дня	час но́чи
2. два (*m. & n.*), две (*f.*)	2:00 два часа́ дня	два часа́ но́чи
3. три	3:00 три часа́ дня	три часа́ но́чи
4. четы́ре	4:00 четы́ре часа́ дня	четы́ре часа́ утра́
5. пять	5:00 пять часо́в дня	пять часо́в утра́
6. шесть	6:00 шесть часо́в ве́чера	шесть часо́в утра́
7. семь	7:00 семь часо́в ве́чера	семь часо́в утра́
8. во́семь	8:00 во́семь часо́в ве́чера	во́семь часо́в утра́
9. де́вять	9:00 де́вять часо́в ве́чера	де́вять часо́в утра́
10. де́сять	10:00 де́сять часо́в ве́чера	де́сять часо́в утра́
11. оди́ннадцать	11:00 оди́ннадцать часо́в ве́чера	оди́ннадцать часо́в утра́
12. двена́дцать	12:00 двена́дцать часо́в но́чи	двена́дцать часо́в дня

Note: The afternoon hours 1:00–5:00 are regarded as hours of the *day* = **дня**; 6:00–11:00 p.m. as hours of the *evening* = **ве́чера**; 12:00 midnight–3:00 a.m. as hours of the *night* = **но́чи**; and 4:00–11:00 a.m. as hours of the *morning* = **утра́**. Twelve noon is considered an hour of the *day* = **дня**.

21-5. Тогда́ and пото́м

Note the difference in the meanings of **тогда́** and **пото́м**:

a. **Тогда́** refers to a specific point in time, past or future, but *not* present. For example:

Я **тогда́** был здоро́в.	I was well *then* (at that time).
Ско́ро мы бу́дем в СССР и **тогда́** бу́дем говори́ть то́лько по-ру́сски.	Soon we shall be in the U.S.S.R. and shall *then* speak only Russian.

b. **Пото́м** refers to an event or situation in a series of successive events or situations. For example:

Сего́дня я иду́ в шко́лу, **пото́м** в библиоте́ку, а **пото́м** в кино́.	Today I am going to school, *then* to the library, and *then* to the movies.

21-6. Plural Subjects with the Instrumental

To express a plural subject, especially in the first person, **с** with the instrumental is often used thus:

Мы **с** Ири́н**ой** хо́дим в кино́.	Irene and I go to the movies.
Мы **с** отцо́м слу́шаем ра́дио.	Father and I are listening to the radio.

21-7. Verbs in -ова́ть and -ава́ть

a. Verbs in **-ова́ть** lose the syllable **-ов** in the *present tense* and in the *imperative*. For example:

INFINITIVE	PRESENT	IMPERATIVE
рисова́ть	рису́**ю**	рису́**й**
	рису́**ешь**	рису́**йте**

b. Verbs in **-ава́ть** lose the syllable **-ва** only in the present; their imperative is formed from the infinitive stem, *not* from the present stem. For example:

вст**ава́ть**	встаю́	встава́**й**
	встаёшь	встава́**йте**

Упражне́ния (Exercises)

A. The following sentences are all affirmative. Use the interrogative **что?** to form questions to which these sentences can serve as

UNIT 21 145

answers. (Master ¶ 21-1 before doing this exercise. **Чему́**, which is used idiomatically, is not included here.) For example:

Учи́тель пи́шет ме́лом на доске́.

Question: **Чем учи́тель пи́шет на доске́?**

1. Я чита́ю рома́н. 2. Ма́ша ду́мает о письме́. 3. Мы говори́м о войне́. 4. Он пи́шет сочине́ние перо́м. 5. Она́ не уме́ет приготовля́ть борщ. 6. Оте́ц пьёт чай из стака́на. 7. Я никогда́ не пью воды́. 8. Лес нахо́дится недалеко́ от фе́рмы.

B. Replace the words in parentheses with the proper form of the pronoun or with an appropriate possessive, as required by the sentence. (Master ¶ 21-2 and 21-3 before doing this exercise.) For example:

Я иду́ к (она́). — Я иду́ к **ней**.

Вот письмо́ от (она́) бра́та. — Вот письмо́ от **её** бра́та.

1. Ты сиди́шь о́коло (он). 2. Он стои́т о́коло (я). 3. Мы сиди́м о́коло (она́) отца́. 4. Мы разгова́риваем с (она́). 5. Вы говори́ли о (он). 6. Она́ была́ с (он) в теа́тре. 7. Вот сочине́ние (он) ученика́. 8. Мать дала́ (она́) письмо́. 9. Письмо́ бы́ло у (она́). 10. Что с (ты)? 11. Почему́ вы так смо́трите на (он)? 12. Я е́ду к (ты). 13. Они́ сего́дня бу́дут у (ты). 14. О ком вы говори́ли, о (он) и́ли о (она́)? 15. Что вы (он) пи́шете обо (я)? 16. Вот ва́ше письмо́, чита́йте (оно́). 17. Здесь темно́. Ты (я) ви́дишь? 18. Да, я (ты) ви́жу, но (она́) я не ви́жу. 19. Мы е́дем в го́род и берём (ты) с собо́й. 20. Учи́тельница то́лько что говори́ла о (ты).

C. Supply Russian equivalents for the English words in italics. Then translate the sentences. (Refer to ¶ 21-4.)

1. Мы встаём в *8:00 a.m.* 2. В *9:00 o'clock* мы за́втракаем. 3. *Then* мы идём в *garden*. 4. Мы рабо́таем *in the garden.* пять и́ли шесть *hours*. 5. At *6:00 o'clock* мы конча́ем рабо́ту. 6. В *8:00 p.m.* мы обе́даем. 7. В Аме́рике *usually* обе́дают в *6:00 p.m.*, но мы обе́даем в *8:00.* 8. Мы обе́даем так по́здно, потому́ что всегда́ ждём *father*. 9. Он рабо́тает но́чью и спит днём *six or seven hours*. 10. Он начина́ет рабо́тать в *2:00 a.m.*

Перево́д (Translation)

A. Omit the words in parentheses and include the words in brackets.

1. Why are you laughing? This is not at all funny! 2. What do you want to know about him? 3. He does not interest me in the least [совсе́м не]. 4. You did not read the end of her letter. 5. We read the book through [прочита́ли] to [up to] the end. I shall read again and you listen carefully. 6. The boy again puts (his) head on the table and begins to cry. 7. What is the matter with you? Why are you screaming? 8. Who is on the phone? You are talking too quietly, and I do not hear anything [and I hear nothing]. 9. Who shouted so loudly in the forest? 10. She was not talking about you (*fam.*), but about another girl.

B. Omit the words in parentheses and include the words in brackets. (See ¶21-6.)

1. My brother and I usually have breakfast at seven o'clock in the morning. 2. We eat eggs, bread, and butter, and drink milk or coffee. 3. We never drink tea in the morning. 4. My sister and I often eat lunch in town. 5. We usually eat sandwiches and drink cold milk. 6. After lunch [по́сле за́втрака] we often go to the library. 7. We have a new library in town, and it is very pleasant to work there. 8. Four years ago we lived in the country, and I did not know then how pleasant (it was) to live in a big town. 9. At 6:00 p.m. the whole family has dinner [dines] in the big dining room. 10. I also have a little brother, Vanya, whom everybody loves very much. 11. He has an intelligent [smart] face, big blue eyes, and a pleasant voice. 12. His teacher (*f.*) says that he is the most diligent pupil in school. 13. He always enters the dining room, gay and happy, and kisses mother and father. 14. He never kisses me, but always wants to sit near me. 15. What a fine [прекра́сный] boy!

Вопро́сы (Questions)

1. Кто вдруг вхо́дит в ко́мнату Ма́ши? 2. Что она́ ви́дит? 3. Почему́ Ма́ша была́ так ра́да де́сять мину́т тому́ наза́д? 4. Почему́ она́ тепе́рь пла́чет? 5. Она́ прочита́ла письмо́ до конца́? 6. Почему́ Ма́ша не хо́чет чита́ть да́льше? 7. Э́то пра́вда, что Аки́м её не интересу́ет? 8. Как Ма́ша слу́шает, когда́ её мать чита́ет письмо́ Аки́ма?

9. Когда́ Аки́м и его́ друг начина́ют рабо́тать? 10. Где
они́ ча́сто рабо́тают? 11. Когда́ они́ конча́ют рабо́ту? 12.
Когда́ вся семья́ обе́дает? 13. Семья́ Ва́си мно́го разгова́ри-
вает в столово́й? 14. Э́то нра́вится Аки́му? 15. Что Ва́ся
обыкнове́нно де́лает в го́роде? 16. А что де́лают Аки́м и
Ири́на? 17. Како́е у Ири́ны лицо́? 18. Каки́е у неё глаза́ и
како́й го́лос? 19. Почему́ Аки́му ску́чно с Ири́ной? 20. А
с Ма́шей ему́ то́же ску́чно? 21. Почему́ Ма́ша целу́ет ма́му?
22. А́нна Па́вловна хоро́шая мать? Почему́?

U N I T 22

REVIEW LESSON

Grammar and Vocabulary Review

A. Supply the proper form of the verb in parentheses and the Russian equivalent for English words, and translate at sight. When two verbs are given, select the one required by the meaning of the sentence.

1. Они́ всегда́ (смея́ться), но вчера́ они́ не (смея́ться).

2. Ма́ша, почему́ ты (смея́ться)? Э́то совсе́м не (funny)!

3. Мой това́рищ мне о́чень (люби́ть, нра́виться), и я зна́ю, что я ему́ то́же (нра́виться, люби́ть).

4. Она́ о́чень (likes) (ходи́ть, е́здить) верхо́м на чёрной (horse).

5. Ма́ша о́чень (хоте́ть) ви́деть (Joachim).

6. Здесь так (dark), что мы ничего́ не (уме́ть, мочь) ви́деть.

7. Три го́да тому́ наза́д он (уме́ть, мочь) говори́ть (Spanish), но тепе́рь он всё забы́л.

8. Она́ тепе́рь больна́ и не (уме́ть, мочь) игра́ть на (piano).

9. Ва́ша тетра́дь всегда́ (лежа́ть) (on the floor). Кто (класть) её (on the floor)?

10. Я вас прекра́сно (слы́шать). Пожа́луйста, не (крича́ть)!

11. Уро́к (конча́ться) в (12:00 noon). По́сле уро́ка (we shall eat lunch).

12. Не (пла́кать) де́ти! Ско́ро (we shall have dinner).

13. Мы (купа́ться) в (lake) ка́ждый день, но вчера́ (идти́, ходи́ть) дождь и мы не (купа́ться).

14. Ма́льчик (встава́ть) в (7:00 a.m.) ка́ждый день и бы́стро (умыва́ться) и (одева́ться).

15. Семья́ (за́втракать) в (dining room) в (1:00 p.m.) и (у́жинать) в (8:00 p.m.).

148

B. Translate the following infinitives, conjugate them in the present, past, and future, and give the imperative.

Group I. (Note that these verbs lose the syllable **-ов** or **-ва**— see ¶ **21-7.**)

1. рисовáть   3. целовáть
2. интересовáть   4. давáть
                5. вставáть

Group II.

1. класть   5. входи́ть   9. продолжáть
2. плáкать   6. одевáться   10. приготовля́ть
3. кричáть   7. умывáться   11. умéть
4. кончáть   8. смея́ться   12. петь

C. Give the time of the day:

1. From 1:00 p.m. through 12:00 midnight.
2. From 1:00 a.m. through 12:00 noon.

D. Decline the following nouns in the singular and give their plural in the *nominative* and the *accusative*.

1. дáча. 2. дождь. 3. крéсло. 4. мóре. 5. сочинéние.
6. окнó. 7. письмó. 8. потолóк. 9. конéц. 10. тетрáдь.
11. столóвая. 12. недéля.

E. Give the nominative and genitive plural of the following nouns. (See ¶ **20-7.**)

1. час. 2. учени́к. 3. журнáл. 4. гóлос. 5. обéд. 6. сáндвич. 7. товáрищ. 8. гарáж. 9. зáвтрак. 10. спортсмéн.

Reading and Comprehension Drill

A. Read the following sentences aloud and translate them orally into idiomatic English.

1. Идёт дождь, и я дóлжен éхать óчень мéдленно.
2. Моя́ мать купи́ла мне нóвый немéцкий словáрь.
3. Мы берём её с собóй, потомý что онá всегдá предпочитáет éздить с нáми.
4. Мой товáрищ прекрáсно игрáет в тéннис.
5. Мáша внимáтельно прочитáла письмó Вáси до концá.
6. Профéссор, у котóрого мы жи́ли три недéли, хорóший друг семьи́.
7. Он рабóтал весь вéчер и приéхал домóй довóльно пóздно.

8. Ты поéхала в гóрод в вóсемь часóв утрá.

9. Мы хотúм пить чай, но у нас нет стакáнов.

10. Мы ждём отвéта от товáрищей.

B. Supply the endings, read aloud, and translate.

1. Мой друг пúшет интерéсные сочинéн_____.

2. У негó никогдá нé было лóшад_____ и он не умéет éздить верхóм.

3. Вы всегдá сидúте у себ_____ в кóмнате и дýмаете тóлько о себ_____.

4. Чéрез недéл_____ мы éдем в дерéвн_____ к дя́д_____.

5. Большóе спасúбо за интерéсн_____ кнúгу.

6. Как вам нрáвятся инострáнн_____ язык_____?

7. Вы пóмните сáмые трýдн_____ францýзск_____, немéцк_____ и испáнск_____ слов_____.

8. Ирúна и Мáша умн_____ и красúв_____ рýсск_____ дéвушк_____.

9. Ýтром мы едúм я́йц_____, хлеб с мáсл_____ и пьём кóфе, а в час дня мы едúм сáндвич_____ и пьём холóдн_____ молокó.

10. Какúе у вас прекрáсн_____ чёрн_____ глазá!

11. Птúц_____ вéсело пéли в лес_____, котóр_____ нахóдится на берег_____ óзера.

12. Мы говорúли с учúтел_____ о послéдн_____ рýсск_____ урóк_____.

13. Мой товáрищи прекрáсн_____ спортсмéн_____.

14. У Ирúны мúл_____ лицó, больш_____ сúн_____ глазá, и прия́тн_____ гóлос.

15. Вáся читáет серьёзн_____ ромáны, как напримéр "Отц_____ и дéти" úли "Американск_____ трагéдия."

Перевóд (Translation)

Omit the words in parentheses and include the words in brackets.

1. Boris wanted to see the teacher (*m.*), but he was not at home.
2. The little boy, whom you saw a week ago, is my younger brother. 3. We shall be very bored in the country. 4. After supper we went [**поéхали**] to grandfather's, but he was not in town. 5. Do not swim in the lake when it is raining. 6. Boris and Ivan are the most diligent pupils in school. 7. A week ago we saw a French tragedy at the new theater. 8. My sister went [**поéхала**] with us, and cried all evening. 9. She is a strange girl.

10. She cries when she is reading a novel, when our little brother is not well, and even when our dog is sick.

Discussion (Бесе́да)

The Russian translation of this text is given on the next page. Translate without looking at the Russian text; then compare your work with the printed version.

Omit the words in parentheses and include words in brackets.

Teacher: 1. "We read a great deal [much] about Joachim, Masha, Vasya, and Irene. 2. How do you like these [э́ти] young men and women [girls]? 3. What are they doing? 4. What interests Joachim, Vasya, or Masha?"

Ivan: 5. "Joachim writes long letters to Vasya. 6. Vasya is very fond of Joachim, but he thinks that Joachim writes too much about Masha and too little about himself."

Vera: 7. "Girls do not interest Vasya, and he does not like (it) that they interest his friend."

Petya: 8. "Masha, of course, does not sing like a bird, and does not swim like a fish. 9. Joachim wrote nothing about this [об э́том], and Vasya does not know how she swims, or how she sings."

Anne: 10. "Vasya is a serious youth. 11. He reads long novels and very often goes to the library, but his letters are not at all serious. 12. He writes, for instance, (to) Joachim, that everybody is waiting for him: [both] the horses and the cows, [and] the dogs and the cats, and (his) sister Irene. . . ."

Tanya: 13. "This is not true! 14. He writes only that the grey horse is waiting for Joachim!"

Teacher: 15. "Tanya, please do not shout!"

Fedya: 16. "It's not true. . . . Vasya is not an odd youth! 17. A person who reads serious novels, as for instance, *War and Peace, Fathers and Sons,* or *An American Tragedy,* is not at all odd, but very, very intelligent [у́мный]!"

Katya: 18. "I do not understand why Joachim is bored (when he is) with Irene. 19. She has a beautiful face, big black eyes, and a pleasant voice. 20. She is a beauty!"

Ivan: 21. "Her eyes are not black, but blue!"

Teacher: 22. "If you want (to), we can continue our conversation [разгово́р] tomorrow. 23. But for [А на] today—(that's) enough [дово́льно]!"

Pupils: 24. "Oh, what a pity!"

Бесе́да (**Discussion**)

(This section of the lesson could also be used as a skit to be put on by the Russian club or in class.)

Учи́тель: 1. Мы мно́го чита́ли об Аки́ме, Ма́ше, Ва́се и Ири́не. 2. Как вам нра́вятся э́ти (these) ю́ноши и де́вушки? 3. Что они́ де́лают? 4. Что интересу́ет Аки́ма, Ва́сю и́ли Ма́шу?

Ива́н: 5. Аки́м пи́шет Ва́се дли́нные пи́сьма. 6. Ва́ся о́чень лю́бит Аки́ма, но он ду́мает, что Аки́м сли́шком мно́го пи́шет о Ма́ше и сли́шком ма́ло о себе́.

Ве́ра: 7. Де́вушки не интересу́ют Ва́сю и ему́ не нра́вится, что они́ интересу́ют его́ дру́га.

Пе́тя: 8. Ма́ша, коне́чно, не поёт как пти́ца и не пла́вает как ры́ба. 9. Аки́м об э́том [about this] ничего́ не писа́л, и Ва́ся не зна́ет, как она́ пла́вает, и́ли как она́ поёт.

А́нна: 10. Ва́ся серьёзный ю́ноша. 11. Он чита́ет дли́нные рома́ны и о́чень ча́сто хо́дит в библиоте́ку, но его́ пи́сьма совсе́м не серьёзные. 12. Он, наприме́р, пи́шет Аки́му, что все его́ ждут: и ло́шади, и коро́вы, и соба́ки, и ко́шки и сестра́ Ири́на. . . .

Та́ня: 13. Э́то не пра́вда! 14. Он пи́шет то́лько, что Аки́ма ждёт се́рая ло́шадь! . . . .

Учи́тель: 15. Та́ня, пожа́луйста, не кричи́те!

Фе́дя: 16. Не пра́вда. . . . Ва́ся не стра́нный ю́ноша! 17. Челове́к, кото́рый чита́ет серьёзные рома́ны, как наприме́р: "Война́ и мир," "Отцы́ и де́ти" и́ли "Америка́нская траге́дия," совсе́м не стра́нный, а о́чень, о́чень у́мный!

Ка́тя: 18. Я не понима́ю, почему́ Аки́му ску́чно с Ири́ной. 19. У неё краси́вое лицо́, больши́е чёрные глаза́ и прия́тный го́лос. 20. Она́ краса́вица!

Ива́н: 21. Её глаза́ не чёрные, а си́ние! . . . .

Учи́тель: 22. Е́сли хоти́те, мы мо́жем продолжа́ть наш разгово́р (conversation) за́втра. 23. А на (for) сего́дня — дово́льно (enough)!

Ученики́: 24. Ах, как жаль!

U N I T 23

THE ASPECTS

This unit presents the basic and most useful information on the aspects. The grammar in this unit should be covered before the reading exercises and is therefore given first.

The text is intended to illustrate and clarify grammatical principles rather than offer connected material. To simplify the study of the aspects, perfective forms of familiar verbs are used. Irregular perfective forms, especially of unfamiliar verbs, will be introduced very sparingly in the remaining units.

Грамма́тика (Grammar)

23-1. The Aspects

We have already learned that verbs of motion have two distinct forms in Russian: the *habitual* and the *actual*. (See ¶ 13-3.) However, there are two other forms that most Russian verbs—not simply those of motion—possess. These two forms are known as the *imperfective aspect* and the *perfective aspect*.

Both aspects designate the same action but they describe different types of performance with respect to the element of time. For example:

imp.	Он ви́дел.	He saw.
pf.	Он **у**ви́дел.	He noticed.
imp.	Она́ пла́кала.	She was crying.
pf.	Она́ **за**пла́кала.	She started crying.

153

a. The *imperfective* describes an action which is in progress and is unfinished.   Such an action is either:

1. continuous *or* ⎫
2. repeated *or* ⎬ No *result* or *time limit* is indicated.
3. of unknown duration ⎭

b. The *perfective* describes an action which is either:

1. completed *or* ⎫
2. just begun *or* ⎪ *Completion, start, result or time*
3. performed only once *or* ⎨ *limit* is emphasized.
4. of limited duration ⎭

c. In English, ideas of continuity or completion of an action are conveyed by means of auxiliary verbs or other words, e.g., *was, used to, began to, finished, once, awhile.*   In Russian, instead of such additional words, the aspects are generally used to describe varieties of the same action.   The following table gives concrete examples of the way the aspects function in this respect.

	Imperfective	Perfective
Infinitive	1. писа́ть to write, to be writing	написа́ть to finish writing (*action completed*)
	2. пла́кать to cry, to be crying	запла́кать to start crying (*action begun*)
	3. крича́ть to shout, to be shouting	кри́кнуть to exclaim once (*single performance*)
	4. рабо́тать to work, to be working	порабо́тать to work awhile (*limited duration*)
Present	1. Он пи́шет кни́гу. He is writing a book. Он пи́шет. He is writing, he writes.	None
	2. Она́ пла́чет. She is crying. Она́ ча́сто пла́чет. She often cries.	
	3. Я кричу́. I shout, am shouting.	
	4. Ты рабо́таешь. You work, you are working.	

	Imperfective	Perfective
Past	1. Он писа́л кни́гу. He was writing a book (*action in progress and unfinished*).	Он написа́л кни́гу. He has written a book (*action completed in the past*).
	2. Она́ пла́кала. She was crying.	Она́ запла́кала. She started crying (*action begun in the past*).
	3. Я крича́л. I was shouting.	Я кри́кнул. I shouted once, I exclaimed (*single performance in the past*).
	4. Ты рабо́тал. You were working.	Ты порабо́тал. You worked awhile (*limited duration in the past*).
Future	1. Он бу́дет писа́ть. He will write, will be writing.	Он напи́шет. He will write (and finish) (*action will be completed*).
	2. Она́ бу́дет пла́кать. She will cry, will be crying.	Она́ запла́чет. She will start crying (*action will be begun*).
	3. Я бу́ду крича́ть. I shall shout, shall be shouting.	Я кри́кну. I shall shout once (*single performance in the future*).
	4. Ты бу́дешь рабо́тать. You will work, will be working.	Ты порабо́таешь. You will work awhile (*limited duration in the future*).
Imperative	1. пиши́! write!	напиши́! write (and finish)!
	2. плачь! cry!	запла́чь! start crying!
	3. кричи́! shout!	кри́кни! exclaim! shout (once)!
	4. рабо́тай! work!	порабо́тай! work awhile!

23-2. Perfective Forms of the Verb

a. Perfective infinitive.

1. All of the infinitives given in prior lessons have been *imperfective* infinitives. The perfective infinitive, however, closely resembles the imperfective infinitive and can be derived from it in one of the following ways:

	IMPERFECTIVE	PERFECTIVE
(a) by adding a prefix	писа́ть	**на**писа́ть (to finish writing)
(b) by dropping a syllable	встава́ть	встать (to get up once)
(c) by changing **-ать** or **-ять** to **-ить**	изуча́ть	изуч**и́ть** (to master something)
(d) irregularly (from different stems).	говори́ть	сказа́ть (to tell, say one thing)

2. Henceforth, perfective infinitives will be designated by the abbreviation *pf.* as they occur in the vocabulary.

b. Present tense—none.

The perfective aspect has no present tense since a completed action cannot be going on in the present. *Never* use the perfective aspect to render the present tense.

c. The perfective past tense is formed from the perfective infinitive in the same way as the imperfective past is formed from its infinitive, and has the same endings. For example:

Imperfective		Perfective	
Infinitive	Past	Infinitive	Past
писа́ть	писа́л	написа́ть	написа́л
встава́ть	встава́ла	встать	вста́ла
изуча́ть	изуча́ли	изучи́ть	изучи́ли
говори́ть	говори́ло	сказа́ть	сказа́ло

d. Perfective future.

1. When the perfective is formed from the imperfective by adding a prefix, the *perfective future* is obtained by merely adding the prefix to the present tense. For example:

PRESENT TENSE	PERFECTIVE FUTURE	
я пишу́	я **на**пишу́	I shall write (and finish)
ты пи́шешь	ты **на**пи́шешь	you will write (and finish)
etc.	*etc.*	
я рабо́таю	я **по**рабо́таю	I shall work *awhile*
ты рабо́таешь	ты **по**рабо́таешь	you will work *awhile*
etc.	*etc.*	

2. All other perfectives form the future tense from the perfective infinitive in accordance with the same rules which determine the formation of the present tense from the imperfective infinitive (see ¶ **4-2, 7-1,** and **8-1**). For example:

IMPERFECTIVE INFINITIVE	PERFECTIVE INFINITIVE
изуча́ть (I) to study	изучи́ть (II) to master
	(*study carried to completion*)

PRESENT	PERFECTIVE FUTURE	
я изуча́**ю**	я изучу́	I shall master
ты изуча́**ешь**	ты изу́ч**ишь**	
он изуча́**ет**	он изу́ч**ит**	
мы изуча́**ем**	мы изу́ч**им**	
вы изуча́**ете**	вы изу́ч**ите**	
они́ изуча́**ют**	они́ изу́ч**ат**	

IMPERFECTIVE INFINITIVE	PERFECTIVE INFINITIVE
говори́ть (II) to speak,	сказа́ть (I) to have told or
to talk	said (once)

PRESENT	PERFECTIVE FUTURE	
я говор**ю́**	я скажу́	I shall tell, say
		(something once)
ты говори́**шь**	ты ска́ж**ешь**	
он говори́**т**	он ска́ж**ет**	
мы говори́**м**	мы ска́ж**ем**	
вы говори́**те**	вы ска́ж**ете**	
они́ говор**я́т**	они́ ска́ж**ут**	

Note: The imperfective of the verb **изуча́ть** belongs to the First Conjugation and the perfective to the Second; thus the present tense and the perfective future differ accordingly.   On the other hand, **говори́ть** is of Conjugation II and **сказа́ть** of Conjugation I.

e. Perfective imperative.

The *perfective imperative* is formed from the *perfective future* in accordance with the same rules which apply to the formation of the *imperfective imperative* from the *present tense* (see ¶ 11-5 and 20-10.
For example:

PERFECTIVE FUTURE   PERFECTIVE IMPERATIVE

ты напи́шешь $\left\{\begin{array}{l}\text{напиши́!}\\\text{напиши́те!}\end{array}\right\}$ write (and finish)!

ты изу́чишь $\left\{\begin{array}{l}\text{изучи́!}\\\text{изучи́те!}\end{array}\right\}$ master (something)!

ты ска́жешь $\left\{\begin{array}{l}\text{скажи́}\\\text{скажи́те!}\end{array}\right\}$ tell, say (one thing)!

23-3. Plural of Nouns in -á or -я́

A few masculine nouns take an accented **-á** or **-я́** in the nominative plural instead of the regular plural ending (see ¶ 20-2).

бе́рег	берега́	shores
ве́чер	вечера́	evenings
глаз	глаза́	eyes
го́лос	голоса́	voices
го́род	города́	towns
до́ктор	доктора́	doctors
дом	дома́	houses
лес	леса́	forests
профе́ссор	профессора́	professors
учи́тель	учителя́	teachers

Приме́ры (Examples)

The perfective verbs in these exercises are all formed from the imperfective by adding one of the following prefixes:

на-, про-, по-, or с-.

The sentences are given in pairs: the first one contains the *imperfective* and the second, the corresponding *perfective* form. Translate the following sentences. *Note:* The perfective meaning of the verbs is *to have done something* (completed action).

A. *Perfective Past*

1. Я две недéли ничегó не писáл. 2. Сегóдня я написáл два письмá. 3. Ученицá дóлго писáла сочинéние. 4. Вáся написáл корóткое, но óчень хорóшее сочинéние. 5. Лéтом, когдá онá жилá на дáче, онá мнóго читáла. 6. Онá прочитáла тринáдцать ромáнов и четы́рнадцать или пятнáдцать журнáлов. 7. Он всегдá рисовáл тóлько берегá Вóлги, городá, домá, и лесá. 8. Сегóдня он в пéрвый раз нарисовáл юношу и дéвушку. 9. Они вчерá весь день дéлали урóки. 10. Сегóдня они сдéлали урóки днём, а вéчером смотрéли телевизор. 11. Когдá мы жили у бáбушки, мы всегдá зáвтракали в вóсемь часóв утрá. 12. Сегóдня мы позáвтракали в дéвять, а потóм всё ýтро игрáли в тéннис. 13. Когдá мы жили в Чикáго, мы чáсто обéдали в рестор́не "Самовáр." 14. Мы тóлько что пообéдали, а тепéрь слýшаем рáдио. 15. Зимóй мы чáсто ýжинаем довóльно пóздно. 16. Сегóдня мы поýжинали óчень рáно и сейчáс же поéхали в теáтр.

B. *Perfective Future*

1. Мой друг пишет длинные письма. 2. Зáвтра я напишý емý корóткое письмó. 3. Онá тепéрь читáет "Войнý и мир." 4. Этот ромáн мне óчень нрáвится и я прочитáю егó ещё раз. 5. Пáпа рисýет кáждый день. 6. Сегóдня вéчером он нарисýет портрéт бáбушки. 7. Мы всегдá зáвтракаем в дéвять часóв утрá и дéлаем урóки в дéсять или в одиннадцать. 8. Зáвтра же мы позáвтракаем в семь и сейчáс же сдéлаем все урóки. 9. Нам óчень нрáвится рестор́н "Синяя птица" и мы там чáсто обéдаем. 10. Éсли хотите, мы сначáла пообéдаем в рестор́не, а потóм бýдем пить чай и разговáривать у меня в кóмнате.

C. *Perfective Imperative*

1. Большóе спасибо за милое письмó, но пишите, пожáлуйста, чáще! 2. Напишите сочинéние сегóдня! 3. Читáйте, пожáлуйста, дáльше! 4. Прочитáйте письмó до концá! 5. Рисýйте всё, что вы видите! 6. Нарисýйте, пожáлуйста, самовáр! 7. Дéлайте урóки кáждый день! 8. Сдéлай урóк до обéда! 9. Ýжинайте дóма! 10. Поýжинайте в рестор́не, котóрый нахóдится óколо библиотéки, а потóм ждите меня в библиотéке.

Слова́рь (Vocabulary)

Verbs are given first.

Prefix +	*Imperfective* =	*Perfective*	(*To have done something*)
на-	писа́ть	= **на**писа́ть	to have written
про-	чита́ть	= **про**чита́ть	to have read
на-	рисова́ть	= **на**рисова́ть	to have drawn
с-	де́лать	= **с**де́лать	to have done
по-	за́втракать	= **по**за́втракать	to have had breakfast
по-	обе́дать	= **по**обе́дать	to have dined
по-	у́жинать	= **по**у́жинать	to have had supper

коро́ткий, -ая, -ое short
трина́дцать thirteen
четы́рнадцать fourteen
пятна́дцать fifteen
Во́лга Volga (river in the U.S.S.R.)
пе́рвый, -ая, -ое first
в пе́рвый раз for the first time
Чика́го (*not decl.*) Chicago
рестора́н restaurant
сейча́с now, presently
сейча́с же immediately, at once
ещё раз once again
па́па (*m.*) papa
портре́т portrait
снача́ла (*adv.*) at first
до *here:* before

Приме́ры (Examples)

The perfective verbs in these exercises are formed from the imperfective by adding the prefix **по-** or **за-**. Note that the same prefix may lend different meanings to a verb. Compare **пообе́дать** (*to have had dinner*) with **погуля́ть** (*to walk awhile*). The first perfective denotes *completed action* whereas the second denotes *short duration*.

A. Translate. Note that in the following sentences all perfectives with **по-** indicate *short duration*.

1. Я немно́го погуля́ю в па́рке, а пото́м весь ве́чер бу́ду чита́ть. 2. Посиди́те ещё немно́го, мы так ре́дко ви́дим друг дру́га. 3. Вчера́ я немно́го порабо́тал в саду́, пото́м полежа́л на дива́не и поспа́л. 4. Ма́льчик постоя́л не́сколько мину́т о́коло две́ри рестора́на и ушёл. 5. Де́вочка поигра́ла с ко́шкой и ушла́. 6. Мы поговори́ли с хозя́йкой и ушли́. 7. Ты иди́ домо́й, а я ещё посижу́ немно́го и поговорю́ с тётей

и с дя́дей.   8. Ты немно́го поигра́ешь на роя́ле, а пото́м
сде́лаешь уро́ки.   9. Мы ещё раз послу́шаем му́зыку, а пото́м
бу́дем танцова́ть.   10. Снача́ла поду́май, а пото́м отвеча́й!

Слова́рь (Vocabulary)

Verbs are given first.

Prefix	+ Imperfective	= Perfective	(To do something for a short time)
по-	гуля́ть	= погуля́ть	to walk awhile
по-	сиде́ть	= посиде́ть	to sit awhile
по-	рабо́тать	= порабо́тать	to work awhile
по-	лежа́ть	= полежа́ть	to lie awhile
по-	спать	= поспа́ть	to sleep a little, to take a nap
по-	стоя́ть	= постоя́ть	to stand awhile
по-	игра́ть	= поигра́ть	to play awhile
по-	говори́ть	= поговори́ть	to have a chat
по-	слу́шать	= послу́шать	to listen awhile
по-	ду́мать	= поду́мать	to think awhile

не́сколько (adv. with gen. pl.) several, a few
мину́т (gen. pl. of **мину́та**)
ушёл, ушла́, ушло́, ушли́ (past of pf. **уйти́**) went away (once)
де́вочка little girl
му́зыка music
танцова́ть (I); танцу́ю, -ешь, -ют to dance

B. Translate.   Note that in the following sentences all perfectives with **за-** indicate the *beginning of an action*.

1. Все вдруг заговори́ли о войне́.   2. Студе́нты закрича́ли
"ура́!"   3. Ученики́ запе́ли весёлую пе́сню.   4. Ве́ра чита́ла
"Войну́ и мир" и вдруг запла́кала.   5. Де́вочка запла́чет,
е́сли она́ прочита́ет письмо́ до конца́.   6. Учени́ца написа́ла
упражне́ние, поду́мала немно́го и вдруг гро́мко засмея́лась.

Слова́рь (Vocabulary)

Verbs are given first.

Prefix	+ Imperfective	= Perfective	(To begin doing something)
за-	говори́ть	= заговори́ть	to begin talking
за-	крича́ть	= закрича́ть	to begin shouting, to exclaim
за-	петь	= запе́ть	to begin singing
за-	пла́кать	= запла́кать	to begin weeping
за-	смея́ться	= засмея́ться	to burst into laughter

пе́сня song
упражне́ние exercise

Перево́д (Translation)

Omit the words in parentheses and include the words in brackets.

1. Write the exercise, please!   2. You have written a very short composition.   3. When will you read (and finish) the novel?   4. He has drawn a samovar for the first time.   5. They have already done the lessons for tomorrow [**на за́втра**].   6. We shall first have dinner, and then listen (for awhile) to the radio.   7. Read (through) your lesson once again.   8. Please write the exercises before [**до**] dinner.   9 There are fourteen or fifteen restaurants in town.   10. Mother began to cry, but father burst into laughter.   11. We listened (awhile) to the music, and then danced all evening.   12. We had a little chat with the host and left [went away].   13. He talked for a long time about Masha, but suddenly he began talking about Irene.   14. Everybody exclaimed: "We do not like this song!"   15. The little girl burst into laughter.   16. We shall sit awhile in the park and have a little chat.   17. This exercise is not difficult.   Think awhile and then write.

МОЙ ЗАНЯ́ТИЯ И МОЙ УЧИТЕЛЯ́

Обыкнове́нно я встаю́ в во́семь часо́в утра́, но сего́дня у меня́ экза́мен по ру́сской исто́рии и я встал в шесть. За́втра я опя́ть вста́ну о́чень ра́но, потому́ что у меня́ экза́мен по матема́тике.

Наш учи́тель, Фёдор Па́влович, говори́т, что матема́тика о́чень лёгкий предме́т, но я ду́маю, что а́лгебра, геоме́трия и да́же арифме́тика о́чень тру́дные предме́ты. Фёдор Па́влович большо́й специали́ст по матема́тике. Когда́ он объясня́ет уро́к в кла́ссе, я всё понима́ю, но че́рез пятна́дцать и́ли два́дцать мину́т я забыва́ю почти́ всё, что он объясни́л. К сча́стью, мы с Оле́гом ча́сто занима́емся вме́сте. Он прекра́сно зна́ет матема́тику и объясня́ет мне все тру́дные уро́ки, а я объясня́ю ему́ ру́сскую грамма́тику. О́чень прия́тно занима́ться с таки́м хоро́шим ученико́м.

Я беру́ уро́ки му́зыки у одно́й ста́рой да́мы. Вчера́, когда́ я шёл на уро́к к мое́й учи́тельнице, я уви́дел Фёдора Па́вловича, кото́рый шёл домо́й. Как то́лько он меня́ уви́дел, он закрича́л: "За́втра бу́дет о́чень тру́дный экза́мен. По́мни э́то, Ми́ша!" Я зна́ю, что он сказа́л пра́вду. К сожале́нию, он всегда́ говори́т то́лько пра́вду.

Слова́рь (Vocabulary)

Verbs are given first. When both aspects are presented, the *imperfective* comes first, then the *perfective* with associated forms.

вставáть (I); *pf.* **встать (I)**; *fut.* **встáну, встáнешь, -нут**; *imper.* **встань, встáньте** to get up, to rise

объяснять (I); **объясня́ю, -ешь, -ют**; *pf.* **объясни́ть (II)**; *fut.* **объясню́, объясни́шь, -я́т** to explain (see ¶ 10-B)

забыва́ть (I); **забыва́ю, -ешь, -ют**; *pf.* **забы́ть (I)**; *fut.* **забу́ду, -ешь, -ут**; *imper.* **забу́дь, забу́дьте** to forget

занима́ться (I) *intrans.*; **занима́юсь, -ешься, -ются** to study, to busy one-self (with)

ви́деть (II) to see; *pf.* **уви́деть (II)**; *fut.* **уви́жу, уви́дишь, -ят**; (*no imper.*) to notice

говори́ть (II); to speak, to say, to talk; *pf.* **сказа́ть (I)**; *fut.* **скажу́, ска́жешь, -ут**; *imper.* **скажи́, -и́те** to say, to tell (once)

заня́тия (*n. pl.*) studies

по (*with dat.*) on, in

исто́рия history

по ру́сской исто́рии in Russian history

матема́тика (*sing. in Russian*) mathematics

Фёдор (*dim.* **Фе́дя**) Theodore

Па́влович Pavlovich (*lit.* Paul's son)

лёгкий, -ая, -ое (*pr.* **лёхкий**) easy

предме́т subject

а́лгебра algebra

геоме́трия geometry

арифме́тика arithmetic

два́дцать twenty

сча́стье luck, happiness

к сча́стью fortunately

Оле́г Oleg

таки́м *instr. of* **тако́й**

да́ма lady

я беру́ уро́ки у одно́й да́мы I am taking lessons *from a* lady

как то́лько as soon as

Ми́ша (*m.*) Misha

сожале́ние regret

к сожале́нию unfortunately

Грамма́тика (Grammar)

24-1. Full Declension of Adjectives in the Singular

The following tables are largely a matter of review, except for the *dative* and the *instrumental*.   (See ¶ **14-2** and **18-3**.)

   a. Hard adjectives.

Group I (**-ый, -ая, -ое**)

	masculine	feminine	neuter
nom.	но́в**ый**	но́в**ая**	но́в**ое**
gen.	но́в**ого**	но́в**ой**	но́в**ого**
dat.	но́в**ому**	но́в**ой**	но́в**ому**
acc.	но́в**ый** *or* но́в**ого**	но́в**ую**	но́в**ое**
instr.	но́в**ым**	но́в**ой (ою)**	но́в**ым**
prep.	о но́в**ом**	о но́в**ой**	о но́в**ом**

Group II (-**о́й**, -**а́я**, -**о́е**)

	masculine	feminine	neuter
nom.	молодо́й	молода́я	молодо́е
gen.	молодо́го	молодо́й	молодо́го
dat.	молодо́му	молодо́й	молодо́му
acc.	молодо́й	молоду́ю	молодо́е
	or молодо́го		
instr.	молоды́м	молодо́й (о́ю)	молоды́м
prep.	о молодо́м	о молодо́й	о молодо́м

b. Soft adjectives.

	masculine	feminine	neuter
nom.	после́дний	после́дняя	после́днее
gen.	после́днего	после́дней	после́днего
dat.	после́днему	после́дней	после́днему
acc.	после́дний or после́днего	после́днюю	после́днее
instr.	после́дним	после́дней (ею)	после́дним
prep.	о после́днем	о после́дней	о после́днем

c. Mixed adjectives.

Group I (-**г**, -**к**, -**х** + -**ий**, -**ая**, -**ое**)

	masculine	feminine	neuter
nom.	ру́сский	ру́сская	ру́сское
*gen.	ру́сского	ру́сской	ру́сского
*dat.	ру́сскому	ру́сской	ру́сскому
*acc.	ру́сский	ру́сскую	ру́сское
	or ру́сского		
instr.	ру́сским	ру́сской (ою)	ру́сским
*prep.	о ру́сском	о ру́сской	о ру́сском

Group II (-**ж**, -**ч**, -**ш**, -**щ** + -**ий**, -**ая**, -**ее**)

	masculine	feminine	neuter
nom.	хоро́ший	хоро́шая	хоро́шее
gen.	хоро́шего	хоро́шей	хоро́шего
dat.	хоро́шему	хоро́шей	хоро́шему
acc.	хоро́ший	хоро́шую	хоро́шее
	or хоро́шего		
instr.	хоро́шим	хоро́шей (ею)	хоро́шим
prep.	о хоро́шем	о хоро́шей	о хоро́шем

* Note that these cases follow the pattern of Group I of hard adjectives.

Group III (-г, -к, -х, -ж, -ч, ш, -щ + -о́й, -а́я, -о́е)

	masculine	*feminine*	*neuter*
nom.	дорого́й	дорога́я	дорого́е
★gen.	дорого́го	дорого́й	дорого́го
★dat.	дорого́му	дорого́й	дорого́му
★acc.	дорого́й *or* дорого́го	дорогу́ю	дорого́е
instr.	дороги́м	дорого́й (о́ю)	дороги́м
★prep.	о дорого́м	о дорого́й	о дорого́м

24-2. Declension of the Demonstrative Pronoun э́тот in the Singular †

	masculine	*feminine*	*neuter*
nom.	э́тот	э́та	э́то
gen.	э́того	э́той	э́того
dat.	э́тому	э́той	э́тому
acc.	э́тот *or* э́того	э́ту	э́то
instr.	э́тим	э́той	э́тим
prep.	об э́том	об э́той	об э́том

24-3. Declension of Possessive Adjective-Pronouns in the Singular

a. The possessives **мой, моя́, моё** and **твой, твоя́, твоё** are both adjectives and pronouns. When used as adjectives, they precede the noun they modify, and mean *my* and *your*; when used as pronouns, they follow the noun and mean *mine* and *yours*. For example:

Э́то **мой** дом.	This is *my* house.
Э́тот дом **мой**.	This house is *mine*.
Э́то **твоя́** ко́мната.	This is *your* room.
Э́та ко́мната **твоя́**.	This room is *yours*.
Э́то **моё** кре́сло.	This is *my* armchair.
Э́то кре́сло **моё**.	This armchair is *mine*.

★ Note that these cases follow the pattern of Group II of hard adjectives.
† See ¶ 14-1.

	masculine	feminine	neuter
nom.	мой	моя́	моё
gen.	моего́	мое́й	моего́
dat.	моему́	мое́й	моему́
acc.	мой	мою́	моё
	or моего́		
instr.	мои́м	мое́й (е́ю)	мои́м
prep.	о моём	о мое́й	о моём

Note: Except for stress and the accusative endings, both are declined like **после́дний**.

b. The possessives **наш, на́ша, на́ше** and **ваш, ва́ша, ва́ше** are also adjectives or pronouns, depending on whether they precede or follow the noun.   When used as adjectives, they mean *our* and *your*; when used as pronouns, they mean *ours* and *yours*.   For example:

Э́то **наш** дом.   This is *our* house.
Э́тот дом **наш.**   This house is *ours*.

	masculine	feminine	neuter
nom.	наш	на́ша	на́ше
gen.	на́шего	на́шей	на́шего
dat.	на́шему	на́шей	на́шему
acc.	наш	на́шу	на́ше
	or на́шего		
instr.	на́шим	на́шей (ею)	на́шим
prep.	о на́шем	о на́шей	о на́шем

Note: Except for the nominative and accusative endings, **наш, на́ша, на́ше** and **ваш, ва́ша, ва́ше** are declined like **хоро́ший**.

Упражне́ния (Exercises)

A. Decline the following in the singular.

1. э́тот ма́льчик.   2. э́та де́вочка.   3. э́то упражне́ние.   4. ми́лый учи́тель.   5. тру́дная рабо́та.   6. коро́ткое письмо́. 7. пуста́я дере́вня.   8. большо́е кре́сло.   9. после́дний обе́д. 10. си́няя дверь.   11. хоро́ший слова́рь.   12. дорого́й оте́ц.

13. хоро́шее сочине́ние.   14. твой портре́т.   15. твоя́ коро́ва.
16. твоё сча́стье.   17. ваш трамва́й.   18. на́ша семья́.   19. ва́ша
ча́шка.   20. на́ше окно́.

B. In place of the blanks, supply the appropriate case endings.

1. Мы сего́дня идём к наш＿＿＿ хоро́ш＿＿＿ това́рищу.
2. В наш＿＿＿ больш＿＿＿ ко́мнате стои́т си́нее кре́сло.   3. Ты
лю́бишь гуля́ть в наш＿＿＿ краси́в＿＿＿ саду́.   4. Она́ не
объясни́ла после́дн＿＿＿ уро́ка по исто́р＿＿＿.   5. Он до́лго
разгова́ривал с э́т＿＿＿ молод＿＿＿ челове́ком.   6. Учи́тельница
всегда́ пи́шет э́т＿＿＿ си́н＿＿＿ карандашо́м.   7. Она́ ча́сто хо́дит
к тво＿＿＿ сестре́ и к тво＿＿＿ бра́ту.   8. Мы говори́ли о ваш＿＿＿
хоро́ш＿＿＿ шко́ле и о ваш＿＿＿ прекра́сн＿＿＿ учи́теле.   9. Она́
лю́бит е́здить верхо́м на э́т＿＿＿ бе́л＿＿＿ ло́шади.   10. Я вам
дал после́д＿＿＿ кни́гу из мо＿＿＿ библиоте́ки.

C. In the following sentences, supply the appropriate verb forms
in place of the English words and translate at sight.

1. Мы всегда́ встаём в семь часо́в утра́, но сего́дня мы *got up*
в шесть.   2. За́втра мы опя́ть *shall get up* ра́но.   3. Наш оте́ц
всегда́ *used to get up* ра́но.   4. Учи́тель всегда́ прекра́сно
explained матема́тику.   5. Сего́дня учи́тельница хорошо́ *explained* уро́к.   6. Мы с Ива́ном занима́емся вме́сте и он *will
explain* мне но́вый уро́к.   7. Что *will say* мой учи́тель, е́сли он
меня́ *will see* (*notice*) в па́рке?   8. Она́ до́лго говори́ла, но я не
по́мню, что она́ *said*.   9. Почему́ ты всегда́ так мно́го занима́лся,
а тепе́рь совсе́м не *study*?   10. Я тебе́ ничего́ не скажу́, потому́
что ты сейча́с же всё *will forget* (*once*).   11. Пожа́луйста, *tell*;
я ничего́ не *will forget* (*once*).   12. К сожале́нию, она́ *forgot* всё,
что я ей *explained*.

Перево́д (Translation)

A. Omit the words in parentheses and include the words in
brackets.   Translate all possessives.

1. I conversed with my hostess (for) a long time.   2. He explained the lesson (to) my brother.   3. Unfortunately, he forgot
the last Russian word.   4. He had a chat with your younger brother.
5. He is going (walking) to our young teacher (*m.*).   6. We told
our hostess that you have to study today.   7. I shall have a chat
with your good friend [дру́гом].   8. You forgot this old lady.
9. Fortunately, I noticed him in the theater, and told him that you

were [are] waiting for him.   10. We were talking about our last examination.   11. Did you see our summer house?   12. Do not forget that tomorrow we shall get up early.   13. We prefer to live in your (*fam.*) big house.   14. You did not write your exercise. 15. Arithmetic, algebra, and geometry are easy subjects.

B. Omit the words in parentheses and include the words in brackets.

1. I do not like to get up early, but today I got up at six.   2. I have an examination in geometry tomorrow morning, and shall be studying all day.   3. Our mathematics teacher [**профéссор матемáтики**] told me that the examination will be (a) very difficult (one).   4. Unfortunately, he always tells the truth.   5. Our teacher explains the lessons very well.   6. A week ago he explained a difficult lesson and I understood [**пóнял**] everything. 7. But in [**чéрез**] two days I forgot everything.   8. He is the smartest pupil in our class.   9. It is very pleasant to study with such a good pupil.

Вопрóсы (Questions)

1. Когдá вы обыкновéнно встаёте?   2. Почемý вы сегóдня встáли в шесть?   3. Когдá вы встáнете зáвтра?   4. По какóму предмéту у вас зáвтра экзáмен?   5. Математика лёгкий или трýдный предмéт?   6. Какúе предмéты лёгкие?   7. А какúе сáмые трýдные?   8. Как ваш учúтель математики объясняет урóки?   9. С кем вы занимáетесь?   10. Вам приятно с ним (с ней) занимáться?   Почемý?   11. Вы любите мýзыку?   12. У когó вы берёте урóки мýзыки?   13. Когдá вы хóдите на урóк к вáшему учúтелю (к вáшей учúтельнице)? 14. Что Фёдор Пáвлович сказáл Мúше, как тóлько он егó увúдел?   15. Фёдор Пáвлович всегдá говорúт прáвду?

U N I T 25

МОИ́ ЗАНЯ́ТИЯ И МОИ́ УЧИТЕЛЯ́ (Continued)

Мы с Оле́гом та́кже изуча́ем тепе́рь ру́сский язы́к, ру́сскую литерату́ру и ру́сскую исто́рию.   Для меня́ э́ти предме́ты са́мые лёгкие и са́мые интере́сные, но для Оле́га они́ са́мые тру́дные.   Поэ́тому они́ ему́ не о́чень нра́вятся, но он о́чень лю́бит Никола́я Ива́новича Орло́ва, кото́рый преподаёт все э́ти предме́ты в на́шей шко́ле.

Никола́й Ива́нович Орло́в прекра́сный преподава́тель и о́чень ми́лый и культу́рный челове́к.   Его́ роди́тели бы́ли о́чень бога́тые лю́ди.   У них был большо́й дом в Москве́, заво́д в Ту́ле и да́ча в Крыму́, на берегу́ Чёрного мо́ря.   Когда́ Никола́й Ива́нович был ма́леньким ма́льчиком, у него́ была́ гуверна́нтка, кото́рая говори́ла с ним то́лько по-францу́зски и́ли по-англи́йски.   Поэ́тому он хорошо́ зна́ет англи́йский язы́к.

Господи́н Орло́в учи́лся в Москве́ и стал инжене́ром.   Пото́м он рабо́тал на фа́брике в Крыму́.   Из Кры́ма он пое́хал на Кавка́з и там рабо́тал на фе́рме.   С Кавка́за он пое́хал на Украи́ну и там снача́ла рабо́тал на по́чте, а пото́м на вокза́ле. Пото́м он до́лго жил в А́нглии и во Фра́нции и наконе́ц уе́хал в США.

Слова́рь (Vocabulary)

литерату́ра literature
для (*with gen.*) for
э́ти (*pl. of* э́тот) these
поэ́тому therefore
Орло́в Orlov
преподава́ть (I); преподаю́, -даёшь, -даю́т; *imper.* преподава́й, - йте
  to teach

170

преподава́тель (*m.*) teacher
культу́рный, -ая, -ое cultured
бога́тый, -ая, -ое rich
лю́ди (*nom. pl. of* челове́к) people, men and women
заво́д plant (industrial)
Ту́ла Tula (an industrial town)
Крым (*prep.* with в = Крыму́) Crimea
Чёрное мо́ре Black Sea
гуверна́нтка governess
англи́йский, -ая, -ое English
учи́ться (**II**) *intrans*; учу́сь, у́чишься, -атся to study, to attend school
стать (**I**) (*pf. of* станови́ться); ста́ну, ста́нешь, -ут; *past* стал, -ла, -ло,
    -ли; *imper.* стань, ста́ньте to become
инжене́р engineer
фа́брика factory
пое́хать (**I**) (*pf. of* е́хать) to go, to set out (by conveyance)
на to, at, in (see ¶25-1)
с from (see ¶25-1)
Кавка́з Caucasus
Украи́на Ukraine
по́чта post office
вокза́л railway station
А́нглия England
во in, to, into (see ¶25-1d)
Фра́нция France
уе́хать (**I**) (*pf. of* е́хать) + в to leave for, depart for
США (*pr.* Сэ Ша А) (Соединённые Шта́ты Аме́рики) U.S.A.

Грамма́тика (Grammar)

25-1. Prepositions в — из, на — с, к — от with Verbs of Motion

This paragraph is largely a review of ¶3-3, 11-1, and 15-5.

a. в — из.

1. We have seen that the preposition в + *accusative* indicates
motion to the interior of an object having enclosed space (see
¶11-1), whereas в + *prepositional* indicates location within such a
space (see ¶3-3).   For example:

Ма́льчик идёт в шко́лу.   The boy is going to school (*is
                                going inside*).

(Answers the question: Куда́ ма́льчик идёт?)

Ма́льчик в шко́ле.   The boy is in school (*inside*).

(Answers the question: Где ма́льчик?)

Ма́льчик рабо́тает в па́рке.   The boy is working *in* the park.

(Answers the question: Где ма́льчик рабо́тает?)

Ма́льчик гуля́ет **в** па́рк**е**.   The boy is taking a walk *in* the
                                                                                       park.

    (Answers the question: **Где** ма́льчик гуля́ет?)

    Note: In the second example, **в** + *prepositional* situates an *object* within an enclosed space, while in the third and fourth examples an *action* is situated within such space.

    2. **из** + *genitive* indicates motion *from within* an object having enclosed space.   For example:

Ма́льчик идёт **из** шко́л**ы**.   The boy is coming from (*out of the*) school.

Ма́льчик е́дет **из** го́род**а**.   The boy is coming (*by vehicle*) from town.

ШКО́ЛА

Ма́льчик идёт **в** шко́лу.

Ма́льчик идёт **из** шко́лы.

в + *acc.* = motion into enclosed space.

из + *gen.* = motion from within enclosed space.

Point of arrival is within enclosed space.

Point of departure is within enclosed space.

Стол **в** шко́л**е**.

в + *prep.* = location within enclosed space.

    b. **на — с.**

    The preposition **на**, governing the *accusative* or the *prepositional*, and its corresponding preposition **с**, governing the *genitive*, are often used instead of **в** and **из** as follows:

1. With nouns designating *occasions* or *events* (see ¶ II-I).   For example:

Ма́льчик идёт **на** уро́к, **на** концéрт.	The boy is going *to* the lesson, *to* the concert.
Ма́льчик идёт **с** уро́ка, **с** концéрта.	The boy is coming *from* the lesson, *from* the concert.

Note: With such nouns that designate no specific physical space, the use of **в** and **из** is inconceivable.

2. With nouns designating some specific surface area.   Motion then is *to within* or *from within* the area.

Я иду́ **на** плóщадь, **на** у́лицу.	I am going *to* the (interior of the) square, *into* the street.
Я иду́ **с** плóщади, **с** у́лицы.	I am coming *from* (within) the square, *from* the street.
Солда́т éдет **на** фронт, **на** аэродрóм, **на** юг.	The soldier is going *to* the front, *to* the airport, south.
Солда́т éдет **с** фрóнта, **с** аэродрóма, **с** ю́га.	The soldier is coming *from* the front, *from* the airport, *from* the south.

ПЛО́ЩАДЬ

Ма́льчик идёт **на** плóщадь.

Ма́льчик идёт **с** плóщади.

на + *acc.* = motion into the area.

с + *gen.* = motion out of the area.

Point of arrival is inside a specific surface area.

Point of departure is inside a specific surface area.

Магази́н **на** плóщади.

на + *prep.* = location within a surface area.

3. With specific nouns, e.g., **Кавка́з, Украи́на, фа́брика, заво́д, по́чта, вокза́л.**

Солда́т е́дет **на** Кавка́з, **на** Украи́ну.	The soldier is going *to* the Caucasus, *to* the Ukraine.
Солда́т живёт **на** Кавка́зе, **на** Украи́не.	The soldier lives *in* the Caucasus, *in* the Ukraine.
Солда́т е́дет **с** Кавка́за, **с** Украи́ны.	The soldier is coming *from* the Caucasus, *from* the Ukraine.
Челове́к идёт **на** фа́брику, **на** заво́д, **на** по́чту, **на** вокза́л.	The man is going *to* the factory, *to* the plant, *to* the post office, *to* the railway station.
Челове́к рабо́тает **на** фа́брике, **на** заво́де, **на** по́чте, **на** вокза́ле.	The man is working *at* the factory, *at* the plant, *at* the post office, *at* the railway station.
Челове́к идёт **с** фа́брики, **с** заво́да, **с** по́чты, **с** вокза́ла.	The man is coming *from* the factory, *from* the plant, *from* the post office, *from* the railway station.

c. **к — от.**

1. We have seen that **к** + *dative* indicates motion toward or up to, but *not inside* an object (see ¶ **15-5**). For example:

Я иду́ **к** о́зеру.	I am going to the lake (*not into it*).
Я иду́ **к** бра́ту.	I am going to brother's.

2. **от** + *genitive* indicates motion away from an object. The point of departure is *outside* the object itself. For example:

Я иду́ **от** о́зера.	I am coming from the lake (*was not in it*).
Я иду́ **от** бра́та.	I am coming from brother's

Note: With **к** and **от** the points of arrival and departure are *outside* the object.

ÓЗЕРО

Я иду́ **к** о́зеру. **к**   **от** Я иду́ **от** о́зера.

к + *dat.* = motion toward or up to an object.

от + *gen.* = motion away from an object.

Point of arrival is outside the object.

Point of departure is outside the object.

d. The prepositions **в, к, с** change to **во, ко, со** before words beginning with certain groups of consonants. For example:

во Фра́нции	in France
во вто́рник	on Tuesday
ко мне	to me
со мно́й	with me

25-2. Predicative Instrumental

a. The instrumental instead of the nominative is usually used in the predicate with forms of **быть** (*infinitive, past, future,* and *imperative*) to indicate a temporary state or change. For example:

Сестра́ хо́чет **быть** учи́тельни-цей.	Sister wants *to be* a teacher.
Господи́н Орло́в **был** инже-не́ром, пото́м учи́телем.	Mr. Orlov *was* an engineer, then a teacher.
Э́тот студе́нт **бу́дет** профе́ссо-ром.	This student *will be* a professor (now he is not).
Будь хоро́шим това́рищем.	*Be* a good friend!

b. When no change or temporary state is implied, the nominative is used.   For example:

Его́ роди́тели бы́ли бога́тые лю́ди.	His parents *were* rich people (*and remained so*).

c. Certain verbs require the instrumental with all forms (especially verbs of *becoming* and *seeming*).

Он де́лается больши́м ма́льчиком	He *is becoming* a big boy.
Он стал до́ктором.	He *became* a doctor.
Он ка́жется ста́рым.	He *seems* old.

25-3. Instrumental Singular of Nouns with Stems in a Sibilant

If the stem of a noun ends in **ж, ч, ш, щ,** or **ц,** it is important to note the stress.

a. When the stress is on the case endings, the instrumental takes the regular endings: **-ой** for the feminine and **-ом** for the masculine and neuter.   For example:

Feminine		Masculine		Neuter	
nom.	*instr.*	*nom.*	*instr.*	*nom.*	*instr.*
госпожа́	госпож**о́й**	каранда́ш	карандаш**о́м**	плечо́ (shoulder)	плеч**о́м**
овца́ (sheep)	овц**о́й**	оте́ц	отц**о́м**	лицо́	лиц**о́м**

b. When the stress is on the stem, the letter **o** in the instrumental endings changes to **e,** i.e., **-ой** becomes **-ей** and **-ом** becomes **-ем.** For example:

Feminine		Masculine		Neuter	
nom.	*instr.*	*nom.*	*instr.*	*nom.*	*instr.*
да́ча	да́ч**ей**	му**ж**	му́ж**ем**	со́лнце (sun)	со́лнц**ем**
Ма́ша	Ма́ш**ей**	това́ри**щ**	това́рищ**ем**	се́рдце (heart)	се́рдц**ем**
пти́ца	пти́ц**ей**	америка́не**ц**	америка́нц**ем**		

Упражнéния (Exercises)

A. Give the instrumental of the following:

1. ýлица.   2. Мѝша.   3. красáвица.   4. Мáша.   5. дáма.
6. áлгебра.   7. дéвочка.   8. мýзыка.   9. ю́ноша.   10. Вóлга.
11. óзеро.   12. гарáж.   13. борщ.   14. учѝтель.   15. америкáнец.   16. товáрищ.   17. Ивáнович.   18. инженéр.

B. Supply Russian equivalents for the English words and translate.

1. Господѝн Орлóв éдет *to Tula*.   2. Госпожá Орлóва недáвно приéхала *from Moscow*.   3. Сегóдня вéчером мы идём *to the theater*.   4. Онѝ приéхали *from New York* в дéвять часóв вéчера.   5. Мы дóлго жѝли *in France*.   6. *From France* мы поéхали *to the U.S.A.*   7. Онѝ два часá гуля́ли *in the garden*.   8. Онá тепéрь должнá идтѝ *to the lesson*.   9. Наш преподавáтель тóлько что приéхал *from the lesson*.   10. Онѝ стоя́т *in the street* и ждут трамвáя.   11. Он поéхал *to the examination*.   12. Онá идёт *from work*.   13. Мы с *husband* и егó *friend* éдем *to the Ukraine*.   14. Мы бýдем *in the Ukraine* две недéли.   15. Наш преподавáтель дóлго преподавáл *in the Caucasus*.   16. Ваш инженéр приéхал *from the Caucasus* год томý назáд.   17. Хотѝте поéхать со мнóй (with me) *to the plant*?   18. *From the factory* мы идём *to town*.   19. Я был *at the post office* сегóдня.   20. *From the post office* я поéхал *to the railway station*.   21. Вы тепéрь идёте *to the doctor*?   22. Нет, я тепéрь идý *from the doctor*.   23. Твой отéц уéхал *for the U.S.A.*   24. Он чáсто éздит *to the lake*.   25. Онѝ шли *from the lake*.

C. Supply the proper case endings for the words in parentheses, and translate the sentences into English.

1. Олéг хóчет стать (инженéр).   2. Мáша хотéла быть (учѝтельница).   3. Я дýмаю, что Ивáн бýдет (хорóший дóктор).   4. Ивáн стáнет (мой хорóший товáрищ).   5. Онá не хóчет быть (гувернáнтка).   6. Мой преподавáтель был (культýрный человéк).   7. Николáй Ивáнович бýдет (америкáнец).   8. Он учѝлся в Крымý и стал (учѝтель).   9. Нáша бéлая лóшадь стáла óчень (красѝвая).   10. Отéц Акѝма был (ýмный человéк).

Перево́д (Translation)

1. Anna Pavlovna Orlova is our Russian teacher. 2. She teaches Russian, Russian literature, and Russian history in our school. 3. She is a very cultured person, and it is always pleasant to converse with her.

4. She speaks French and German excellently, because she had [**у неё бы́ли**] two governesses when she was a little girl [**ма́ленькой де́вочкой**]. 5. Her father was a very rich man [person]. 6. He had a plant in the Ukraine, a factory in the Caucasus, and a summer house in the Crimea on the shore of the Black Sea.

7. Anna Pavlovna's husband is also a very cultured person. 8. He studied in the Ukraine and became an engineer. 9. From the Ukraine he went [**пое́хал**] to the Caucasus, and there worked in a plant (for) two years. 10. From the Caucasus he went to France and studied in a French university. 11. He finally went to the U.S.A.

12. Anna Pavlovna Orlova and Nicholas Ivanovich Orlov are very happy people. 13. They have lovely children—one boy and two (little) girls. 14. In the summer the whole family lives in the country. 15. There they have a beautiful summer house on the sea shore. 16. Oleg and I like to go to their summer home [**к ним на да́чу**]. 17. My sister said yesterday that we like Anna Pavlovna because she prepares for us borshch, cutlets, and Russian dessert. 18. Fortunately, my sister does not always tell the truth.

Вопро́сы (Questions)

1. Каки́е предме́ты Ми́ша и Оле́г тепе́рь изуча́ют? 2. Для кого́ э́ти предме́ты са́мые лёгкие? 3. Для кого́ они́ са́мые тру́дные? 4. Почему́ они́ не о́чень нра́вятся Оле́гу? 5. Каки́е предме́ты он лю́бит? 6. Кто преподаёт все э́ти предме́ты? 7. Никола́й Ива́нович хоро́ший преподава́тель? 8. Где он жил, когда́ он был ма́леньким ма́льчиком? 9. Где он учи́лся? 10. Кем он стал снача́ла, инжене́ром и́ли преподава́телем? 11. Где он рабо́тал, когда́ он был инжене́ром? 12. Куда́ он пое́хал из Кры́ма? 13. Где он рабо́тал на Кавка́зе? 14. Куда́ он пое́хал с Кавка́за? 15. Как Никола́й Ива́нович говори́т по-англи́йски? 16. Когда́ и где он изуча́л англи́йский язы́к? 17. А где он изуча́л францу́зский язы́к, до́ма и́ли во Фра́нции?

UNIT 26

ЕВРОПÉЙСКИЕ ТУРÍСТЫ В США

Господи́н Смит встреча́ет парохо́д, на кото́ром прие́хали тури́сты из Евро́пы.

Смит: — Здра́вствуйте.   Вы господи́н Никола́ев?

Никола́ев: — Да, я Никола́ев.   А вы господи́н Смит, наш гид?

Смит: — Да, моя́ фами́лия Смит.   Óчень прия́тно с ва́ми познако́миться.

Никола́ев: — Мне то́же о́чень прия́тно.   Как э́то ми́ло, что вы нас встреча́ете!

Смит: — Ско́лько тури́стов в ва́шей гру́ппе?

Никола́ев: — Девятна́дцать челове́к — оди́ннадцать мужчи́н и во́семь же́нщин.

Смит: — Вы все ру́сские?

Никола́ев: — О нет!   То́лько госпожа́ Бра́ун и я ру́сские. Мы преподаём ру́сский язы́к в Пари́же.

Смит: — А кто э́ти ю́ноши и де́вушки?

Никола́ев: — Это на́ши студе́нты и студе́нтки.   Они́ говоря́т друг с дру́гом то́лько по-ру́сски.   Им нельзя́ говори́ть ни по-францу́зски, ни по-англи́йски.

Смит: — А! тепе́рь я понима́ю, почему́ вам да́ли ги́да, кото́рый говори́т по-ру́сски.   А вам мо́жно говори́ть по-англи́йски?

Никола́ев: — Мне и госпоже́ Бра́ун, коне́чно, мо́жно.

179

Словарь (Vocabulary)

европе́йский, -ая, -ое European
тури́ст tourist
Смит Smith
встреча́ть (I); встреча́ю, -ешь, -ют to meet
парохо́д steamer
Евро́па Europe
Никола́ев Nikolaev
гид guide
фами́лия surname
знако́миться (II); знако́млюсь, знако́мишься, -ятся; *pf.* **познако́-
    миться (II)** to become acquainted
о́чень прия́тно с ва́ми познако́миться very pleased to meet you
ми́ло it is nice
ско́лько (*with gen. pl. of objects that can be counted*) how much, how many
ско́лько тури́стов? how many tourists? (**ско́лько молока́?** how much
    milk?)
гру́ппа group
девятна́дцать nineteen
мужчи́на (*m.*) man
же́нщина woman
Бра́ун Brown
Пари́ж Paris
на́ши (*pl. of* **наш**) our
друг с дру́гом with each other
нельзя́ (it is) impossible, one may not (see ¶ 16-1)
ни . . . ни neither . . . nor
мо́жно (it is) possible, one may (see ¶ 16-1)

II

ЕВРОПЕ́ЙСКИЕ ТУРИ́СТЫ В США (Continued)

Смит: — Вы сказа́ли, что госпожа́ Бра́ун ру́сская?

Никола́ев: — Да, она́ ру́сская, но её муж англича́нин, по-
э́тому её фами́лия Бра́ун.   Скажи́те, пожа́луйста, ско́лько дней
мы бу́дем в Нью-Йо́рке и ско́лько в Вашингто́не?

Смит: — Вы бу́дете в Нью-Йо́рке три дня — в четве́рг, в
пя́тницу и в суббо́ту.   В воскресе́нье вы пое́дете в Вашингто́н
и бу́дете там в понеде́льник и во вто́рник.   В сре́ду вы е́дете
да́льше.

Никола́ев: — Куда́ мы пое́дем из Вашингто́на?

Смит: — Из Вашингто́на вы пое́дете на юг, а зате́м в Кали-
фо́рнию.   Что вы хоти́те ви́деть в Нью-Йо́рке?

Николаев: — Всё! Никто из нас ещё не видел Нью-Йорка; мы в США в первый раз. В журналах и газетах мы много читали о театрах, музеях, универмагах, гостиницах и ресторанах Нью-Йорка. Наконец, мы всё это увидим!

Смит: — Вы, конечно, не всё увидите. Помните, что вы приехали в Нью-Йорк только на три дня. Но я покажу вам главные музеи, библиотеки, университеты, Уолл-стрит, Центральный вокзал, Рокфеллеровский центр, Эмпайр стейт билдинг и Кони-Айленд.

Николаев: — Когда наша первая экскурсия?

Смит: — Завтра утром. Итак, до завтра!

Николаев: — До завтра, господин Смит!

Словарь (Vocabulary)

The days of the week are given first. Note that в + name of day in the accusative means *on*.

понедельник	в понедельник	*on* Monday
вторник	во вторник	*on* Tuesday
среда	в среду	*on* Wednesday
четверг	в четверг	*on* Thursday
пятница	в пятницу	*on* Friday
суббота	в субботу	*on* Saturday
воскресенье	в воскресенье	*on* Sunday

англичанин (*nom. pl.* **англичане**, *gen. pl.* **англичан**) Englishman
юг south
затем after that, then
Калифорния California
никто (*pron.*) nobody, no one
никто из нас none of us
музей (*m.*) museum
универмаг department store
гостиница hotel
показывать (I); показываю, -ешь, -ют; *pf.* **показать (I);** *fut.* **покажу, покажешь, покажут;** *imper.* **покажи, -ите** to show
главный, -ая, -ое main, chief
Уолл-стрит Wall Street
Центральный вокзал Grand Central Station
Рокфеллеровский центр Rockefeller Center
Эмпайр стейт билдинг Empire State Building
Кони-Айленд Coney Island
экскурсия excursion, trip

Грамма́тика (Grammar)

Part I

26-1. Declension of Personal Pronouns in the Plural

For the *singular*, see ¶ 21-2.

Case	Plural: All Genders			
	First person	Second person	Third person	
				With governing prepositions
nom.	мы	вы	они́	
gen.	нас	вас	их	у них
dat.	нам	вам	им	к ним
acc.	нас	вас	их	на них
instr.	на́ми	ва́ми	и́ми	с ни́ми
prep.	о нас	о вас	о них	о них

26-2. Declension of the Demonstratives э́тот, э́та, and э́то in the Plural

For the *singular*, see ¶ 24-2.

PLURAL : ALL GENDERS

nom.	э́ти	*acc.*	э́ти *or* э́тих
gen.	э́тих	*instr.*	э́тими
dat.	э́тим	*prep.*	об э́тих

26-3. First Declension of Nouns in the Plural

For the *singular*, see ¶ 15-7c; for the formation of the *nominative plural*, see ¶ 20-2; for the *accusative plural* of inanimate nouns, see ¶ 20-3; and for plurals ending in -á or -я́, see ¶ 23-3.

Case	Hard	Soft		
	-а (*nom. sing.*)	-я (*nom. sing.*)		-ия (*nom. sing.*)
nom.	ка́рты	неде́ли	дя́ди	а́рмии
gen.	карт	неде́ль	дя́дей	а́рмий
dat.	ка́ртам	неде́лям	дя́дям	а́рмиям
acc.	ка́рты	неде́ли	дя́дей	а́рмии
instr.	ка́ртами	неде́лями	дя́дями	а́рмиями
prep.	о ка́ртах	о неде́лях	о дя́дях	об а́рмиях

a. The *accusative* of inanimate nouns is the same as the nominative; the accusative of animate nouns is the same as the genitive. For example:

$$\textit{nom. \& acc.} \begin{cases} \text{ка́рты} \\ \text{а́рмии} \end{cases} \qquad \textit{gen. \& acc.} \begin{cases} \text{дя́дей} \\ \text{коро́в} \end{cases}$$

b. The genitive.

1. The genitive of nouns in **-а** is their stem, i.e., they lose the ending of the nominative singular. For example: **ка́рта — карт**.

2. The genitive of nouns in **-я** is their stem, but **-ь** is added to retain the softness of the preceding consonant. For example: **неде́ля — неде́ль**.

3. Nouns in **-ия** take **-ий**. For example: **а́рмия — а́рмий**.

4. *Exceptions*. The following nouns thus far studied take **-ей**:

nom.	*gen.*
дя́дя	дя́дей
тётя	тётей
семья́	семе́й
ю́ноша	ю́ношей

c. The genitive with fleeting **-о** or **-е**. A number of nouns with stems ending in two consonants insert the letter **о** or **е** before the last consonant to make pronunciation easier.

1. *Hard* nouns usually insert **о**:

nom.	*gen.*
студе́нтка	студе́нток
доска́	досо́к

2. *Soft* nouns usually insert **е**:

nom.	*gen.*
пе́сня	пе́сен
дере́вня	дереве́нь

3. The **е** is also inserted when the consonant next to the last in the stem ending is a sibilant:

nom.	*gen.*
ча́шка	ча́шек
де́вочка	де́вочек

Part II

26-4. Second Declension of Masculine Nouns in the Plural

For the *singular*, see ¶ 18-4d; for the formation of the *nominative plural*, see ¶ 20-2.

Case	Hard Consonant (*nom. sing.*)	Soft -ь (*nom. sing.*)		-й (*nom. sing.*)
		Stress on stem	Stress on ending	
nom.	журна́лы	автомоби́ли	дожди́	трамва́и
gen.	журна́лов	автомоби́лей	дожде́й	трамва́ев
dat.	журна́лам	автомоби́лям	дождя́м	трамва́ям
acc.	журна́лы	автомоби́ли	дожди́	трамва́и
instr.	журна́лами	автомоби́лями	дождя́ми	трамва́ями
prep.	о журна́лах	об автомоби́лях	о дождя́х	о трамва́ях

a. The genitive.

1. Nouns in a consonant take **-ов**. For example: журна́л — журна́л**ов**.

2. Nouns in **-ь** take **-ей**. For example: автомоби́ль — автомоби́л**ей**.

3. Nouns in **-й** take **-ев**. For example: трамва́й — трамва́**ев**. When stressed on the ending, they take **-ёв**: чай — ча**ёв**.

4. Nouns in **-ц** take **-ов** when ending is stressed: оте́ц — отц**о́в**. When the stem is stressed, they take **-ев**: ме́сяц (*month*) — ме́сяц**ев**.

5. *Exceptions.*

(a) Nouns in **ж, ч, ш,** or **щ** take **-ей** instead of **-ов**:

гара́ж	гараж**е́й**
каранда́ш	карандаш**е́й**
това́рищ	това́рищ**ей**

(b) The following nouns are identical in the nominative singular and the genitive plural:

nom. sing.	*gen. pl.*	
глаз	глаз	eye
раз	раз	time (occasion)
солда́т	солда́т	soldier
челове́к	челове́к★	man, person

b. The *accusative* of inanimate nouns is the same as the nominative; the accusative of animate nouns is the same as the genitive. For example:

nom. & acc.   { журна́лы
                 { автомоби́ли

gen. & acc.   { студе́нтов
                 { учителе́й

Упражне́ния (Exercises)

A. Decline the following nouns in singular and plural.

1. по́чта.   2. фа́брика (see ¶ 20-2a).   3. де́душка.   4. студе́нтка.   5. ча́шка.   6. гости́ница (see ¶ 25-3b).   7. фами́лия.   8. тётя.   9. вокза́л.   10. коне́ц.   11. универма́г.   12. са́ндвич.   13. америка́нец.   14. преподава́тель.   15. музе́й.

B. Supply equivalents for the English words and translate. (Memorize ¶ 26-1 and 26-2 before doing this exercise.)

1. Кто *these* тури́сты?   2. Я хочу́ познако́миться с *these* студе́нтами.   3. Как до́лго вы разгова́ривали с *them*?   4. Мы вчера́ говори́ли о *them*, а не о *you* (*pl.*).   5. Мы показа́ли *them* парохо́д.   6. Я ви́дел *these* же́нщин, когда́ мы бы́ли в музе́е.   7. Мы *you* (*pl.*) о́чень хорошо́ ви́дим, но *them* мы совсе́м не ви́дим.   8. Нельзя́ разгова́ривать с *us*, когда́ мы занима́емся.   9. Что вы чита́ли *about these* ю́ношах?   10. Не дава́йте ничего́ (*to*) *these* де́вочкам.   11. Вы (*to*) *us* да́ли о́чень интере́сную кни́гу.   12. (*To*) *you* мо́жно говори́ть по-англи́йски на уро́ке францу́зского языка́?

C. Replace all nouns in parentheses with plurals in the required cases.   (Master ¶ 26-3 and 26-4 before doing this exercise.)

1. (Ка́рта) (учени́к) лежа́т на (стол).   2. Мы девятна́дцать (день) рабо́тали в (сад).   3. Господи́н Смит до́лго говори́л об (универма́г), (гости́ница) и (музе́й) США.   4. В на́шем го́роде

★ This form is used after definite and some indefinite numbers.

нет (трамва́й), но есть мно́го (автомоби́ль). 5. Вы ещё не по-
знако́мились с э́тими (студе́нт) и (студе́нтка). 6. В э́тих
(магази́н) нет ни (кни́га), ни (журна́л), ни (газе́та) и ни (каран-
да́ш). 7. В на́шей шко́ле пятна́дцать (учи́тель) и два́дцать
(учи́тельница). 8. Ско́лько (ю́ноша) и (де́вушка) в ва́шем
кла́ссе? 9. Я не зна́ю (фами́лия) э́тих (тури́ст). 10. Господи́н
Никола́ев лю́бит разгова́ривать с (америка́нец).

Перево́д (Translation)

A. Translate, including words in brackets.

1. Today is Wednesday. 2. On Wednesday I have a music
lesson at five o'clock. 3. Yesterday was Tuesday. 4. On
Tuesday morning I was at the railway station. 5. Tomorrow is
Thursday. 6. On Thursday I go to the post office. 7. On
Friday we dine in a restaurant. 8. On Saturday we shall be in
Washington. 9. On Sunday we usually rest. 10. On Monday
our class is going on [на] an excursion.

B. Omit the words in parentheses and include the words in
brackets.

1. The guide is meeting the tourists who arrived from France.
2. His surname is Smith. 3. He [ему́] is very pleased to become
acquainted with these tourists. 4. Mr. Nikolaev and Mrs. Brown
teach Russian in a French university. 5. Their students speak
only Russian. 6. They may not speak French or English. 7. The
teachers (*use dat.*), of course, may speak French or English. 8. The
French tourists have not yet seen the theaters, museums, libraries,
and hotels of New York. 9. They will be in New York on Sunday,
Monday, and Tuesday. 10. On Wednesday they will leave for
[пое́дут] California.

Вопро́сы (Questions)

1. Како́й сего́дня день, понеде́льник и́ли вто́рник? 2. Како́й
день был вчера́? 3. Како́й день бу́дет за́втра? 4. Что вы
де́лали во вто́рник? 5. Где вы бы́ли в сре́ду? 6. Куда́ вы
пое́дете в суббо́ту? 7. Что вы бу́дете де́лать в четве́рг?
8. Вы всегда́ отдыха́ете в воскресе́нье?

9. Кого́ встреча́ет господи́н Смит?   10. С кем он разгова́ривает?   11. Ско́лько мужчи́н и ско́лько же́нщин в гру́ппе тури́стов?   12. Что господи́н Никола́ев преподаёт в Пари́же? 13. Кому́ нельзя́ говори́ть по-англи́йски?   14. Кому́ мо́жно говори́ть и по-англи́йски и по-францу́зски?   15. Кто муж госпожи́ Бра́ун, ру́сский, англича́нин и́ли америка́нец?   16. Куда́ европе́йские тури́сты пое́дут из Вашингто́на?   17. О чём э́ти тури́сты так мно́го чита́ли в журна́лах и газе́тах? 18. Что господи́н Смит хо́чет показа́ть тури́стам?

U N I T 27

I

ИНТЕРВЬЮ́ С ЕВРОПЕ́ЙСКИМИ ТУРИ́СТАМИ

Репортёры студе́нческой газе́ты "На́ше вре́мя" встреча́ют европе́йских тури́стов в гости́нице. Тури́сты всю ночь е́хали по́ездом из Чика́го в Нью-Йо́рк и о́чень уста́ли, но они́ всё-таки ра́ды познако́миться и поговори́ть с америка́нскими студе́нтами.

Молоды́е тури́сты уже́ бы́ли в Вашингто́не, в Но́вом Орлеа́не, в Лос-А́нжелосе, в Сан-Франци́ско, в Чика́го и в други́х больши́х и интере́сных города́х Соединённых Шта́тов. Всю́ду они́ знако́мились и разгова́ривали с ученика́ми и учени́цами сре́дних школ и с их учителя́ми и учи́тельницами. Они́ та́кже ча́сто бесе́довали с мужчи́нами и же́нщинами, кото́рых встреча́ли в гости́ницах, универма́гах, теа́трах и́ли в поезда́х и трамва́ях. Они́ прекра́сно провели́ вре́мя и Соединённые Шта́ты им о́чень нра́вятся.

Молоды́е америка́нские репортёры никогда́ ещё не́ были в Евро́пе и им интере́сно поговори́ть о шко́лах, университе́тах, и о жи́зни ученико́в в ра́зных европе́йских стра́нах. Среди́ тури́стов есть францу́зы, англича́не, испа́нцы и не́мцы, а господи́н Никола́ев и госпожа́ Бра́ун, их учителя́, ру́сские.

Слова́рь (Vocabulary)

интервью́ (*n.*; *not decl.*; *pr.* **интэрвью́**) interview
репортёр reporter
студе́нческий, -ая, -ое student (*adj.*)
вре́мя (*n.*) (*gen.* **вре́мени**) time

188

ночь (*f.*) night
по́езд (*pl.* поезда́) train
е́хать по́ездом to go by train
уста́л, уста́ла, -ло, -ли tired
всё-таки́ all the same
ра́ды (*pl. of* рад) glad
Но́вый Орлеа́н New Orleans
Лос-А́нжелос Los Angeles
Сан-Франци́ско (*not decl.*) San Francisco
соединённый, -ая, -ое united
штат state
всю́ду (*adv.*) everywhere
сре́дний, -яя, -ее middle (*adj.*)
сре́дняя шко́ла high school
бесе́довать (I); бесе́дую, бесе́дуешь, -ют to chat, to talk; *pf.* побесе́довать
  (I) to have a talk
проводи́ть (II); провожу́, прово́дишь, -ят; *pf.* провести́ (I); *fut.* про-
  веду́, -ёшь, -у́т; *past* провёл, провела́, -ло́, -ли́ to spend (time)
они́ прекра́сно провели́ вре́мя they had a wonderful time
о about, concerning
жизнь (*f.*) life
ра́зный, -ая, -ое various
страна́ (*pl.* стра́ны) country
среди́ (*with gen.*) among
францу́з Frenchman
испа́нец*fl* (pl. испа́нцы) Spaniard
не́мец*fl* (*pl.* не́мцы) German

II

ИНТЕРВЬЮ́ С ЕВРОПЕ́ЙСКИМИ ТУРИ́СТАМИ
(Continued)★

Пе́рвый репортёр: — Мы зна́ем, что вы час тому́ наза́д
прие́хали из Чика́го и о́чень уста́ли.

Господи́н Го́фман: — Мы уста́ли, но нам всё-таки о́чень
прия́тно с ва́ми побесе́довать.

Второ́й репортёр: — Нам то́же о́чень прия́тно. Скажи́те,
пожа́луйста, как ва́ша фами́лия?

Г-н. Го́фман: — Я не́мец. Моя́ фами́лия Го́фман. А как
ва́ша?

Вт. реп.: — Моя́ фами́лия Го́пкинс, а фами́лия моего́ това́ри-
ща — Уа́йт.

Пер. реп.: — Ско́лько студе́нтов в ва́шей гру́ппе?

Г-н. Шаро́н: — Нас бы́ло семна́дцать, но тепе́рь нас то́лько
шестна́дцать, потому́ что одна́ из на́ших тури́сток уже́ уе́хала.

★ This material may be used for dramatization in class.

Вт. реп.: — Вы о́чень хорошо́ говори́те по-англи́йски.

Г-н. Шаро́н: — О, нет! У меня́ плохо́е произноше́ние. Я изуча́л англи́йский язы́к без учи́теля. По-ру́сски я говорю́ лу́чше, чем по-англи́йски. Мы все лу́чше говори́м по-ру́сски.

Пер. реп.: — Как э́то мо́жет быть?

Госпожа́ Го́мес: — Мы мно́го занима́емся и всё вре́мя говори́м друг с дру́гом то́лько по-ру́сски. Ка́ждый день мы пи́шем ру́сские упражне́ния и́ли сочине́ния.

Г-жа. Фо́стер: — У меня́ уже́ есть восемна́дцать тетра́дей с ру́сскими упражне́ниями и сочине́ниями.

Г-жа. Бра́ун: — Мы ещё не рассказа́ли репортёрам о на́шей пое́здке по Соединённым Шта́там.

Вт. реп.: — Ва́ша пое́здка нас о́чень интересу́ет. Пожа́луйста, расскажи́те, где вы бы́ли, что вы де́лали, и как вам нра́вится на́ша страна́?

Г-н. Шаро́н: — Мне о́чень нра́вится Вашингто́н с его́ краси́выми у́лицами, прекра́сными зда́ниями и па́рками.

Г-жа. Го́мес: — А я люблю́ Нью-Йо́рк! Нигде́ я ещё не ви́дела таки́х больши́х магази́нов и замеча́тельных зда́ний и гости́ниц.

Г-жа. Фо́стер: — А мне бо́льше нра́вится Ло́ндон. Вы ещё не́ были в Ло́ндоне, госпожа́ Го́мес. Как жаль!

Г-н. Го́фман: — А я полюби́л Калифо́рнию. Каки́е краси́вые па́рки, у́лицы, дома́ и сады́ в Лос-А́нжелосе и в Сан-Франци́ско! И како́й там кли́мат! — всегда́ светло́ и тепло́, и не́бо всегда́ я́сное.

Пер. реп.: — Ну, в Сан-Франци́ско иногда́ о́чень хо́лодно, и ча́сто идёт дождь.

Вт. реп.: — Мы о́чень ра́ды, что вы так хорошо́ провели́ вре́мя в США, и что всё вам так нра́вится. Ита́к, до свида́ния, и большо́е спаси́бо за прия́тный и интере́сный разгово́р.

Слова́рь (Vocabulary)

Го́фман Hoffmann
второ́й, -а́я, -о́е second
как ва́ша фами́лия? what is your last name?
Го́пкинс Hopkins
Уа́йт White (*surname*)

семна́дцать seventeen
Шаро́н Charon
нас бы́ло семна́дцать there were seventeen of us
шестна́дцать sixteen
тури́стка (*gen. pl.* **тури́сток**) tourist (*f.*)
произноше́ние pronunciation
без (*with gen.*) without
чем (*conj.*) than
как э́то мо́жет быть? how is this possible?
Го́мес (*foreign names of women not decl.*) Gomez
Фо́стер (*foreign names of women not decl.*) Foster
восемна́дцать eighteen
рассказа́ть (**I**) (*pf. of* **расска́зывать**); *fut.* **расскажу́, расска́жешь, -ут**
  to relate, to tell
пое́здка (*gen. pl.* **пое́здок**) trip
зда́ние building
бо́льше (*adv.*) more
Ло́ндон London
полюби́ть (**II**) (*pf. of* **люби́ть**) to fall in love, to become fond of
кли́мат climate
отдохну́ть (**I**) (*pf. of* **отдыха́ть**); *fut.* **отдохну́, отдохнёшь, -у́т**; *imper.*
  отдохни́, -йте to rest

Грамма́тика (Grammar)

Part I

27-1. Second Declension of Neuter Nouns in the Plural

For the *singular*, see ¶**18-4e**; for the formation of the *nominative plural*, see ¶**20-2**; for the *accusative plural* of inanimate nouns, see ¶**20-3**.

Case	Hard	Soft	
	-o (*nom. sing.*)	**-e** (*nom. sing.*)	**-ие** (*nom. sing.*)
nom.	слова́	моря́	сочине́ния
gen.	слов	море́й	сочине́ний
dat.	слова́м	моря́м	сочине́ниям
acc.	слова́	моря́	сочине́ния
instr.	слова́ми	моря́ми	сочине́ниями
prep.	о слова́х	о моря́х	о сочине́ниях

a. The genitive (note resemblances to First Declension):

1. The genitive of nouns in **-o** is their stem; e.g., сло́во — слов.
2. Nouns in **-e** take **-ей**; e.g., мо́ре — море́й.
3. Nouns in **-ие** take **-ий**; e.g., сочине́ние — сочине́ний.

b. The genitive with fleeting **-o** and **-e**. A number of neuter nouns with stems ending in two consonants insert an **o** or **e** before the last consonant.

nom. sing.	*gen. pl.*
окно́	о́кон
кре́сло	кре́сел
письмо́	пи́сем (**e** replaces **ь**)

27-2. Third Declension in the Plural

For the *singular*, see ¶ **19-2**; for the formation of the *nominative plural*, see ¶ **20-2**.

Case	Stress on oblique case endings		Stress on stem
	-ь (*nom. sing.*)	Sibilant (**ж, ч, ш, щ**) + **-ь** (*nom. sing.*)	**-ь** (*nom. sing.*)
nom.	ло́шади	но́чи	тетра́ди
gen.	лошаде́й	ноче́й	тетра́дей
dat.	лошадя́м	ноча́м	тетра́дям
acc.	лошаде́й	но́чи	тетра́ди
instr.	лошадя́ми *or* лошадьми́	ноча́ми	тетра́дями
prep.	о лошадя́х	о ноча́х	о тетра́дях

a. The *accusative* of inanimate nouns is the same as the nominative; the accusative of animate nouns is the same as the genitive. For example: *gen.* and *acc.* **лошаде́й.**

b. Nouns with stems in **ж, ч, ш,** or **щ** have hard endings in the *dative, instrumental,* and *prepositional,* as in **ночь.**

Part II

27-3. Full Declension of Adjectives in the Plural

For the *singular*, see ¶ **24-1.**

Note: The accusative of adjectives modifying inanimate nouns is

the same as the nominative; that of adjectives modifying animate
nouns is the same as the genitive.

ALL GENDERS

a. Hard:

	Group I	Group II
	(**-ый, -ая, -ое**)	(**-о́й, -а́я, -о́е**)
nom.	но́в**ые**	молод**ы́е**
gen.	но́в**ых**	молод**ы́х**
dat.	но́в**ым**	молод**ы́м**
acc.	но́в**ые** *or* но́в**ых**	молод**ы́е** *or* молод**ы́х**
instr.	но́в**ыми**	молод**ы́ми**
prep.	о но́в**ых**	о молод**ы́х**

b. Soft (**-н + ий, -н + яя, -н + ее**):   *Compare with Pers.*
                                                Pron. Pl. (¶26-1)

nom.	после́дн**ие**	они́
gen.	после́дн**их**	их
dat.	после́дн**им**	им
acc.	после́дн**ие** *or* после́дн**их**	их
instr.	после́дн**ими**	и́ми
prep.	о после́дн**их**	о них

c. Mixed:

	Group I	Group II	Group III
	(**-г, -к, -х +** **-ий, -ая, -ое**)	(**-ж, -ч, -ш, -щ** **+ -ий, -ая, -ее**)	(**-г, -к, -х, -ж, -ч, -ш, -щ + -о́й, -а́я, -о́е**)
nom.	ру́сск**ие**	хоро́ш**ие**	дорог**и́е**
gen.	ру́сск**их**	хоро́ш**их**	дорог**и́х**
dat.	ру́сск**им**	хоро́ш**им**	дорог**и́м**
acc.	ру́сск**ие** *or* ру́сск**их**	хоро́ш**ие** *or* хоро́ш**их**	дорог**и́е** *or* дорог**и́х**
instr.	ру́сск**ими**	хоро́ш**ими**	дорог**и́ми**
prep.	о ру́сск**их**	о хоро́ш**их**	о дорог**и́х**

27-4. Possessive Adjective-Pronouns in the Plural

For the *singular*, see ¶24-3.

мой, *m.*; моя, *f.*;   наш, *m.*; наша, *f.*;
      моё, *n.*   наше, *n.*

nom.	мой	наши
gen.	моих	наших
dat.	моим	нашим
acc.	мой *or* моих	наши *or* наших
instr.	моими	нашими
prep.	о моих	о наших

Note: The possessives **твой, твоя, твоё** and **ваш, ваша, ваше** are declined respectively like **мой, моя, моё** and **наш, наша, наше.**

27-5. Cardinal Numerals 1 through 20

a. Formation of 11 to 20.

Note how these numerals are formed: **-на-** (meaning *plus*) and **дцать** (a contraction of **десять**) are added to the numerals **один** through **девять**. Thus, **одиннадцать**, for example, is composed of **один + -на- + дцать** (pr. **ццать**), and literally means *one above (plus) ten*. On the other hand, **двадцать** is composed of **два + дцать**, and means *two tens*.

1. один (*m.*)	+ на + дцать = одиннадцать	= 11
2. две (*f.*)	+ на + дцать = двенадцать	= 12
3. три	+ на + дцать = тринадцать	= 13
4. четыр(е)	+ на + дцать = четырнадцать	= 14
5. пят(ь)	+ на + дцать = пятнадцать	= 15
6. шест(ь)	+ на + дцать = шестнадцать	= 16
7. сем(ь)	+ на + дцать = семнадцать	= 17
8. восем(ь)	+ на + дцать = восемнадцать	= 18
9. девят(ь)	+ на + дцать = девятнадцать	= 19
два	+ дцать = двадцать	= 20

b. Agreement with adjectives and nouns.

Два, три, and **четыре** require the adjective in the *genitive plural* and the noun in the *genitive singular*. The numbers **пять** through **двадцать** require both the adjective and the noun in the *genitive plural*. (See ¶9-3 and 20-8.)

For example:

> два ру́сск**их** журна́л**а**; две ру́сск**их** ка́р**ты**; два но́в**ых**
> сло́в**а**; пять ру́сск**их** журна́л**ов**; двена́дцать ру́сск**их** карт;
> два́дцать но́в**ых** слов.

Упражне́ния (Exercises)

A. Decline the following nouns in the plural. (Master ¶27-1 first.)

1. лицо́. 2. окно́. 3. кре́сло. 4. письмо́. 5. зда́ние.
6. произноше́ние. 7. о́зеро (*nom. pl.* озёра).

B. Decline the following adjectives in all genders, singular and plural. (Master ¶27-3 first.)

1. ра́зный. 2. сре́дний. 3. пусто́й. 4. плохо́й. 5. америка́нский.

C. Decline the following adjectives and nouns in the singular and plural. (Master ¶27-2 and 27-4 first.)

1. хоро́ший това́рищ. 2. большо́е зда́ние. 3. твоя́ ло́шадь.
4. ва́ша тетра́дь. 5. сре́дняя шко́ла.

D. Count from 1 through 20 with each of the following adjectives and nouns. (Master ¶27-5 first.) For example:
одна́ молода́я тури́стка, две молоды́х тури́стки . . . пять молоды́х тури́сток, etc.

1. хоро́ший това́рищ. 2. лёгкое сло́во. 3. пусто́е зда́ние.
4. прекра́сный день. 5. бе́лая ло́шадь. 6. дли́нная ночь.
7. сре́дняя шко́ла. 8. коро́ткое письмо́. 9. гла́вный музе́й.
10. интере́сная экску́рсия.

E. In place of the blanks supply the appropriate case endings in the plural, and translate.

1. В гости́ниц_____ Нью-Йо́рка мно́го тури́ст_____ и тури́ст_____ (*f.*). 2. Европе́йск_____ студе́нт_____ хоте́ли побесе́довать с америка́нск_____ репортёр_____. 3. Мы ещё никогда́ не ви́дели таки́х больш_____ и краси́в_____ зда́н_____. 4. Ва́ш_____ това́рищ_____ неда́вно познако́мились с учени́к_____ и учени́ц_____ сре́дн_____ школ. 5. Всю́ду мы встреча́ли счастли́в_____ и весёл_____ ма́льчик_____ и

де́воч_____. 6. Вы сказа́ли, что ва́ш_____ роди́тели изуча́ют иностра́нн_____ язык_____ без учител_____, без книг и без словар_____. Как э́то мо́жет быть? 7. В на́ш_____ теа́тр _____, музе́_____ и библиоте́к_____ нельзя́ кури́ть (smoke). 8. Мы ещё никогда́ не ви́дели таки́х больш_____ и хоро́ш _____ трамва́_____. 9. Среди́ тури́ст_____ бы́ло мно́го доктор_____, профессор_____ и инжене́р_____. 10. В одну́ неде́лю мои́ приле́жн_____ ученик_____ написа́ли двена́дцать упражне́н_____ и шесть сочине́н_____. 11. Репортёры разгова́ривали с европе́йск_____ юнош_____ об их заня́т_____, преподава́тел_____, и о ра́зн_____ предме́т _____, кото́р_____ они́ тепе́рь изуча́ют в сре́дн_____ школ _____. 12. Америка́нск_____ тури́стки полюби́ли Пари́ж с его́ краси́в_____ у́лиц_____, хоро́ш_____ теа́тр_____ и замеча́тельн_____ универма́г_____ и музе́_____.

Перево́д (Translation)

Include the words in brackets and omit the words in parentheses.

An Interview with American Tourists

1. The reporters of the French magazine *Our Life* are meeting American tourists who just arrived from England. 2. The Americans are very tired [**о́чень уста́ли**] but are glad to become acquainted and to have a talk with the French reporters. 3. The tourists had a wonderful time in England. 4. Everywhere they were making the acquaintance of [**знако́мились с**] pupils and teachers. 5. They also often chatted with men and women whom they met in theaters, restaurants, museums, libraries, and [at] railway stations. 6. They like Europe very much. 7. Mr. White has fallen in love with London, and Mr. Hopkins with Paris. 8. They all [**Все**] think that Paris is a remarkable city. 9. They have never seen such beautiful streets, buildings, and parks, and have never dined in such excellent restaurants. 10. They also like the climate of France. 11. It is always warm and bright, and the sky is clear. 12. They will be in Paris sixteen days. 13. The tourists prefer to speak French, but the reporters want to speak English. 14. Unfortunately, both the Americans and the Frenchmen (have) a very bad pronunciation. 15. Therefore, they often do not understand each other. 16. But all the same, the conversation is very pleasant and interesting.

Вопро́сы (Questions)

1. Кто встреча́ет европе́йских тури́стов? 2. Где репортёры их встреча́ют? 3. Как до́лго тури́сты е́хали по́ездом из Чика́го в Нью-Йо́рк? 4. Каки́е америка́нские города́ они́ уже́ ви́дели? 5. С кем они́ всю́ду знако́мились и разгова́ривали? 6. С кем они́ разгова́ривали в поезда́х и в трамва́ях? 7. Как они́ провели́ вре́мя в Соединённых Шта́тах? 8. Соединённые Шта́ты нра́вятся европе́йским тури́стам? 9. Репортёры студе́нческой газе́ты уже́ бы́ли в Евро́пе? 10. О чём им интере́сно поговори́ть с европе́йскими тури́стами? 11. Как фами́лия ру́сского учи́теля? 12. Почему́ фами́лия ру́сской учи́тельницы "Бра́ун"? 13. Как фами́лия не́мца? Францу́за? Пе́рвого репортёра? Второ́го репортёра? 14. Ско́лько челове́к в гру́ппе тури́стов? 15. Ско́лько студе́нтов в э́той гру́ппе? 16. Почему́ господи́н Шаро́н лу́чше говори́т по-ру́сски, чем по-англи́йски? 17. Почему́ господи́ну Шаро́ну так нра́вится Вашингто́н? 18. Почему́ госпожа́ Го́мес лю́бит Нью- Йо́рк? 19. Почему́ господи́н Го́фман полюби́л Калифо́рнию? 20. Пого́да всегда́ хоро́шая в Лос-А́нжелосе? 21. А в Сан-Франци́ско не́бо всегда́ я́сное?

U N I T 28

REVIEW LESSON

Grammar Review

A. Conjugate the following verbs in full, in the *imperfective* (present, past, compound future, and imperative) and *perfective* (past, future, and imperative) aspects.

1. писа́ть — написа́ть.   2. объясня́ть — объясни́ть.   3. рисова́ть — нарисова́ть.   4. встава́ть — встать.   5. люби́ть — полюби́ть.   6. забыва́ть — забы́ть.   7. бесе́довать — побесе́довать.   8. проводи́ть — провести́.   9. говори́ть — сказа́ть. 10. пока́зывать — показа́ть.

B. Conjugate the following verbs in the present, past, and compound future.

1. смея́ться.   2. занима́ться.   3. знако́миться.

C. Decline the following adjectives and nouns in the plural.

1. лёгкий уро́к.   2. большо́й гара́ж.   3. хоро́ший инжене́р. 4. ти́хая у́лица.   5. бога́тая же́нщина.   6. си́нее кре́сло. 7. дли́нное упражне́ние.   8. прия́тная экску́рсия.   9. ста́рый трамва́й.   10. молодо́й не́мец.

D. Supply the nominative plural of the following.

1. пусто́й дом.   2. друго́й бе́рег.   3. культу́рный учи́тель. 4. прия́тный ве́чер.   5. большо́й лес.   6. си́ний глаз.   7. хоро́ший до́ктор.   8. стра́нный го́лос.   9. ру́сский го́род.   10. европе́йский профе́ссор.

198

E. Count from 1 through 20 with each of the following adjectives and nouns.

1. но́вая ка́рта.   2. си́ний дива́н.   3. ру́сское сло́во.   4. хоро́ший преподава́тель.   5. тру́дное сочине́ние.

Reading and Comprehension Drill

A. Read the following sentences aloud and translate them orally into idiomatic English.

1. Сего́дня моя́ сестра́ в пе́рвый раз написа́ла хоро́шее сочине́ние.   2. Мы сде́лали все уро́ки, пообе́дали и пото́м пое́хали к на́шим това́рищам.   3. Е́сли хоти́те, мы снача́ла поу́жинаем, а пото́м поговори́м о на́шей экску́рсии.   4. Посиди́те немно́го в э́том кре́сле и отдохни́те, а пото́м пое́дем на рабо́ту.   5. Все вдруг заговори́ли об испа́нских тури́стках.   6. Когда́ на́ша учи́тельница объясня́ет геоме́трию в кла́ссе, я всё понима́ю.   К сожале́нию, че́рез де́сять мину́т я забыва́ю всё, что она́ объясни́ла.   7. К сча́стью, мы с Ири́ной занима́емся вме́сте, и она́ объясни́т мне уро́к по геоме́трии.   8. Я вам ничего́ не скажу́, потому́ что вы сейча́с же всё забу́дете.   9. За́втра у нас экза́мен по исто́рии Соединённых Шта́тов Аме́рики.   10. Вы всегда́ встаёте в де́вять часо́в утра́. Почему́ вы сего́дня вста́ли в семь?

B. Supply the endings or Russian equivalents of English words; then read aloud and translate.

1. Америка́нские тури́ст_____ и европе́йск_____ репортёр_____ о́чень полюби́ли друг дру́г_____.   2. Мои́ роди́тели бы́ли о́чень бога́т_____ и культу́рн_____ (people).   3. Когда́ мы бы́ли ма́леньк_____ де́вочк_____, у нас бы́ли гуверна́нтк_____, кото́р_____ говори́ли (with us) то́лько по-францу́зски.   4. С Кавка́з_____ мы пое́хали на Украи́н_____ и там рабо́тали на фа́брик_____ не́сколько (weeks).   5. Мы с му́ж_____ ча́сто е́здим (by train) в Калифо́рн_____.   6. О́чень прия́тно с (you) познако́миться.   7. Как фами́лия ва́шего англи́йск_____ преподава́тел_____?   8. Мы говори́м друг с дру́г_____ то́лько (Spanish).   9. В журна́лах и кни́г_____ мы мно́го чита́ли о больши́х универма́г_____, библиоте́к_____ и музе́_____ Ло́ндона.   10. Среди́ тури́ст_____ есть мно́го францу́з_____, испа́нц_____, не́мц_____ и ру́сск_____.

Перево́д (Translation)

Include the words in brackets and omit the words in parentheses.

1. The American reporters arrived from California. 2. Our friends are going to the Ukraine. 3. Tomorrow my sister and I are going to the factory. 4. From the post office, the tourists (*f.*) went (by vehicle) to the railway station. 5. I am now coming from the doctor. 6. Our students will become good engineers. 7. Masha always wanted to be a teacher. 8. One may not converse with us when we are studying. 9. What did you read about these little girls? 10. Your pupils' books were lying on the floor. 11. The European tourists conversed for a long time with the Americans about the big buildings, the excellent hotels, and remarkable museums of Paris. 12. In this store there are neither books, newspapers, pencils, nor notebooks. 13. In our class there are seventeen girls and eighteen boys. 14. We do not know the surnames of these ladies. 15. On Monday, [on] Tuesday, and [on] Wednesday I work in Washington. 16. On Thursday, [on] Friday, and [on] Saturday I work in New York. On Sunday I rest. 17. The pupils of our high school wanted to have a chat with the European boys and girls. 18. The American tourists (*f.*) fell in love with London—with its beautiful streets, big department stores, and remarkable museums. 19. We are very glad that you had such a good time in the country. 20. You are very tired and have to have a rest.

Вопро́сы (Questions)

1. Как ва́ша фами́лия? 2. Где живёт ва́ша семья́? 3. А где вы живёте? 4. Где вы у́читесь? 5. Вы мно́го занима́етесь? 6. Ско́лько часо́в в день (a day) вы занима́етесь? 7. Вы хоро́ший учени́к? (Вы хоро́шая учени́ца?) 8. Когда́ вы вста́ли сего́дня у́тром? 9. Когда́ вы обыкнове́нно встаёте? 10. Вы уже́ поза́втракали? 11. Куда́ вы вчера́ пое́хали по́сле за́втрака? 12. Куда́ вы за́втра пое́дете по́сле у́жина? 13. Како́й сего́дня день, среда́ и́ли четве́рг? 14. Что вы обыкнове́нно де́лаете в сре́ду? 15. У кого́ вы берёте уро́ки му́зыки? 16. Каки́е предме́ты вы изуча́ете в шко́ле? 17. Каки́е предме́ты вас о́чень интересу́ют? 18. Каки́е иностра́нные языки́ вы уже́ зна́ете дово́льно хорошо́? 19. Как вы обыкнове́нно прово́дите вре́мя в суббо́ту ве́чером? 20. Вы

лю́бите танцова́ть?   21. С кем вы предпочита́ете танцова́ть? Почему́?   22. Каки́е больши́е города́ Соединённых Шта́тов вы уже́ ви́дели?   23. Вы уже́ бы́ли в Евро́пе?   24. Каки́е европе́йские города́ нра́вятся америка́нским тури́стам?   25. Как им нра́вится кли́мат А́нглии?

APPENDIX

EVERYDAY EXPRESSIONS

The following expressions deal with everyday situations and provide material for oral drill and conversation.

A. In the Classroom

1. Откро́йте, пожа́луйста, дверь.	1. Open the door, please.
2. Закро́йте, пожа́луйста, окно́.	2. Please close the window.
3. Откро́йте, пожа́луйста, кни́гу.	3. Please open the book.
4. Чита́йте, пожа́луйста.	4. Please read.
5. Переведи́те с ру́сского на англи́йский.	5. Translate from Russian into English.
6. Иди́те к доске́.	6. Go to the blackboard.
7. Пиши́те перево́д на доске́.	7. Write the translation on the blackboard.
8. Пиши́те упражне́ние в тетра́ди.	8. Write the exercise in the notebook.
9. Напиши́те коро́ткое сочине́ние на за́втра.	9. Write a short composition for tomorrow.
10. Пригото́вьте уро́к на за́втра.	10. Prepare the lesson for tomorrow.
11. Отвеча́йте на все вопро́сы по-ру́сски.	11. Answer all the questions in Russian.
12. Пожа́луйста, повтори́те отве́т ещё раз.	12. Please repeat the answer again.
13. Слу́шайте внима́тельно.	13. Listen attentively.
14. Чита́йте ме́дленнее, пожа́луйста.	14. Please read more slowly.
15. Пиши́те быстре́е.	15. Write faster.
16. Говори́те гро́мче.	16. Speak louder.
17. Чита́йте ти́ше.	17. Read more quietly.
18. Бу́дем чита́ть все вме́сте.	18. Let us all read together.
19. Э́то пра́вильно.	19. This is correct.
20. Э́то непра́вильно. Вот оши́бка.	20. This is incorrect. Here is a mistake.

B. Greetings and Good Wishes

1. Здра́вствуйте.
2. До́брое у́тро.
3. До́брый день.
4. До́брый ве́чер.
5. О́чень рад вас ви́деть.
6. Как вы пожива́ете?
7. Спаси́бо, о́чень хорошо́. А вы?
8. Та́к себе.
9. Сади́тесь, пожа́луйста.
10. Бу́дьте как до́ма.
11. Что у вас но́вого?
12. До свида́ния.
13. Споко́йной но́чи.
14. До за́втра.

15. Всего́ хоро́шего.

16. Счастли́вого пути́.
17. Жела́ю вам успе́ха.
18. С днём рожде́ния!
19. С Рождество́м Христо́вым!
20. С Но́вым Го́дом!

1. Hello.   How do you do?
2. Good morning.
3. Good day.
4. Good evening.
5. I am very glad to see you.
6. How are you?
7. Very well, thank you. And you?
8. So so.
9. Please have a seat.
10. Make yourself at home.
11. What's new with you?
12. Goodbye.
13. Good night.
14. See you tomorrow (*lit.* until tomorrow)

15. Good luck (*lit.* the best of everything).

16. Happy journey.
17. I wish you success.
18. Happy birthday!
19. Merry Christmas!
20. Happy New Year!

C. Politeness

1. Спаси́бо!
2. Большо́е спаси́бо!
3. Не́ за что!

4. Извини́те, пожа́луйста.
5. Бу́дьте добры́.
6. Переда́йте, пожа́луйста, соль.

1. Thank you!
2. Many thanks!
3. Don't mention it!   That's nothing!

4. Pardon me, please.
5. Be so kind!
6. Please pass the salt.

D. Introductions

1. Позвóльте вам представить Вéру Ивáновну.
2. Как вáше имя?
3. Как вáша фамúлия?
4. Как вáше имя и óтчество?
5. Óчень приятно познакóмиться.

1. Permit me to introduce to you Vera Ivanovna.
2. What is your name?
3. What is your last name?
4. What is your first name and patronymic?
5. I am very pleased to meet you.

E. Health

1. Как вáше здорóвье?
2. Спасúбо.   Я здорóв.
3. Я бóлен.
4. У меня головá болúт.
5. У меня нáсморк.

6. Сегóдня мне лýчше.
7. Вчерá мне бы́ло хýже.

1. How is your health?
2. Thank you.   I am well.
3. I am ill.
4. I have a headache.
5. I have a cold (in the head).
6. Today I feel better.
7. Yesterday I felt worse.

F. Time

1. Котóрый тепéрь час?
2. Тепéрь пять часóв.
3. В котóром часý вы бýдете дóма?
4. Я бýду дóма в два часá.

1. What time is it now?
2. It is now five o'clock.
3. At what time will you be home?
4. I shall be home at two o'clock.

G. Weather

1. Какáя сегóдня погóда?
2. Сегóдня óчень хорóшая погóда.
3. Вчерá былá плохáя погóда.
4. Хóлодно сегóдня.
5. Вчерá бы́ло óчень теплó.
6. Сегóдня идёт снег.
7. Вчерá шёл дождь.

1. How is the weather today?
2. The weather is very fine today.
3. The weather was bad yesterday.
4. It is cold today.
5. It was very warm yesterday.
6. It is snowing today.
7. It rained yesterday.

МАТЕРИА́Л ДЛЯ ЧТЕ́НИЯ

The following short selections are offered as additional reading material and are intended to increase the students' passive vocabulary. Hence, no grammatical explanations or questions in Russian accompany the text.

The selections have been taken from readers published in Russia for Russian pupils, but are here retold in simpler language and with the introduction of few new words. Unfamiliar words and expressions are translated in the footnotes.

I

Чле́ны[1] челове́ческого[2] те́ла[3]

Одна́жды[4] чле́ны челове́ческого те́ла поссо́рились[5] и не хоте́ли служи́ть[6] друг дру́гу.[7]

— Не хоти́м ходи́ть, говоря́т но́ги;[8] ходи́те са́ми![9]

— Не хоти́м рабо́тать для вас, говоря́т ру́ки;[10] рабо́тайте са́ми!

— Не хочу́ корми́ть[11] вас, кричи́т рот.[12]

— Не хоти́м смотре́ть! крича́т глаза́.

Так как[13] рот не корми́л те́ло, ру́ки не рабо́тали, но́ги не ходи́ли, а глаза́ не смотре́ли, то[14] все чле́ны ста́ли о́чень сла́быми.[15] Наконе́ц, все по́няли,[16] что нельзя́ ссо́риться,[17] а что ну́жно помога́ть[18] друг дру́гу. Ско́ро по́сле э́того всё те́ло ста́ло здоро́вым[19] и кре́пким.[20, 21]

Слова́рь (Vocabulary)

1. **член** member
2. **челове́ческий** human
3. **те́ло** body
4. **одна́жды** once
5. **поссо́риться (II)** *pf.* to have a quarrel
6. **служи́ть (II)** to serve
7. **друг дру́гу** (*dat.*) each other
8. **нога́** foot, leg
9. **сам** (*pron.*) myself, yourself, himself, *etc.*
10. **рука́** hand
11. **корми́ть (II)** to feed
12. **рот** mouth

13. **так как** since, as
14. **то** then, so
15. **сла́бый** weak
16. **поня́ть** (**I**) *pf.* to understand, to grasp
17. **ссо́риться** (**II**) to quarrel
18. **помога́ть** (**I**) to help
19. **здоро́вый** healthy
20. **кре́пкий** strong
21. **ста́ло здоро́вым и кре́пким** (*pred. instr.* is used with **стать**) became healthy and strong.

II

Бога́ч[1] и портно́й[2]

В го́роде в одно́м[3] до́ме жи́ли бога́тый купе́ц[4] и бе́дный[5] портно́й — купе́ц наверху́,[6] а портно́й внизу́.[7] Портно́й всегда́ рабо́тал о́чень по́здно и за рабо́той[8] пел[9] пе́сни. У портно́го был хоро́ший го́лос и он обыкнове́нно пел о́чень весёлые пе́сни. Эти пе́сни нра́вились купцу́. К несча́стью,[10] портно́й ча́сто пел так гро́мко, что купе́ц не мог спать.

Одна́жды[11] купе́ц дал портно́му мно́го де́нег.[12] Бе́дный портно́й тепе́рь стал богачо́м и переста́л[13] рабо́тать. Он та́кже переста́л[13] петь, потому́ что он всё[14] вре́мя боя́лся,[15] что украду́т[16] у него́ де́ньги. Он ма́ло спал но́чью, а иногда́ всю ночь совсе́м не спал.

Наконе́ц портно́й по́нял,[17] что он несча́стен,[18] потому́ что бога́т. Тогда́ он верну́л[19] де́ньги купцу́, и сказа́л: "Я лу́чше бу́ду рабо́тать и пе́сни петь."

Слова́рь (Vocabulary)

1. **бога́ч** rich man
2. **портно́й** tailor
3. **оди́н** one
4. **купе́ц** merchant
5. **бе́дный** poor
6. **наверху́** upstairs
7. **внизу́** downstairs
8. **за рабо́той** at work
9. **петь** (**I**) to sing
10. **к несча́стью** unfortunately
11. **одна́жды** once
12. **де́ньги** (*pl. only*) money
13. **переста́ть** (**I**) *pf.* to cease, to stop
14. **всё вре́мя** all the time

15. **боя́ться (II)**   to fear
16. **укра́сть (I)** *pf.*   to steal
    что украду́т   that one will steal
17. **поня́ть (I)** *pf.*   to understand
18. **несча́стен** (*m.*)   unhappy
19. **верну́ть (I)** *pf.*   to return, to give back

III

Москва́

Москва́ — столи́ца¹ СССР. Э́то полити́ческий,² экономи́-
ческий³ и культу́рный центр⁴ страны́.

В це́нтре Москвы́ нахо́дится Кремль,⁵ а о́коло Кремля́ —
Кра́сная⁶ пло́щадь.⁷ На Кра́сной пло́щади нахо́дятся Храм
Васи́лия Блаже́нного⁸ — замеча́тельный па́мятник⁹ ру́сской
архитекту́ры,¹⁰ мавзоле́й Ле́нина и Ста́лина,¹¹ огро́мный¹²
универма́г ГУМ,¹³ гости́ница "Москва́" и други́е больши́е
зда́ния.

В Москве́ мно́го библиоте́к, музе́ев, теа́тров и карти́нных
галере́й.¹⁴ Библиоте́ка и́мени Ле́нина¹⁵ в Москве́ — са́мая
больша́я библиоте́ка СССР. В Москве́ та́кже нахо́дится
Всесою́зная Акаде́мия нау́к,¹⁶ Консервато́рия¹⁷ и Моско́вский
университе́т — са́мый ста́рый университе́т в стране́.

Слова́рь (Vocabulary)

1. **столи́ца**   capital
2. **полити́ческий**   political
3. **экономи́ческий**   economic
4. **центр**   center
5. **Кремль**   the Kremlin
6. **Кра́сная**   red
7. **пло́щадь**   square
8. **Храм Васи́лия Блаже́нного**   Saint Basil's Cathedral
9. **па́мятник**   monument
10. **архитекту́ра**   architecture
11. **мавзоле́й Ле́нина и Ста́лина**   the Lenin and Stalin Mausoleum
12. **огро́мный**   huge
13. **Госуда́рственный универса́льный магази́н**   State Department
    Store
14. **карти́нная галере́я**   picture gallery
15. **Библиоте́ка и́мени Ле́нина**   the Lenin Library
16. **Всесою́зная Акаде́мия нау́к**   the All-Union Academy of Sciences
17. **Консервато́рия**   the Conservatory

IV

Перча́тки *

Потеря́ли котя́тки
На доро́ге перча́тки
И в слеза́х прибежа́ли домо́й.
— Ма́ма, ма́ма, прости́,
Мы не мо́жем найти́
Перча́тки!

— Потеря́ли перча́тки?
Вот дурны́е котя́тки!
Я вам ны́нче не дам пирога́.
Мя́у-мя́у, не дам
Мя́у-мя́у, не дам
Я вам ны́нче не дам пирога́!

Побежа́ли котя́тки,
Отыска́ли перча́тки
И смея́сь, прибежа́ли домо́й.
— Ма́ма, ма́ма, не злись,
Потому́ что нашли́сь,
Потому́ что нашли́сь
Перча́тки!

— Отыска́ли перча́тки?
Вот спаси́бо, котя́тки!
Я за э́то вам дам пирога́.
Мур-мур-мур, пирога́,
Мур-мур-мур, пирога́,
Я за э́то вам дам пирога́!

* From **Плывёт, плывёт кора́блик** by С. Марша́к—his version of *Three Little Kittens*. An English translation appears on page 212.

Three Little Kittens

The three little kittens
They lost their mittens,
And they began to cry,
Oh! mommy dear,
We sadly fear,
Our mittens we have lost.

What! lost your mittens?
You naughty kittens,
Then you shall have no pie.
Mi-ew, mi-ew, mi-ew, mi-ew,
Then you shall have no pie.

The three little kittens
They found their mittens,
And they began to cry,
Oh! mommy dear,
See here, see here,
Our mittens we have found.

What! found your mittens?
You darling kittens,
Then you shall have some pie.
Mi-ew, mi-ew, mi-ew, mi-ew,
Then you shall have some pie.

ПОСЛО́ВИЦЫ (Proverbs)

1. **В гостя́х хорошо́, а до́ма ещё лу́чше.**
   There's no place like home.

2. **Век живи́ — век учи́сь.**
   Live and learn.

3. **Куй желе́зо пока́ горячо́.**
   Strike while the iron's hot.

4. **Лу́чше по́здно, чем никогда́.**
   Better late than never.

5. **Не всё то зо́лото, что блести́т.**
   All is not gold that glitters.

6. **Не откла́дывай на за́втра, то что мо́жно сде́лать сего́дня.**
   Never put off till tomorrow what can be done today.

7. **Повторе́нье — мать уче́нья.**
   Practice makes perfect.

8. **Пра́вда доро́же зо́лота.**
   Truth is dearer than gold.

9. **Рука́ ру́ку мо́ет.**
   One hand washes the other.

10. **Сло́во — серебро́, молча́ние — зо́лото.**
    Speech is silver, but silence is golden.

11. **Ти́ше е́дешь — да́льше бу́дешь.**
    Haste makes waste.

12. **Что посе́ешь, то и пожнёшь.**
    As ye sow, so shall ye reap.

213

ЗАГА́ДКИ (Riddles)

1. Что э́то ?*

Нет ног,[1] а хожу́
рта нет,[2] а скажу́:
когда́ спать,
когда́ встава́ть,
когда́ рабо́ту начина́ть.

[1] I have no feet   [2] I have no mouth

2. Что э́то ?*

В огне́[1] не гори́т,[2] в воде́[3] не то́нет.[4]

[1] In fire   [2] does not burn   [3] in water   [4] does not sink

3. Что э́то ?*

Ска́терть[1] бе́ла,[2] всё поле[3] оде́ла.[4]

[1] tablecloth   [2] white   [3] field   [4] dressed, covered

4. Что э́то ?*

Овсо́м[1] не ко́рмят,[2]
кнуто́м[3] не го́нят,[4]
а как па́шет,[5] —
семь плуго́в[6] та́щит.[7]

[1] with oats   [2] they do not feed   [3] with a whip   [4] they do not drive
[5] plows   [6] seven plows   [7] pulls, drags

* For answer, see p. 216.

5. **Что э́то ?***

Два бра́та спе́реди[1] бегу́т,[2] два бра́та сза́ди[3] догоня́ют.[4]

[1] in front   [2] are running   [3] behind   [4] are catching up, are chasing

6. **Что э́то ?***

Без рук,[1] без ног,[2] а дом сторожи́т.[3]

[1] without hands   [2] without feet   [3] guards, watches over

7. **Что э́то ?***

Тóнкая[1] девчóнка,[2]
Бéлая юбчóнка,[3]
Крáсный[4] нос.[5]

Чем длиннéе[6] нóчи
Тем онá корóче[7]
От[8] горю́чих слёз.[9]

[1] thin   [2] little girl   [3] little skirt   [4] red   [5] nose   [6] the longer   [7] the shorter she is   [8] from   [9] scalding tears

* For answer, see p. 216.

Answers to Загáдки (**Riddles**)

1. **Часы́** — clock.

2. **Лёд** — ice.

3. **Снег** — snow.

4. **Трáктор** — tractor.

5. **Четы́ре колесá** — four wheels.

6. **Замóк** — lock.

7. **Свечá** — candle.

РУ́ССКИЕ ПЕ́СНИ

Брат Ива́н (Кано́н)

(Printed by arrangement with the Thrift Press, Ithaca, New York)

Брат И - ван, Брат И - ван,

спишь - ли ты, спишь-ли ты?

Звони в коло - ко - ла, звони в коло - ко - ла,

Динь, динь, динь, динь, динь, динь!

Харитóша

(Printed by arrangement with Leeds Music Corporation)

Е - ду, е - ду, е - ду, е - ду, е - ду,

пись-ма раз-да - ю... Не схо - дя с ве - ло - си -

пе - да, я с у - лыб - кой всем по - ю: Не ску -

чай - те, по - лу - чай - те, кто за - ждал-ся, кто влюб -

лен. Пись-ма неж-ны-е, род - ны-е, де - ло -

вы-е, за - каз - ны - е — Всем вру - ча - ет Ха - ри -

то - ша, ак - ку - рат - ный поч - та - льон.

1. Еду, еду, еду, еду,
   Еду, письма раздаю . . .
   Не сходя с велосипеда,
   Я с улыбкой всем пою:

2. Я везу любовь и радость
   И дыхание весны
   Из Москвы и Ленинграда
   И со всех концов страны.

3. Здесь конверты разной масти
   И газетные листы . . .
   В этой сумке смех и счастье
   И надежды и мечты.

4. Я берусь письмо доставить,
   Чтобы в срок оно пришло.
   Я хочу собой прославить
   Почтальона ремесло.

   Припев:
   Не скучайте, получайте,
   Кто заждался, кто влюблен.
   Письма нежные, родные,
   Деловые, заказные —
   Всем вручает Харитоша,
   Аккуратный почтальон.

Катю́ша

(Printed by arrangement with Leeds Music Corporation)

Рас - цве - та - ли   я - бло - ни и

гру - ши,   по - плы - ли   ту - ма - ны над ре -

кой.   Вы - хо - ди - ла

на бе - рег Ка - тю - ша,   на вы -

со - кий бе - рег на кру - той.

1. Расцветали яблони и груши,
   Поплыли туманы над рекой.
   Выходила на берег Катюша,
   На высокий берег на крутой.

2. Выходила, песню заводила
   Про степного сизого орла,
   Про того, которого любила,
   Про того, чьи письма берегла.

3. Ой ты, песня, песенка девичья,
   Ты лети за ясным солнцем вслед
   И бойцу на дальнем пограничье
   От Катюши передай привет.

4. Пусть он вспомнит девушку простую,
   Пусть услышит, как она поёт,
   Пусть он землю бережёт родную,
   А любовь Катюша сбережёт.

Во ку́знице

(Printed by arrangement with Leeds Music Corporation)

Во ку ... во куз - ни - це. Во

ку ... во куз - ни - це. Во куз -

ни - це мо - ло - ды - е куз - не - цы, во куз -

ни - це мо - ло - ды - е куз - не - цы.

Во ку . . . во кузнице,
Во кузнице молодые кузнецы.
Они, они куют,
Они куют, приговаривают:
"Пойдём, пойдём, Дуня,
Пойдём Дуня, в огород, в огород.
Сорвём, сорвём Дуне,
Сорвём Дуне лопушок, лопушок,
Сошьём, сошьём Дуне,
Сошьём Дуне сарафан, сарафан.
Носи, носи, Дуня,
Носи Дуня, не марай, не марай.
По пра . . . по праздничкам,
По праздничкам надевай, надевай.

Each line is repeated twice.

Вечёрний звон

(*Printed by arrangement with the Thrift Press, Ithaca, New York*)

Вечерний звон, вечерний звон,
Как много дум наводит он!

О юных днях в краю родном,
Где я любил, где отчий дом!

И как я с ним навек простясь
Там слышал звон в последний раз.

Вечерний звон, вечерний звон,
Как много дум наводит он!

Эй у́хнем

(Printed by arrangement with the Thrift Press, Ithaca, New York)

ра - зовьём мы кудря - ву.

Ай да, да, ай да, ай да, да ай да,

ра - зовьём кудря-ву - ю!

Эй ухнем, эй ухнем!

Колокóльчик

(Printed by arrangement with Leeds Music Corporation)

1. Од - но - звуч-но гре-мит ко - ло -
2. Столь - ко чувс-тва в той пе - сне у -
3. И при - пом-нил я в но - чи дру -

- коль - чик, и до - ро - га пы -
- ны - лой, Столь-ко чувс - тва в на -
- ги - е И род - ны - е по -

- лит-ся слег-ка,_____ И у-ны-ло по ро - вно-му
- пе-ве род-ном,_____ Что в гру-ди мо-ей хлад-ной, ос -
- ля и ле-са _____ И на о-чи, дав-но уж су -

по - лю За-ли - ва-ет-ся песнь ям - щи - ка.
- ты - лой Раз-го - ре-ло-ся сер - дце ог - нём.
- хи - е На-бе - жа-ла, как ис - кра, сле - за.

4. Однозвучно гремит колокольчик
   И дорога пылится слегка
   И замолк мой ямщик, а дорога,
   Предо мной далека, далека.

Вниз по ма́тушке по Во́лге

(Printed by arrangement with Leeds Music Corporation)

Бодро, Широко

Один · Все

1. Вниз__ по ма - туш - ке__ по Во-лге по
2. По__ ши-ро - ко - му__ раз-до-лью раз-
3. Ни - че-го__ ввол - нах__ не ви-дно не

Во - - - лге по ши -
до - - - лью под - ни -
ви - - - дно, о - дна

- ро - ко - му__ раз-до - - - лью.
- ма - ла-ся__ по - го - - - да.
ло - до-чка__ чер-не - - - ет.

PRONUNCIATION CHARTS

The charts on pages 230–234 represent only an approximation of Russian sounds, as it is impossible to give exact English equivalents. Therefore, when consulting the charts, refer to the more detailed rules on pronunciation.

Chart 1. Hard and Soft Vowels (See ¶1-A)

hard: а э о у ы

soft: я е ё ю и

The first four *soft* vowels represent a combination of the *y* sound in *yes* and the corresponding *hard* vowels; thus:

$$y + a = я$$
$$y + э = e$$
$$y + o = ё$$
$$y + y = ю$$

Chart 2. Voiced and Voiceless Consonants (See ¶9-A)

Voiced:	б	в	г	д	ж	з
Voiceless:	п	ф	к	т	ш	с

The consonants л, м, н and р are always voiced.

The consonants ц, ч, and щ are always voiceless.

Chart 3. Pronunciation of Vowels

For the pronunciation of **a**, see **¶2-A**; for **я**, **¶10-A**; for **e**, **¶4-A**; for **o**, **¶3-A**; for **ë**, *The Written Alphabet* (p. 8) and **¶8-D**; after sibilants, **¶8-C**.

Vowel	Stressed	Unstressed	After some letters (unstressed)	In connected speech
A a	As *a* in c*a*r: Ива́н она́	As *a* in ciga-rette: сады́ Ве́ра	After **ч** or **щ**, like *e* in ch*e*root: часы́ пло́щадь	
Я я	As *ya* in *ya*rd: мо*я́*, *я*	As *ye* in *ye*ar: *я*зы́к, *я*нва́рь	тся = ца ться = ца	
Э э	As *e* in *e*gg: э́та ду*э́*т	As *e* in *e*vict: *э*та́ж *э*кра́н		
E e	As *ye* in *ye*s (when initial or after a vowel): *е́*сли у*е́*хал	As *e* in *e*vent: сестра́ стена́	After **ж**, **ш**, and **щ**, like *e* in *e*gg: то́же пи́шет	
Ы ы	As *y* in s*y*l-lable: ты, вы забы́ть	Same as stressed		
И и	As *e* in *e*vil: пить И́да	Same as stressed	After **ж**, **ш**, and **ц**, like ы: жить маши́на	As **ы** (when pre-ceded by hard con-sonant): брат **и** я бу́дем **и**гра́ть
O o	As *o* in sp*o*rt: заво́д стол	As *o* in c*o*me: когда́ Москва́		
Ё ё	As *yo* in *yo*lk: её, ёлка своё	Always stressed		
У у	As *oo* in b*oo*ty: у́тро	Same as stressed		
Ю ю	As *u* in *u*se: ю́мор, юг, даю́	Same as stressed		
Й й	This letter always stands after a vowel, and forms the second part of a diphthong. Compare with *y* in bo*y*.			

Chart 4.   Pronunciation of Consonants

For final **в**, see **¶4-B**; for final **д**, see **¶3-B**.   For hard and soft consonants, see **¶8-B**.   For voiced and voiceless consonants, see **¶9-A**.   For **ъ** and **ь**, see **¶10-B**.

Con- so- nant	Hard	Soft	Voiced	Voiceless
Б б	As *b* in *b*ook: брат бумáга собáка	As *b* in *b*eauty: библиотéка бéлый		In final position or before voiceless consonant, like *p* in *p*art: хлеб, клуб, трýбка
В в	As *v* in *v*ote: Вóлга вáза	As *v* in *v*iew: вúдеть Вéра		In final position or before voiceless consonant, like *f* in *f*our: Иванóв, студéн- тов, вчерá, в час
Г г	As *g* in *g*lad: гóлос гóрод	As *g* in *g*eese: гид	As *v* in *v*ote: in genitive case ending егó, óго	In final position or before voiceless consonant, like *k* in *k*eep: друг As *ch* in lo*ch* before **к**: легкó, мя́гко
Д д	As *d* in *d*o: да	As *d* in *d*ew: дя́дя		In final position or before voiceless consonant, like *t* in *t*ake: вид, сад
Ж ж	As *s* in plea*s*-ure: журнáл	Always hard		In final position or before voiceless consonant, like *sh* in *sh*ip: муж, мужскóй
З з	As *z* in *z*one: завóд вáза	As *z* in cra*z*ier: зимá взять		In final position or before voiceless consonant, like *s* in *s*alt: раз, глаз без карт
К к	As *k* in *k*ing: как кóфе	As *c* in *c*ue: урóки кем	Before voiced consonant, like *g* in *g*ood: к дя́де так же	

Chart 4 (continued).

Con-so-nant	Hard	Soft	Voiced	Voiceless
Л л	As *ll* in we*ll:* ла́мпа Ло́ндон	As *ll* in mi*ll*ion лицо́ люби́ть		
М м	As *m* in *m*y: Москва́ ма́ленький	As *m* in *m*usic: мя́со мел		
Н н	As *n* in *n*o: на, наш ночь	As *n* in ge*n*ial: нет, не́бо		
П п	As *p* in *p*ark: парк по́чта	As *p* in *p*ew: пить, пе́сня пять		
Р р	As *r* in *r*ose: рад ра́дио, ру́сский	As *r* in seri-ously: ряд, река́ орёл		
С с	As *s* in *s*top: солда́т Сталингра́д	As *s* in *s*eek: си́ний всё	Before voiced consonant, like *z* in *z*one: сде́лать сдава́ть: про́сьба	
Т т	As *t* in *t*ip: там, то́лько тут	As *t* in *s*teel: ти́хо тётя		
Ф ф	As *f* in *f*our: фами́лия фронт, факт	As *f* in *f*ew: Фе́дя		
Х х	As *ch* in lo*ch* (Scotch): хорошо́ са́хар	As *h* in *h*uge (with strong breath): хи́мия		
Ц ц	As *ts* in boo*ts:* центр цвет	Always hard		
Ч ч	Always soft	As *ch* in *ch*eck: час, чем чита́ть		
Ш ш	As *sh* in *sh*ip: шко́ла штат	Always hard		
Щ щ	Always soft	As *shch* in fre*sh ch*eese: ещё, борщ		

Chart 5.   Vowel Changes

The replacement of one vowel by another when preceded by certain consonants often occurs in Russian. The chart below summarizes the most important rules governing such changes, and should prove valuable in explaining many irregularities in the inflection of nouns, adjectives, pronouns, and verbs. Remember this chart and refer to it frequently.

The sign > stands for *is replaced by*.

After gutturals г, к, х	After sibilants ж, ч, ш, щ	After ц
ь can never stand	е, ё are pronounced *eh, oh*, not *yeh, yo*	и > ы (except in words of foreign origin)
ы > и ю > у я > а	ы > и ю > у я > а	ы (remains) ю > у я > а
	unstressed о > е	unstressed о > е

For **ы > и**, see ¶7-A and ¶7-B.   For **ю > у**, see ¶5-A.

TABLES

Declension of Nouns

Table 1. First Declension

Case	Hard	Soft		
	-а	**-я**		**-ия**
nom.	ка́рта	неде́ля	дя́дя	а́рмия
gen.	ка́рты	неде́ли	дя́ди	а́рмии
dat.	ка́рте	неде́ле	дя́де	а́рмии
acc.	ка́рту	неде́лю	дя́дю	а́рмию
instr.	ка́рт**ой** (**-ою**)	неде́л**ей** (**-ею**)	дя́д**ей** (**-ею**)	а́рми**ей** (**-ею**)
prep.	о ка́рте	о неде́ле	о дя́де	об а́рмии

PLURAL†

Case	Hard	Soft		
	-а (*nom. sing.*)	**-я** (*nom. sing.*)		**-ия** (*nom. sing.*)
nom.	ка́рт**ы**	неде́ли	дя́ди	а́рмии
gen.	карт	неде́ль	дя́дей	а́рмий
dat.	ка́рт**ам**	неде́л**ям**	дя́д**ям**	а́рми**ям**
acc.	ка́рт**ы**	неде́ли	дя́дей	а́рмии
instr.	ка́рт**ами**	неде́л**ями**	дя́д**ями**	а́рми**ями**
prep.	о ка́рт**ах**	о неде́л**ях**	о дя́д**ях**	об а́рми**ях**

* For membership, see ¶ 15-7a. For classification into *hard* and *soft*, see ¶ 15-7b. For the *accusative* of animate objects, see ¶ 15-7 c-2. For irregularities in declension, see ¶ 25-3b.

† For formation of the *nominative plural*, see ¶ 20-2a, b. For the *accusative plural* of animate and inanimate nouns, see ¶ 26-3a. For the *genitive plural*, see ¶ 26-3b. For the *genitive plural* with fleeting **-о** or **-е**, see ¶ 26-3c.

Table 2.   Second Declension

MASCULINE SINGULAR*

Case	Hard	Soft		
	Consonant	-ь		-й
		Stress on stem	Stress on ending	
nom.	журна́л	автомоби́ль	дождь	трамва́й
gen.	журна́ла	автомоби́ля	дождя́	трамва́я
dat.	журна́лу	автомоби́лю	дождю́	трамва́ю
acc.	журна́л	автомоби́ль	дождь	трамва́й
instr.	журна́лом	автомоби́лем	дождём	трамва́ем
prep.	о журна́ле	об автомоби́ле	о дожде́	о трамва́е

MASCULINE PLURAL†

Case	Hard	Soft		
	Consonant (nom. sing.)	-ь (nom. sing.)		-й (nom. sing.)
		Stress on stem	Stress on ending	
nom.	журна́лы	автомоби́ли	дожди́	трамва́и
gen.	журна́лов	автомоби́лей	дожде́й	трамва́ев
dat.	журна́лам	автомоби́лям	дождя́м	трамва́ям
acc.	журна́лы	автомоби́ли	дожди́	трамва́и
instr.	журна́лами	автомоби́лями	дождя́ми	трамва́ями
prep.	о журна́лах	об автомоби́лях	о дождя́х	о трамва́ях

* † See notes at the end of this table on p. 237.

Table 2.   Second Declension (Continued)

NEUTER SINGULAR *

Case	Hard	Soft	
	-o	**-e**	**-ие**
nom.	сло́во	мо́ре	сочине́ние
gen.	сло́ва	мо́ря	сочине́ния
dat.	сло́ву	мо́рю	сочине́нию
acc.	сло́во	мо́ре	сочине́ние
instr.	сло́вом	мо́рем	сочине́нием
prep.	о сло́ве	о мо́ре	о сочине́нии

NEUTER PLURAL †

Case	Hard	Soft	
	-o (*nom. sing.*)	**-e** (*nom. sing.*)	**-ие** (*nom. sing.*)
nom.	слова́	моря́	сочине́ния
gen.	слов	море́й	сочине́ний
dat.	слова́м	моря́м	сочине́ниям
acc.	слова́	моря́	сочине́ния
instr.	слова́ми	моря́ми	сочине́ниями
prep.	о слова́х	о моря́х	о сочине́ниях

* For membership, see ¶ 18-4a.   For classification into *hard* and *soft*, see ¶ 18-4b.   For the *accusative* of animate objects, see ¶ 18-4 d-2.

† For formation of the *nominative plural*, see ¶ 20-2.   For the *accusative plural* of animate and inanimate nouns, see ¶ 26-4b.   For formation of the *genitive plural* of masculine nouns, see ¶ 26-4a; for neuter nouns, see ¶ 27-1a. For the *genitive plural* of neuter nouns with fleeting **-o** or **-e**, see ¶ 27-1b.

Table 3.   Third Declension

SINGULAR*

Case	-ь	Sibilant (ж, ч, ш, щ) + -ь	-ь
nom.	ло́шадь	ночь	тетра́дь
gen.	ло́шади	но́чи	тетра́ди
dat.	ло́шади	но́чи	тетра́ди
acc.	ло́шадь	ночь	тетра́дь
instr.	ло́шадью	но́чью	тетра́дью
prep.	о ло́шади	о но́чи	о тетра́ди

PLURAL †

Case	Stress on oblique case endings		Stress on stem
	-ь (*nom. sing.*)	Sibilant (ж, ч, ш, щ) + -ь (*nom. sing.*)	-ь (*nom. sing.*)
nom.	ло́шади	но́чи	тетра́ди
gen.	лошаде́й	ноче́й	тетра́дей
dat.	лошадя́м	ноча́м	тетра́дям
acc.	лошаде́й	но́чи	тетра́ди
instr.	лошадя́ми *or* лошадьми́	ноча́ми	тетра́дями
prep.	о лошадя́х	о ноча́х	о тетра́дях

* For membership, see ¶ **19-2a**.   For the *accusative* of animate objects, see ¶ **19-2b**.

† For formation of the *nominative plural*, see ¶ **20-2b**.   For the *accusative plural* of animate and inanimate nouns, see ¶ **27-2a**.   For nouns with stems in ж, ч, ш, or щ, see ¶ **27-2b**.

Declension of Adjectives

For classification of adjectives, see ¶ 14-2a, b. For agreement of adjectives in the *accusative singular* with nouns, see ¶ 14-1 *note*. For formation of the *nominative plural*, see ¶ 20-4. For agreement of adjectives in the *accusative plural* with nouns, see ¶ 27-3.

Table 4. Hard Declension

GROUP I (-ый, -ая, -ое)

Case	Singular			Plural for all genders
	m.	*f.*	*n.*	
nom.	но́вый	но́вая	но́вое	но́вые
gen.	но́вого	но́вой	но́вого	но́вых
dat.	но́вому	но́вой	но́вому	но́вым
acc.	но́вый *or* но́вого	но́вую	но́вое	но́вые *or* но́вых
instr.	но́вым	но́вой (ою)	но́вым	но́выми
prep.	о но́вом	о но́вой	о но́вом	о но́вых

GROUP II (-о́й, -а́я, -о́е)

Case	Singular			Plural for all genders
	m.	*f.*	*n.*	
nom.	молодо́й	молода́я	молодо́е	молоды́е
gen.	молодо́го	молодо́й	молодо́го	молоды́х
dat.	молодо́му	молодо́й	молодо́му	молоды́м
acc.	молодо́й *or* молодо́го	молоду́ю	молодо́е	молоды́е *or* молоды́х
instr.	молоды́м	молодо́й (о́ю)	молоды́м	молоды́ми
prep.	о молодо́м	о молодо́й	о молодо́м	о молоды́х

Table 5. Soft Declension

(-н + -ий; -н + -яя; -н + -ее)

Case	Singular			Plural for all genders
	m.	*f.*	*n.*	
nom.	после́дний	после́дняя	после́днее	после́дние
gen.	после́днего	после́дней	после́днего	после́дних
dat.	после́днему	после́дней	после́днему	после́дним
acc.	после́дний *or* после́днего	после́днюю	после́днее	после́дние *or* после́дних
instr.	после́дним	после́дней (ею)	после́дним	после́дними
prep.	о после́днем	о после́дней	о после́днем	о после́дних

Table 6.   Mixed Declension

GROUP I (-г, -к, -х + -ий, -ая, -ое)

Case	Singular			Plural for all genders
	m.	*f.*	*n.*	
nom.	ру́сский	ру́сская	ру́сское	ру́сские
gen.	ру́сского	ру́сской	ру́сского	ру́сских
dat.	ру́сскому	ру́сской	ру́сскому	ру́сским
acc.	ру́сский *or* ру́сского	ру́сскую	ру́сское	ру́сские *or* ру́сских
instr.	ру́сским	ру́сской (ою)	ру́сским	ру́сскими
prep.	о ру́сском	о ру́сской	о ру́сском	о ру́сских

GROUP II (-ж, -ч, -ш, -щ + -ий, -ая, -ее)

Case	Singular			Plural for all genders
	m.	*f.*	*n.*	
nom.	хоро́ший	хоро́шая	хоро́шее	хоро́шие
gen.	хоро́шего	хоро́шей	хоро́шего	хоро́ших
dat.	хоро́шему	хоро́шей	хоро́шему	хоро́шим
acc.	хоро́ший *or* хоро́шего	хоро́шую	хоро́шее	хоро́шие *or* хоро́ших
instr.	хоро́шим	хоро́шей (ею)	хоро́шим	хоро́шими
prep.	о хоро́шем	о хоро́шей	о хоро́шем	о хоро́ших

GROUP III (-г, -к, -х; -ж, -ч, -ш, -щ; + -ой, -а́я, -ое)

Case	Singular			Plural for all genders
	m.	*f.*	*n.*	
nom.	дорого́й	дорога́я	дорого́е	дороги́е
gen.	дорого́го	дорого́й	дорого́го	дороги́х
dat.	дорого́му	дорого́й	дорого́му	дороги́м
acc.	дорого́й *or* дорого́го	дорогу́ю	дорого́е	дороги́е *or* дороги́х
instr.	дороги́м	дорого́й (ою)	дороги́м	дороги́ми
prep.	о дорого́м	о дорого́й	о дорого́м	о дороги́х

Declension of Adjective-Pronouns

Table 7. Possessive

The possessives **его́**, **её**, and **их**, are not declined.

Case	Singulars (modifying singulars)			Singulars (modifying plurals, all genders)
	m.	*f.*	*n.*	
nom.	мой	моя́	моё	мои́
gen.	моего́	мое́й	моего́	мои́х
dat.	моему́	мое́й	моему́	мои́м
acc.	мой *or* моего́	мою́	моё	мои́ *or* мои́х
instr.	мои́м	мое́й (е́ю)	мои́м	мои́ми
prep.	о моём	о мое́й	о моём	о мои́х

твой is declined like **мой**.

Case	Plurals (modifying singulars)			Plurals (modifying plurals, all genders)
	m.	*f.*	*n.*	
nom.	наш	на́ша	на́ше	на́ши
gen.	на́шего	на́шей	на́шего	на́ших
dat.	на́шему	на́шей	на́шему	на́шим
acc.	наш *or* на́шего	на́шу	на́ше	на́ши *or* на́ших
instr.	на́шим	на́шей (е́ю)	на́шим	на́шими
prep.	о на́шем	о на́шей	о на́шем	о на́ших

ваш is declined like **наш**.

Declension of Pronouns

Table 8.   Personal Pronouns

SINGULAR

Case	First person (m., f., & n.)	Second person (m., f., & n.)
nom.	я	ты
gen.	меня́	тебя́
dat.	мне	тебе́
acc.	меня́	тебя́
instr.	мной (мно́ю)	тобо́й (тобо́ю)
prep.	обо мне́	о тебе́

Case	Third person* (m. & n.)		Third person * (f.)	
		With governing prepositions		With governing prepositions
nom.	он оно́		она́	
gen.	его́	у него́	её	у неё
dat.	ему́	к нему́	ей	к ней
acc.	его́	на него́	её	на неё
instr.	им	с ним	ей, е́ю	с ней, с не́ю
prep.	о нём	о нём	о ней	о ней

* Pronouns of the third person take the prefix **н-** when they are governed by a preposition.

Table 8 is continued on the next page.

Table 8. Personal Pronouns (Continued)

PLURAL

Case	All genders			
	First person	Second person	Third person*	
				With governing prepositions
nom.	мы	вы	они́	
gen.	нас	вас	их	у них
dat.	нам	вам	им	к ним
acc.	нас	вас	их	на них
instr.	на́ми	ва́ми	и́ми	с ни́ми
prep.	о нас	о вас	о них	о них

  * Pronouns of the third person take the prefix **н-** when they are governed by a preposition.

Table 9.   Relative and Interrogative Pronouns*

nom.	кто	что
gen.	кого́	чего́
dat.	кому́	чему́
acc.	кого́	что
instr.	кем	чем
prep.	о ком	о чём

★ See ¶ 12-2, 21-1.

Table 10.   Demonstrative*

Case	Singular			Plural for all genders
	m.	*f.*	*n.*	
nom.	э́тот	э́та	э́то	э́ти
gen.	э́того	э́той	э́того	э́тих
dat.	э́тому	э́той	э́тому	э́тим
acc.	э́тот *or* э́того	э́ту	э́то	э́ти *or* э́тих
instr.	э́тим	э́той (ою)	э́тим	э́тими
prep.	об э́том	об э́той	об э́том	об э́тих

★ For agreement of the masculine **э́тот** in the *accusative singular with nouns,* see ¶ 14-1. For agreement of the *accusative plural* of **э́ти** with nouns, see ¶ 27-3.

Table 11.   Reflexive Pronoun Singular and Plural (All Genders and Persons)*

nom.	none
gen.	себя́
dat.	себе́
acc.	себя́
instr.	собо́й (ою)
prep.	о себе́

★ See ¶ 19-1.

Numerals

Table 12. Cardinal Numerals 1 through 20*

1. один, одна, одно	11. одиннадцать
2. два (*m. and n.*), две (*f.*)	12. двенадцать
3. три	13. тринадцать
4. четы́ре	14. четы́рнадцать
5. пять	15. пятнадцать
6. шесть	16. шестнадцать
7. семь	17. семнадцать
8. во́семь	18. восемнадцать
9. де́вять	19 девятнадцать
10. де́сять	20. два́дцать

* For formation of 11 through 20, see ¶ **27-5a**. For nouns and adjectives governed by cardinal numerals, see ¶ **9-3. 20-8**. and **27-5b**.

Table 13. Time of Day—On the Hour

P.M.	A.M.
1:00 час дня	час но́чи
2:00 два часа́ дня	два часа́ но́чи
3:00 три часа́ дня	три часа́ но́чи
4:00 четы́ре часа́ дня	четы́ре часа́ утра́
5:00 пять часо́в дня	пять часо́в утра́
6:00 шесть часо́в ве́чера	шесть часо́в утра́
7:00 семь часо́в ве́чера	семь часо́в утра́
8:00 во́семь часо́в ве́чера	во́семь часо́в утра́
9:00 де́вять часо́в ве́чера	де́вять часо́в утра́
10:00 де́сять часо́в ве́чера	де́сять часо́в утра́
11:00 оди́надцать часо́в ве́чера	оди́ннадцать часо́в утра́
12:00 двена́дцать часо́в но́чи	двена́дцать часо́в дня

The afternoon hours 1:00–5:00 are regarded as hours of the *day* = **дня**; 6:00–11:00 p.m. as hours of the *evening* = **ве́чера**; 12:00 midnight–3:00 a.m. as hours of the *night* = **но́чи**; and 4:00–11:00 a.m. as hours of the *morning* = **утра́**. Twelve noon is considered an hour of the *day* = **дня**.

Verbs

Forms of verbs deviating from the regular conjugations are given in the *Russian-English Vocabulary*, pages 253-271.

For *classification* of verbs, see ¶4-2, 7-1, and 7-2.

For the *habitual* and *actual* forms of verbs, see ¶13-3.

For details on the *perfective* and *imperfective aspects*, see ¶23-1 and 23-2.

For *reflexive* verbs, see ¶16-6.

For formation of *present* tense, see ¶4-2 and 7-1; of *past* tense, see ¶10-8 and 23-2; for *compound future*, see ¶11-3; for *perfective future*, see ¶23-2; for *imperative*, see ¶11-5, 20-10, and 23-2e.

Table 14.   Conjugation of Быть (to be)

Singular   Plural

PRESENT

я (есмь)⎫   мы (éсмы)⎫
ты (еси) ⎬ *obsolete*   вы (éсте) ⎬ *obsolete*
он есть   они суть   *seldom used*

PAST

я, ты, он был   мы ⎫
я, ты, онá былá   вы ⎬ бы́ли
онó бы́ло   они ⎭

FUTURE

я бу́ду   мы бу́дем
ты бу́дешь   вы бу́дете
он бу́дет   они бу́дут

IMPERATIVE

будь   бу́дьте

Table 15. Regular Conjugations

CONJUGATION I   CONJUGATION II

INFINITIVE

чита́ть *to read*   **говори́ть** *to speak*

PRESENT TENSE

я чита́**ю**	я говор**ю́**
ты чита́**ешь**	ты говор**и́шь**
он чита́**ет**	он говор**и́т**
мы чита́**ем**	мы говор**и́м**
вы чита́**ете**	вы говор**и́те**
они́ чита́**ют**	они́ говор**я́т**

PAST TENSE

я, ты, он чита́**л**	я, ты, он говори́**л**
я, ты, она́ чита́**ла**	я, ты, она́ говори́**ла**
оно́ чита́**ло**	оно́ говори́**ло**
мы, вы, они́ чита́**ли**	мы, вы, они́ говори́**ли**

COMPOUND FUTURE TENSE

я бу́д**у**		я бу́д**у**	
ты бу́д**ешь**		ты бу́д**ешь**	
он бу́д**ет**	**чита́ть**	он бу́д**ет**	**говори́ть**
мы бу́д**ем**		мы бу́д**ем**	
вы бу́д**ете**		вы бу́д**ете**	
они́ бу́д**ут**		они́ бу́д**ут**	

IMPERATIVE

чита́**й**	говори́
чита́**йте**	говори́**те**

Table 16.   Reflexive Verbs

INFINITIVE

купа́ться   *to bathe* (*oneself*)

PRESENT TENSE

я купа́ю**сь**
ты купа́ешь**ся**   (*pr.* купа́ешь**са**)
он, она́, оно́ купа́ет**ся**   (*pr.* купа́е**ца**)
мы купа́ем**ся**   (*pr.* купа́ем**са**)
вы купа́ете**сь**
они́ купа́ют**ся**   (*pr.* купа́ю**ца**)

PAST TENSE

я, ты, он купа́л**ся**   мы ⎤
я, ты, она́ купа́ла**сь**   вы ⎬ купа́ли**сь**
оно́ купа́ло**сь**   они́ ⎦

COMPOUND FUTURE TENSE

я бу́ду купа́ть**ся**, *etc.*

IMPERATIVE

купа́й**ся**   купа́йте**сь**

Table 17. Impersonal Expressions*

PRESENT TENSE

Affirmative	хо́лодно it *is* cold	мне тебе́ ему́ ей } хо́лодно	I am you are he is she is } cold
		нам вам } хо́лодно им	we are you are } cold they are
Negative	**не** хо́лодно it *is not* cold	мне **не** хо́лодно	I am not cold, *etc.*

PAST TENSE

Affirmative	бы́ло хо́лодно it *was* cold	мне тебе́ } бы́ло ему́ хо́лодно ей	I was you were } cold he was she was
		нам вам } бы́ло им хо́лодно	we were you were } cold they were

Negative	**не́** было хо́лодно
	  it *was not* cold
		мне **не́** было
		    хо́лодно
			I was not cold, *etc.*

FUTURE TENSE

Affirmative	бу́дет хо́лодно it *will be* cold	мне тебе́ } бу́дет ему́ хо́лодно ей	I shall be you will be } cold he will be she will be
		нам вам } бу́дет им хо́лодно	we shall be you will be } cold they will be

Negative	**не** бу́дет хо́лодно
	  it *will not* be cold
		мне **не** бу́дет
		    хо́лодно
			I shall not be cold, *etc.*

* See ¶ **10-5**, **16-1**, and **16-5**.

VOCABULARIES

The following abbreviations are used throughout the text and in the vocabularies. Ordinarily, an italicized word in parentheses applies to the Russian word it follows; for example, **автомоби́ль** (*m.*) means that **автомоби́ль** is a masculine noun. Parts of speech are indicated only when confusion might arise; gender only when it is not obvious from the ending. Important grammatical references are also included.

Abbreviations

acc.	accusative	*irr.*	irregular
act.	actual verb	*lit.*	literally
adj.	adjective	*m.*	masculine
adv.	adverb	*n.*	neuter
colloq.	colloquial	*nom.*	nominative
comp.	comparative	*not decl.*	not declined
conj.	conjugation	*pers.*	personal
dat.	dative	*pf.*	perfective
decl.	declension, declined	*pl.*	plural
		pol.	polite
dim.	diminutive	*pred.*	predicative
f.	feminine	*prep.*	prepositional
fam.	familiar	*pr.*	pronounced
fut.	future	*pron.*	pronoun
gen.	genitive	*reflex.*	reflexive
hab.	habitual	*rel. pron.*	relative pronoun
imper.	imperative	*sing.*	singular
imp.	imperfective	*v.*	verb
instr.	instrumental	*fl*	fleeting **o** or **e**
interr.	interrogative	I	First Conjugation
intrans.	intransitive	II	Second Conjugation

RUSSIAN–ENGLISH VOCABULARY

See this vocabulary for references to rules on grammar and pronunciation; for verb forms, especially irregular ones; and for all irregularities in the declensions of nouns, adjectives, and pronouns.

This vocabulary also includes both the imperfective and perfective aspects if both have been used in this book. Therefore, if only the imperfective aspect is known, consult the vocabulary to find the perfective, and vice versa.

А

а   and, but
автомобиль (*m.*)   automobile
Аки́м   Joachim
а́лгебра   algebra
алло́   hello
Аме́рика   America (*colloq.* the U.S.A.)
америка́нец[fl] (*noun, m.*) (*gen.* **америка́нца**)   American
америка́нский, -ая, -ое   American (*adj.*)
англи́йский, -ая, -ое   English (*adj.*)
англича́нин (*nom. pl.* **англича́не;** *gen. pl.* **англича́н**)   Englishman
А́нглия   England
А́нна   Anne
аппети́т (*only in sing.*)   appetite
арифме́тика   arithmetic
ах!   oh!

Б

ба́бушка   grandmother
баскетбо́л   basketball
без (*with gen.*)   without
бейзбо́л   baseball
бе́лый, -ая, -ое   white
бе́рег (*prep.* **берегу́,** see ¶ **20-6;** *pl.* **берега́**)   shore
    на берегу́   on the shore
бесе́довать (**I**); **бесе́дую, бесе́дуешь, -ют;** *imper.* **бесе́дуй, -йте**   to chat, to talk
   pf. **побесе́довать** (**I**)   to have a talk
библиоте́ка   library
бли́зко (*adv. with* **от**)   near
бога́тый, -ая, -ое   rich
бо́лен (*m.*), **больна́** (*f.*), **больны́** (*pl.*)   sick

болит   aches (*v*.)
    у него болит голова   his head aches
больше (*adv*.)   more
большой, -ая, -ое ; *pl*. -ие   big
    большое спасибо   many thanks
Борис   Boris
борщ (*gen*. борща, *pl*. борщи)   borshch (beet soup)
брат   brother
брать (I); беру, берёшь, берут; *past* брал, -ла, -ло, -ли; *imper*. бери,
    -ите   to take
Браун   Brown (surname)
будет   will be (see ¶ 11-2)
буду   I shall be
бумага   paper
быстро (*adv*.)   rapidly
быть (*irr*.); буду, -ешь, -ут; *past* был, -ла, -ло, -ли (see *Unit* 11);
    imper. будь, будьте   to be
    не может быть   (it is) impossible

В

в (во)   (*with acc*.) to, into (direction); (*with acc*.) at, per (time); (*with prep*.)
    in, at (location)
ваза   vase
Ваня   Vanya
Вася   Basil
ваш, ваша, ваше; *pl*. ваши   your, yours
Вашингтон   Washington
вдруг   suddenly
Вера   Vera
верхом (*adv*.)   astride (a horse); *see* ездить верхом
весело   it is cheerful, gay; cheerfully, gaily
весёлый, -ая, -ое   cheerful, gay
весной (*adv*.)   in the spring
весь, вся, всё (*pron. & adj*.)   entire, whole
    все (*pl*.)   all, everybody
вечер (*pl*. вечера)   evening
    вечером   in the evening
    добрый вечер   good evening
    сегодня вечером   this evening, tonight
видеть (II) (*pf*. увидеть, II); вижу, видишь, видят; (*no imper*.)   to see
вместе (*adv*.)   together
внимательно   carefully, attentively
во (*see* в)   in, to (see ¶ 25-1d)
вода   water
война (*pl*. войны)   war
вокзал   railway station (see ¶ 25-1 b-3)
вокруг (*with gen*.)   around
волейбол   volleyball
Волга   Volga (*river in the U.S.S.R.*)

вопро́с question
восемна́дцать eighteen
во́семь eight
воскресе́нье Sunday
  в воскресе́нье on Sunday
вот here is, here are (see ¶4-1)
вре́мя (*n.*) (*gen.* **вре́мени**) time
  проводи́ть вре́мя to spend time
все (*pl. of* **весь, вся, всё**) all, everybody
  всё э́то all this
  всё-таки all the same
всегда́ always
встава́ть (**I**) (*pf.* **встать, I**); **встаю́, встаёшь, встаю́т** to get up, to rise
встать (**I**) (*pf. of* **встава́ть, I**); *fut.* **вста́ну, вста́нешь, -ут**; *imper.* **встань, вста́ньте** to get up, to rise
встреча́ть (**I**); **встреча́ю, -ешь, -ют** to meet
всю́ду (*adv.*) everywhere
вто́рник Tuesday
  во вто́рник on Tuesday (see ¶25-1d)
второ́й, -а́я, -о́е second
входи́ть (**II**); **вхожу́, вхо́дишь, вхо́дят** to go in, to enter
вчера́ yesterday
вы you (*pl. & polite sing.*)

Г

газе́та newspaper
гара́ж (*gen.* **гаража́**) garage
где where
геоме́трия geometry
гид guide
гла́вный, -ая, -ое main, chief
глаз (*gen.* **гла́за,** *pl.* **глаза́,** *gen. pl.* **глаз**) eye
глу́пый, -ая, -ое stupid
говори́ть (**II**); **говорю́, -и́шь, -я́т** to speak, to say, to talk
  pf. **сказа́ть** (**I**); *fut.* **скажу́, ска́жешь, -ут**; *imper.* **скажи́, -и́те** to say, to tell (once)
говоря́т one says, people say
год year
голова́ head
го́лос (*pl.* **голоса́**) voice
Го́мес Gomez
Го́пкинс Hopkins
го́род (*pl.* **города́,** see ¶23-3) town
господи́н Mister, gentleman
госпожа́ Mrs., Miss
гости́ница hotel
Го́фман Hoffman
грамма́тика grammar
гро́мко loudly
гру́ппа group
гуверна́нтка (*gen. pl.* **гуверна́нток**) governess
гуля́ть (**I**) (*pf.* **погуля́ть, I**) to walk (for pleasure), to take a walk

Д

да   yes

дава́ть (I); даю́, даёшь, даю́т; *past* **дава́л, -ла, -ло, -ли**   to give

да́же   even

дал (*past of pf.* **дать**)   gave

далеко́ (*adv.*)   far

да́льше (*adv.*)   further

да́ма   lady

да́ча   summer house

    на да́че   at a summer house

два (*m. & n.*); **две** (*f.*)   two

два́дцать   twenty

две (*f.*)   two

двена́дцать   twelve

дверь (*f.*)   door

де́вочка (*gen. pl.* **де́вочек**)   little girl

де́вушка (*gen. pl.* **де́вушек**)   girl

девятна́дцать   nineteen

де́вять   nine

де́душка (*gen. pl.* **де́душек**)   grandfather

де́лать (I)   to do

    pf. **сде́лать (I)**   to have done

деньᴵᴵ (*m.*) (*gen.* **дня,** *pl.* **дни**)   day

    до́брый день   good afternoon

    хоро́ший день   beautiful day

дере́вня   village, country

десе́рт   dessert

    на десе́рт   for dessert

де́сять   ten

де́ти (*pl. of* **дитя́**)   children

дива́н   divan

дли́нный, -ая, -ое   long

дневни́к (*gen.* **дневника́**)   diary

днём   in the daytime

до (*with gen.*)   to, up to, until; before

до свида́ния   goodbye

до́брый   good, kind

    до́брый день   good afternoon

    до́брое у́тро   good morning

дово́льно (*adv.*)   quite, rather

дождь (*m.*) (*pl.* **дожди́**)   rain

    идёт дождь   it is raining

    шёл дождь   it was raining

до́ктор (*pl.* **доктора́,** see ¶ **23-3**)   doctor

до́лго (*adv.*)   for a long time

до́лжен, должна́, -о́   obliged to, have to, must

    я до́лжен был   I had to

дом (*nom. pl.* **дома́,** see ¶ **23-3**)   house

до́ма (*adv.*)   at home (location)

домо́й (*adv.*)   home, homeward (direction) (see ¶ **10-6**)

дорого́й, -а́я, -о́е; *pl.* -и́е dear
доска́ (*pl.* **до́ски,** *gen. pl.* **досо́к**) blackboard
друг friend
    друг дру́га each other
    друг с дру́гом with each other
друго́й, -а́я, -о́е; *pl.* други́е (*adj. & pron.*) other, another
ду́мать (I) (*pf.* **поду́мать, I**); **ду́маю, -ешь, -ют** to think
дя́дя (*m.*) (*gen. pl.* **дя́дей**) uncle

Е

Евро́па Europe
европе́йский, -ая, -ое European
его́ his, him
    его́ ещё нет he is not here yet (see ¶16-3)
её her
е́здить (II) *hab.*; **е́зжу, е́здишь, -ят** to go (by conveyance) (see ¶13-3)
    е́здить верхо́м ⎫
    е́здить верхо́м на ло́шади ⎬ to ride horseback
    е́здить на ло́шади ⎭
    е́здить на автомоби́ле to go by automobile
    е́здить на трамва́е to go by streetcar
ей (*dat. of* **она́**) to her
е́сли if (*never means* whether)
есть there is
есть (*irr.*); **ем, ешь, ест, еди́м, еди́те, едя́т** to eat (see ¶15-2)
е́хать (I) *act.*; **е́ду, е́дешь, -ут** to go (by conveyance) (see ¶11-4 & 13-3)
    pf. **пое́хать (I)** to go, to set out (by conveyance)
ещё more, still
    что ещё? what else?

Ж

жаль it is a pity
    о́чень жаль it is a great pity, it is too bad
    как жаль! what a pity!
ждать (I); жду, ждёшь, ждут; *past* **ждал, -ла́, -ло, -ли** to wait (see ¶16-4)
же then, but (*emphatic*), however
    что же what then
жена́ (*pl.* **жёны**) wife
же́нщина woman
жизнь (*f.*) life
жить (I); живу́, живёшь, -у́т; *past* **жил, жила́, жи́ло, -ли** to live
журна́л magazine

З

за (*with acc.*) for
забыва́ть (I) (*pf.* **забы́ть, I**); **забыва́ю, -ешь, -ют** to forget

забы́ть (**I**) (*pf. of* **забыва́ть, I**); *fut.* **забу́ду, -ешь, -ут;** *imper.* **забу́дь, забу́дьте**   to forget

заво́д   plant (industrial)

за́втра   tomorrow

    за́втра у́тром   tomorrow morning

за́втрак   breakfast

за́втракать (**I**) (*pf.* **поза́втракать, I**); **за́втракаю, -ешь, -ют**   to have breakfast, to have lunch (noon)

заговори́ть (**II**) (*pf. of* **говори́ть, II**); *fut.* **заговорю́, -и́шь, -я́т;** *imper.* **заговори́, -и́те**   to begin to talk

закрича́ть (**II**) (*pf. of* **крича́ть, II**); *fut.* **закричу́, -и́шь, -а́т;** *imper.* **закричи́, -и́те**   to begin shouting

замеча́тельный, -ая, -ое   remarkable

занима́ться (**I**) *intrans.*; **занима́юсь, -ешься, -ются**   to study, to busy oneself with

заня́тия (*n. pl.*)   studies

запе́ть (**I**) (*pf. of* **петь, I**); *fut.* **запою́, -ёшь, -ю́т;** *imper.* **запо́й, запо́йте**   to begin singing

запла́кать (**I**) (*pf. of* **пла́кать, I**); *fut.* **запла́чу, -ешь, -ут;** *imper.* **запла́чь, запла́чьте**   to burst out crying, to begin weeping

засмея́ться (**I**) (*pf. of* **смея́ться, I**); *fut.* **засмею́сь, -ёшься, -ю́тся;** *imper.* **засме́йся, засме́йтесь**   to burst into laughter

зате́м   after that, then

заче́м   why, wherefore

зда́ние   building

здесь   here

здоро́в (*m.*)   well (*adj.*)

здоро́ва (*f.*)   well (*adj.*)

здра́вствуйте   how do you do? hello

зимо́й (*adv.*)   in the winter

знако́миться (**II**) (*pf.* **познако́миться, II**); **знако́млюсь, знако́мишься, -ятся;** *imper.* **знако́мься, знако́мьтесь**   to become acquainted

знать (**I**)   to know

зна́чит   (that) means

И

и   and, even

и ... и ...   both ... and ...

Ива́н   Ivan

Ивано́ва   Ivanova

Ива́нович   Ivanovich (see ¶ 15-1)

игра́ть (**I**)   to play

    pf. **поигра́ть** (**I**)   to play awhile

    игра́ть в те́ннис   to play tennis (see ¶ 16-2)

    игра́ть на роя́ле   to play the piano (see ¶ 16-2)

идти́ (**I**); *past* **шёл, шла, шло, шли**   to go, to walk (see ¶ 10-7)

    идём   let's go

из (*with gen.*)   from, out of

изуча́ть (**I**)   to study (see ¶ 10-1)

и́ли   or

инженéр   engineer
иногдá   sometimes
инострáнный, -ая, -ое   foreign
интервью́ (*n.*; *not decl.*; *pr.* **интэрвью́**)   interview
интерéсно   it is interesting
интерéсный, -ая, -ое   interesting; attractive (of a person)
интересовáть (**I**); интересу́ю, -ешь, -ют   to interest
Ири́на   Irene
испáнецᶠˡ (*pl.* испáнцы)   Spaniard
испáнский, -ая, -ое; *pl.* -ие   Spanish
истóрия   history
итáк   well then

К

к (*with dat.*)   to, towards (see ¶ **15-5**)
Кавкáз   Caucasus
кáждый, -ая, -ое   every, each
как   how
    как вы поживáете?   how are you?
    как дóлго?   how long?
какóй, -áя, -óе; *pl.* -и́е   what a, what kind of
Калифóрния   California
карандáш   pencil
кáрта   map
карти́на   picture
Кáтя (*f.*)   Katya
кинó (*n.*; *not decl.*)   movies, movie theater
класс   class
класть (**I**); кладу́, -ёшь, -у́т   to put
кли́мат   climate
кни́га   book
когдá   when
кóмната   room
компóт   stewed fruit
конéцᶠˡ (*pl.* концы́)   end
конéчно (*pr.* конéшно)   of course, certainly
Кóни-Áйленд   Coney Island
контóра   office
кончáть (**I**); кончáю, -ешь, -ют   to finish
кончáться (**I**) (*intrans., used mostly in the third person*); кончáется, кон-
    чáются   to end, to come to an end
корóва   cow
корóткий, -ая, -ое; *pl.* -ие   short
котлéты (*pl. of* котлéта)   cutlets, Russian meat balls
котóрый, -ая, -ое (*rel. & interr. pron.*)   which, who (see ¶ **18-2**)
кóфе (*m.*; *not decl.*)   coffee
кóшка (*gen. pl.* кóшек)   cat
красáвица   beauty, a beautiful woman
краси́вый, -ая, -ое   pretty
крéсло (*gen. pl.* крéсел)   armchair

крича́ть (**II**) (*pf.* закрича́ть, **II**); кричу́, -и́шь, -а́т   to shout, to scream
Крым   Crimea
    в Крыму́   in the Crimea
кто   who (see ¶ 12-2)
    кто э́то?   who is this?
    кто у телефо́на?   who is on the phone?
куда́   where to, whither
культу́рный, -ая, -ое   cultured
купа́ться (**I**) (*pr.* купа́ца); купа́юсь, -ешься (*pr.* купа́ешьса), купа́ют-
    ся (*pr.* купа́юца)   to bathe (oneself)   (see ¶ 16-6)
купи́л   bought
ку́шать (**I**); ку́шаю, -ешь, -ют   to eat (see ¶ 15-6)

Л

ла́мпа   lamp
лежа́ть (**II**) (*pf.* полежа́ть, **II**); лежу́, -и́шь, -а́т   to lie, to lie awhile
лёгкий, -ая, -ое; *pl.* -ие (*pr.* лёхкий)   easy
лес (*pl.* леса́, see ¶ 23-3)   forest
    в лесу́ (*prep. with* в)   in the forest (see ¶ 20-6)
ле́том (*adv.*)   in the summer
литерату́ра   literature
лицо́ (*pl.* ли́ца)   face
Ло́ндон   London
Лос-А́нжелос   Los Angeles
ло́шадь (*f.*)   horse
лу́чше (*adv.*; *comp. of* хорошо́)   better
    мне лу́чше   I feel better
люби́ть (**II**); люблю́, лю́бишь, -ят   to love, to like
    pf. полюби́ть (**II**)   to fall in love, to become very fond of
    не люби́ть   to dislike
лю́ди (*nom. pl. of* челове́к)   people, men and women

М

магази́н   store
Макси́м   Maxim
ма́ленький, -ая, -ое; *pl.* -ие (*adj.*)   small, little
ма́ло (*adv.*)   little (not much)
ма́льчик   boy
ма́ма   mama
ма́сло   butter
матема́тика (*sing. in Russian*)   mathematics
мать   mother
Ма́ша   Masha, Mary
ме́дленно (*adv.*)   slowly
мел   chalk
ми́ло   it is nice
ми́лый, -ая, -ое   nice, dear, lovely
    он тако́й ми́лый   he is such a dear
мину́та   minute

мир peace
Ми́ша (*m.*) Misha
мла́дший, -ая, -ее; *pl.* **-ие**   younger, junior
мне (*dat. of* **я**)   to me
мно́го (*adv.*) much
мо́жет быть   perhaps
   не мо́жет быть   (it is) impossible
мо́жно   it is possible, one may (see ¶ 16-1b)
мой, моя́, моё; *pl.* **мои́** (*adj. & pron.*)   my, mine
молодо́й, -а́я, -о́е   young
молоко́ milk
мо́ре (*n.*) (*pl.* **моря́**)   sea
Москва́ Moscow
мочь (**I**); **могу́, мо́жешь, мо́гут;** *past* **мог, могла́, могло́, могли́;** (*no*
   fut. & no imper.)   to be able to, to be in a position to (see ¶ 9-6 &
   19-3)
муж husband
мужчи́на (*m.*)   man
музе́й (*m.*) museum
му́зыка music
мы we

Н

на (*with acc.*)   to (direction); (*with prep.*)   on, at (location); (see ¶ 25-1b)
наве́рно   surely, most likely
На́дя (*f.*)   Nadya
наконе́ц   at last
на́ми *instr. of* **мы**
наприме́р   for instance
   как наприме́р   as for instance
написа́ть (**I**) (*pf. of* **писа́ть, I**); *fut.* **напишу́, напи́шешь, -ут;** *imper.*
   напиши́, -йте   to have written
нарисова́ть (**I**) (*pf. of* **рисова́ть, I**); *fut.* **нарису́ю, -ешь, -ют;** *imper.*
   нарису́й, -йте   to have drawn
нас *gen. & acc. of* **мы**
   нас бы́ло семна́дцать   there were seventeen of us
нахо́дится   is situated
начина́ть (**I**); **начина́ю, -ешь, -ют**   to begin
наш, -а, -е; *pl.* **на́ши** (*adj. & pron.*)   our, ours
не not
не́бо sky
неда́вно   recently
недалеко́   not far
неде́ля (*f.*)   week
   це́лую неде́лю   a whole week (see ¶ 15-3 & 15-4)
некраси́вый, -ая, -ое   unattractive, ugly
нельзя́   (it is) impossible, one may not (see ¶ 16-1)
не́мец[fl] (*pl.* **не́мцы**)   German (*noun*)
неме́цкий, -ая, -ое; *pl.* **-ие**   German (*adj.*)
немно́го   a little

не́сколько (*adv. with gen. pl.*)   several, a few
нет   no
ни . . . ни . . .   neither . . . nor . . .
нигде́   nowhere
никогда́   never
Никола́ев   Nikolaev
Никола́евна   Nikolaevna (see ¶15-1)
Никола́й   Nicholas
никто́ (*pron.*)   nobody, no one
ничего́   nothing
но   but
но́вый, -ая, -ое   new
Но́вый Орлеа́н   New Orleans
ночь (*f.*)   night (see ¶27-2)
    но́чью   at night
нра́виться (**II**); **нра́влюсь, нра́вишься, нра́вятся**   to like, to please (see
      ¶ 13-5, 14-4, & 18-1)
ну   well
ну́жен, нужна́, -о   necessary (see ¶13-6)
    ну́жно бы́ло   it was necessary (see ¶16-5)
Нью-Йо́рк   New York

О

о   oh!; about
обе́д   dinner
обе́дать (**I**); **обе́даю, -ешь, -ют**   to dine, to have dinner
    pf. **пообе́дать** (**I**)   to have dined
объясни́ть (**II**) (*pf. of* **объясня́ть, I**); *fut.* **объясню́, -и́шь, -я́т** to explain
    (see ¶10-В)
объясня́ть (**I**) (*pf.* **объясни́ть, II**); **объясня́ю, -ешь, -ют**   to explain (see
    ¶10-В)
обыкнове́нно   usually
одева́ться (**I**); **одева́юсь, -ешься, -ются**   to dress oneself
оди́н, одна́, одно́   one
оди́ннадцать   eleven
о́зеро (*pl.* **озёра**)   lake
    на о́зере   at the lake
окно́ (*pl.* **о́кна,** *gen. pl.* **о́кон**)   window
о́коло (*with gen.*)   near
Оле́г   Oleg
О́льга   Olga
он   he
она́   she
они́   they
оно́   it
опя́ть   again
Орло́в   Orlov
о́сенью (*adv.*)   in the fall
от (*with gen.*)   from
отве́т   answer
    что э́то за отве́т?   what kind of an answer is that?

отвеча́ть (I); отвеча́ю, -ешь, -ют   to answer
отдохну́ть (I) (*pf. of* отдыха́ть, I); *fut.* отдохну́, отдохнёшь, -у́т; *imper.*
    отдохни́, -йте   to rest
отдыха́ть (I) (*pf.* отдохну́ть, I)   to rest
оте́ц*fl* (*gen.* отца́)   father (see ¶ 9-5)
о́чень   very

<h2 style="text-align:center">П</h2>

Па́вел*fl* (*gen.* Па́вла)   Paul
Па́влович   Pavlovich
Па́вловна   Pavlovna
па́па (*m.*)   papa
парохо́д   steamer
Пари́ж   Paris
парк   park
пе́рвый, -ая, -ое   first
    в пе́рвый раз   for the first time
перо́   pen
пе́сня   song
Пётр*fl* (*gen.* Петра́)   Peter
Петро́в   Petrov
петь (I); пою́, поёшь, пою́т; *imper.* пой, по́йте   to sing
    pf. запе́ть (I)   to begin to sing
Пе́тя (*m.*)   Petya
пешко́м (*adv.*)   on foot
    ходи́ть пешко́м   to go on foot
писа́ть (I) (*pf.* написа́ть, I); пишу́, пи́шешь, -ут   to write
письмо́ (*pl.* пи́сьма, *gen. pl.* пи́сем)   letter
пить (I); пью, пьёшь, пьют; *past* пил, -ла́, -ло, -ли; *imper.* пей, пе́йте
    to drink
пла́вать (I) *hab.*   to swim
пла́кать (I); пла́чу, -ешь, -ут; *imper.* плачь, пла́чьте   to weep
    pf. запла́кать (I)   to burst out crying
пло́хо (*adv.*)   poorly, badly
плохо́й, -а́я, -о́е; *pl.* -и́е   bad, poor
по (*with dat.*)   on, in
по-англи́йски (*adv.*)   English, in English
побесе́довать (I) (*pf. of* бесе́довать, I); *fut.* побесе́дую, -ешь, -ют;
    imper. побесе́дуй, -йте   to have a talk
поговори́ть (II) (*pf. of* говори́ть, II)   to have a chat
пого́да   weather
погуля́ть (I) (*pf. of* гуля́ть, I)   to walk awhile
поду́мать (I) (*pf. of* ду́мать, I)   to think awhile
по́езд (*pl.* поезда́)   train
    е́хать по́ездом   to go by train
пое́здка (*gen. pl.* пое́здок)   trip
пое́хать (I) (*pf. of* е́хать, I)   to go, to set out (by conveyance)
пожа́луйста   please
пожива́ть (I); пожива́ю, -ешь, -ют   to get on
    как вы пожива́ете?   how are you?
поза́втракать (I) (*pf. of* за́втракать, I)   to have had breakfast

по́здно (*adv.*) late

познако́миться (**II**) (*pf. of* знако́миться, **II**); *fut.* познако́млюсь,
    -ишься, -ятся; *imper.* познако́мься, познако́мьтесь to become
    acquainted

поигра́ть (**I**) (*pf. of* игра́ть, **I**)   to play awhile

по-испа́нски (*adv.*)   Spanish, in Spanish

пока́   for the time being

    пока́ ещё   as yet, still

показа́ть (**I**) (*pf. of* пока́зывать, **I**); *fut.* покажу́, пока́жешь, -ут;
    imper. покажи́, -и́те   to show

пока́зывать (**I**) (*pf.* показа́ть, **I**); пока́зываю, -ешь, -ют   to show

пол (*pl.* полы́)   floor

    на полу́ (*prep. with* на)   on the floor

полежа́ть (**II**) (*pf. of* лежа́ть, **II**)   to lie awhile

полюби́ть (**II**) (*pf. of* люби́ть, **II**); *fut.* полюблю́, полю́бишь, -ят; *imper.*
    полюби́, -и́те   to fall in love, to become fond of

по́мнить (**II**); по́мню, -ишь, -ят   to remember

понеде́льник   Monday

    в понеде́льник   on Monday

по-неме́цки (*adv.*)   German, in German

понима́ть (**I**); понима́ю, -ешь, -ют   to understand

пообе́дать (**I**) (*pf. of* обе́дать, **I**)   to have dined

порабо́тать (**I**) (*pf. of* рабо́тать, **I**)   to work awhile

портре́т   portrait

по-ру́сски (*adv.*)   Russian, in Russian

посиде́ть (**II**) (*pf. of* сиде́ть, **II**); *fut.* посижу́, посиди́шь, -я́т; *imper.*
    посиди́, -и́те   to sit awhile

по́сле (*with gen.*)   after

после́дний, -яя, -ее   last, final

послу́шать (**I**) (*pf. of* слу́шать, **I**)   to listen awhile

поспа́ть (**II**) (*pf. of* спать, **II**); *fut.* посплю́, поспи́шь, -я́т; *imper.* поспи́,
    -и́те   to sleep a little, to take a nap

постоя́ть (**II**) (*pf. of* стоя́ть, **II**)   to stand awhile

потоло́к*fl* (*gen.* потолка́, *pl.* потолки́)   ceiling

пото́м   then, afterwards

потому́ что   because

поу́жинать (**I**) (*pf. of* у́жинать, **I**)   to have had supper

по-францу́зски (*adv.*)   French, in French

почему́   why

по́чта   post office

почти́   almost

поэ́тому   therefore

пра́вда   truth

    э́то не пра́вда   this is not true

предме́т   subject (of study)

предпочита́ть (**I**); предпочита́ю, -ешь, -ют   to prefer

прекра́сно   very well, excellently

прекра́сный, -ая, -ое   excellent

преподава́тель (*m.*)   teacher

преподава́ть (**I**); преподаю́, -ёшь, -ю́т; *imper.* преподава́й, -йте   to
    teach

приготовля́ть (**I**); приготовля́ю, -ешь, -ют   to prepare

приéхал (*past of pf.* **приéхать**)   arrived
прилéжный, -ая, -ое   diligent
приятно (*adv.*)   it is pleasant
приятный, -ая, -ое   pleasant
провестú (**I**) (*pf. of* **проводúть**, **II**); *fut.* **проведу́, -ёшь, -у́т**; *past* **провёл,
    провела́, -ло́, -лú**   to spend (time)
проводúть (**II**) (*pf.* **провестú**, **I**); **провожу́, провóдишь, -ят**   to spend
    (time)
продолжáть (**I**); **продолжáю, -ешь, -ют**   to continue
произношéние   pronunciation
профéссор (*pl.* **профессорá**, see ¶ **23-3**)   professor
прочитáть (**I**) (*pf. of* **читáть**, **I**)   to have read
птúца   bird
пустóй, -áя, -óе   empty, desolate
пя́тница   Friday
    в пя́тницу   on Friday
пятнáдцать   fifteen
пять   five

Р

рабóта   work
рабóтать (**I**) (*pf.* **порабóтать**, **I**); **рабóтаю, -ешь, -ют**   to work
рад, -а, -о; *pl.* **рáды**   glad
рáдио (*not decl.*)   radio
раз   time (occasion)
    в пéрвый раз   for the first time
    ещё раз   once again
    одúн раз   once
разговáривать (**I**); **разговáриваю, -ешь, -ют**   to converse
рáзный, -ая, -ое   various
рáно (*adv.*)   early
рассказáть (**I**) (*pf. of* **расскáзывать**, **I**); *fut.* **расскажу́, расскáжешь,
    -ут**; *imper.* **расскажú, -úте**   to relate, to tell
рéдко (*adv.*)   seldom, rarely
репортёр   reporter
ресторáн   restaurant
рисовáть (**I**) (*pf.* **нарисовáть**, **I**); **рису́ю, -ешь, -ют**   to draw
родúтели (*m., pl.*)   parents (father and mother)
Рокфéллеровский центр   Rockefeller Center
ромáн   novel
роя́ль (*m.*)   piano
    игрáть на роя́ле   to play the piano (see ¶ **16-2**)
ру́сский (*noun & adj.*)   Russian
    ру́сский язы́к   Russian (language) (see ¶ **10-2**)
ры́ба   fish

С

с (*with instr.*)   with; (*with gen.*)   from (see ¶ **25-1b**)
сад   garden
    в саду́ (*prep. with* **в**)   in the garden (see ¶ **20-6**)
салáт   salad

самова́р   samovar
са́мый, -ая, -ое *(used with adj. to form superlative)*   the most
Сан-Франци́ско *(not decl.)*   San Francisco
са́ндвич   sandwich
са́хар   sugar
светло́ *(adv.)*   it is bright
сде́лать (I) *(pf. of* де́лать, I)   to have done
себя́ *(reflex. pron.)*   self, oneself (see ¶ 19-1)
    у себя́   at one's (own) . . .
сего́дня *(pr.* сево́дня)   today
    сего́дня ве́чером   tonight, this evening
сейча́с   now, presently
    сейча́с же   immediately, at once
секре́т   secret
семна́дцать   seventeen
семь   seven
семья́   family (see ¶ 10-B)
серьёзно   seriously
серьёзный, -ая, -ое   serious
се́рый, -ая, -ое   gray
сестра́   sister
сиде́ть (II) *(pf.* посиде́ть, II); сижу́, сиди́шь, сидя́т   to sit
    сиде́ть до́ма   to stay home
си́него цве́та   (of) blue (color)
си́ний, -яя, -ее   blue
сказа́ть (I) *(pf. of* говори́ть, II); *fut.* скажу́, ска́жешь, -ут; *imper.*
    скажи́, -и́те   to say, to tell (once)
ско́лько *(used with gen. pl. of objects that can be counted)*   how much, how
    many
ско́ро   soon
ску́чно (мне ску́чно)   I am bored (see ¶ 16-1)
сла́ва бо́гу!   thank goodness!
сли́шком *(adv.)*   too (much)
слова́рь *(m.)* *(gen.,* словаря́, *pl.* словари́)   dictionary
сло́во *(pl.* слова́)   word
слу́шать (I) *(pf.* послу́шать, I); слу́шаю, -ешь, -ют   to listen to
слы́шать (II); слы́шу, слы́шишь, слы́шат   to hear
смешно́   it is funny
смея́ться (I); смею́сь, смеёшься, смею́тся; *imper.* сме́йся, сме́йтесь
      to laugh (see ¶ 18-1)
    pf. засмея́ться (I)   to burst into laughter
Смирно́в   Smirnov
Смит   Smith
смотре́ть (II); смотрю́, смо́тришь, смо́трят   to look
    смотре́ть на *(with acc.)*   to look at
    смотре́ть телеви́зор   to look at television
снача́ла *(adv.)*   at first
соба́ка   dog
совсе́м *(adv.)*   entirely
    совсе́м не   not at all, not in the least
сожале́ние   regret
    к сожале́нию   unfortunately

соединённый, -ая, -ое   united
Соединённые Штáты   United States
сочинéние (*n.*)   composition
спасúбо   thanks, thank you
    большóе спасúбо   many thanks
спать (**II**) (*pf.* **поспáть,** **II**); **сплю, спишь, спят;** *past* **спал, спалá, -ло,**
    -ли   to sleep
специалúст   specialist
спокóйной нóчи   good night
спорт   sport
спортсмéн   sportsman
спортсмéнка   sportswoman
спрáшивать (**I**)   to ask (questions)
средá   Wednesday
    в срéду   on Wednesday
средú (*with gen.*)   among
срéдний, -яя, -ее   middle
срéдняя шкóла   high school, secondary school
СССР   U.S.S.R.
стакáн   glass
Сталингрáд   Stalingrad
стáрый, -ая, -ое   old
стать (**I**) (*pf. of* **становúться**); *fut.* **стáну, -ешь, -ут;** *past* **стал, -ла, -ло,**
    -ли; *imper.* **стань, стáньте**   to become
стенá (*pl.* **стéны**)   wall
стол (*gen.* **столá,** *pl.* **столы́**)   table
столóвая (*noun, f.*; see ¶**20-9**)   dining room
стоя́ть (*pf.* **постоя́ть, II**); **стою́, -úшь, -я́т;** *imper.* **стой, -йте**   to stand
странá (*pl.* **стрáны**)   country
стрáнный, -ая, -ое   strange, odd
студéнт   student (*m.*)
студéнтка (*gen. pl.* **студéнток**)   student (*f.*)
студéнческий, -ая, -ое; *pl.* **-ие**   student (*adj.*)
стул   chair
суббóта   Saturday
    в суббóту   on Saturday
суп (*pl.* **супы́, -óв**)   soup
счастлúвый, -ая, -ое (*pr.* **щастлúвый**)   happy
счáстье (*pr.* **щáстье**)   luck, happiness
    к счáстью   fortunately
США (*pr.* **Сэ Ша А**) (**Соединённые Штáты Амéрики**)   U.S.A.
сюрпрúз   surprise

Т

так (*adv.*)   so
тáкже   also, in addition, likewise
такóй, -áя, -óе; *pl.* **-úе**   such a
там   there
танцовáть (**I**); **танцýю, -ешь, -ют**   to dance
Тáня (*f.*)   Tanya
твой, твоя́, твоё; *pl.* **твоú** (*adj. & pron.*)   your, yours (*fam. sing.*)
теáтр   theater

телеви́зор   television set
    смотре́ть телеви́зор   to look at television
телефо́н   telephone
    кто у телефо́на?   who is on the phone?
темно́   it is dark (see ¶ 16-1)
тепе́рь   now
те́ннис   tennis
    игра́ть в те́ннис   to play tennis (see ¶ 16-2)
тепло́   it is warm (see ¶ 16-1)
тетра́дь (*f.*)   notebook
тётя (*gen. pl.* **тётей**)   aunt
ти́хо (*adv.*)   quiet, quietly
това́рищ (*instr.* **това́рищем**, see ¶ 25-3b)   comrade, friend
тогда́   then, at that time (see ¶ 21-5)
то́же   also
то́лько   only
    то́лько что   just now
    как то́лько   as soon as
тому́ наза́д   ago
траге́дия   tragedy
трамва́й (*m.*)   streetcar
    е́хать на трамва́е   to go by streetcar
три   three
трина́дцать   thirteen
тру́дный, -ая, -ое   difficult
Ту́ла   Tula (*an industrial town*)
тури́ст   tourist
тури́стка (*gen. pl.* **тури́сток**)   tourist (*f.*)
тут   here
ты   you (*fam. sing.*)

У

у (*with gen.*)   by, at
    у меня́ нет   I do not have (see ¶ 13-1)
    у себя́   at one's (own) . . .
Уа́йт   White (*surname*)
уви́деть (**II**) (*pf. of* **ви́деть, II**); *fut.* **уви́жу, уви́дишь, -ят**; (*no imper.*)   to
    notice
уе́хать (**I**) (*pf. of* **е́хать, I**)   to leave, to depart
    уе́хать в   to leave for, to depart for
уже́   already
у́жин   supper
у́жинать (**I**) (*pf.* **поу́жинать, I**); **у́жинаю, -ешь, -ют**   to have supper
Украи́на   Ukraine
у́лица (*instr.* **у́лицей**, see ¶ 25-3b)   street
уме́ть (**I**); **уме́ю, -ешь, -ют**   to know how (see ¶ 19-3)
у́мный, -ая, -ое   clever, smart
    како́й он у́мный   how clever he is
умыва́ться (**I**); **умыва́юсь, -ешься, -ются**   to wash oneself

универма́г department store
университе́т university
упражне́ние exercise
Уо́лл-стрит Wall Street
ура́ hurrah
уро́к lesson
уста́л, -ла, -ло, -ли tired
у́тро morning
    до́брое у́тро good morning
у́тром in the morning
учени́к pupil (*m.*)
учени́ца pupil (*f.*)
учи́тель (*m.*) (*pl.* **учителя́,** see ¶ **23-3**) teacher
учи́тельница teacher (*f.*)
учи́ться (**II**) *intrans.* ; **учу́сь, у́чишься, -атся** to study, to attend school
ушёл, ушла́, ушло́, ушли́ (*past of pf.* **уйти́**) went away (once)

Ф

фа́брика factory
фами́лия surname
    как ва́ша фами́лия ? what is your last name?
Фёдор (*dim.* **Фе́дя**) Theodore
Фе́дя (*dim. of* **Фёдор**) Fedya, Teddy
фе́рма farm
    на фе́рме at the farm
Фо́стер Foster
Фра́нция France
францу́з Frenchman
францу́зский, -ая, -ое; ** *pl.* **-ие French

X

хлеб bread
ходи́ть (**II**) *hab.*; **хожу́, хо́дишь, -ят** to walk (see ¶ **13-2 & 13-3**)
    ходи́ть пешко́м to go on foot
хозя́йка owner, mistress, hostess, housekeeper
    хозя́йка до́ма owner of the house, hostess
хозя́ин master, owner, host
хо́лодно it is cold (see ¶ **16-1**)
холо́дный, -ая, -ое cold
хоро́ший, -ая, -ее; *pl.* **-ие** good
    хоро́ший день beautiful day
хорошо́ well, good, O.K., all right
хоте́ть (*irr.*); **хочу́, хо́чешь, хо́чет, хоти́м, -и́те, -я́т;** *past* **хоте́л, -ла,
    -ло, -ли;** (*no imper.*) to want, to wish
ху́же worse
    мне ху́же I feel worse

Ц

цвет color
целова́ть (**I**); **целу́ю, -ешь, -ют** to kiss (see ¶ **21-7**)

це́лый, -ая, -ое   whole
    це́лую мину́ту   a whole minute
    це́лую неде́лю   a whole week (see ¶ **15-3 & 15-4**)
Центра́льный вокза́л   Grand Central Station

Ч

чай (*m.*) (*pl.* **чай**)   tea
час (*pl.* **часы́**)   hour
ча́сто   often
ча́шка (*gen. pl.* **ча́шек**)   cup
ча́ще   oftener, more frequently
челове́к   man, person
чем (*instr. of* **что**)   with what; (*conj.*)   than
че́рез (*with acc.*)   in (*lit.*, after the lapse of)
Чёрное мо́ре   Black Sea
чёрный, -ая, -ое   black
четве́рг   Thursday
    в четве́рг   on Thursday
четы́ре   four
    на четы́ре дня   for four days
четы́рнадцать   fourteen
Чика́го (*not decl.*)   Chicago
чита́ть (**I**) (*pf.* **прочита́ть, I**); **чита́ю, -ешь, -ют**   to read
что   what, that (see ¶ **21-1**)
    что ещё   what else
    что же   what then
    что с тобо́й ?   what's the matter with you?
    что э́то за   what kind of
что́бы   in order to

Ш

шестна́дцать   sixteen
шесть   six
шко́ла   school
шокола́д   chocolate
штат   state

Э

экза́мен   examination
экску́рсия   excursion, trip
Э́мпайр стейт би́лдинг   Empire State Building
эне́ргия (*pr.* **энэ́ргия**)   energy
э́то   this is, that is
    э́то всё   that is all
э́тот, э́та, э́то; *pl.* э́ти (*adj. & pron.*)   this (see ¶ **14-1**)

Ю

юг south
юноша (*m.*)   youth, young man

Я

я I
язык   language
яйцо (*pl.* **яйца**)   egg
ясный, -ая, -ое   clear

ENGLISH-RUSSIAN VOCABULARY

See the *Russian–English Vocabulary* for references to rules on grammar and pronunciation; for verb forms, especially irregular ones; and for all irregularities in the declensions of nouns, adjectives, and pronouns.

The *Russian–English Vocabulary* also includes the imperfective and perfective aspects if both have been used in this book. In this case, the two aspects are always given together. Therefore, if only the imperfective aspect is known, consult the *Russian–English Vocabulary* to find the perfective, and vice versa.

A

able, to be **мочь (I)**
aches (*v.*) **болит**
    his head aches **у него́ боли́т голова́**
acquainted, to become **знако́миться (II)**; *pf.* **познако́миться (II)**
addition, in ... **та́кже**
after **по́сле** (*with gen.*)
after that **зате́м**
afterwards **пото́м**
again **опя́ть**
    once again **ещё раз**
ago **тому́ наза́д**
algebra **а́лгебра**
all **все**
    all this **всё э́то**
    that is all **э́то всё**
all right **хорошо́**
all the same **всё-таки**
almost **почти́**
already **уже́**
also **та́кже, то́же**
always **всегда́**
America **Аме́рика**
American (*noun, m.*) **Америка́нец**[fl]; (*adj.*) **америка́нский, -ая, -ое;**
    pl. **-ие**
among **среди́** (*with gen.*)
and **и, а**
Anne **А́нна**
another **друго́й, -а́я, -о́е;** *pl.* **-и́е** (*adj. & pron.*)
answer (*noun*) **отве́т**
answer, to **отвеча́ть (I)**

appetite **аппети́т**
arithmetic **арифме́тика**
armchair **кре́сло**
around **вокру́г** (*with gen.*)
arrived **прие́хал**
ask (questions), to **спра́шивать** (**I**)
astride (a horse) **верхо́м** (*adv.*)
at **у** (*with gen.*)
at last **наконе́ц**
attentively **внима́тельно**
attractive (of a person) **интере́сный, -ая, -ое**
aunt **тётя**
automobile **автомоби́ль** (*m.*)

B

bad (*adj.*) **плохо́й**
   it is too bad **о́чень жаль**
badly (*adv.*) **пло́хо**
baseball **бейзбо́л**
Basil **Ва́ся**
basketball **баскетбо́л**
bathe (oneself), to **купа́ться** (**I**)
be, to **быть** (*irr.*)
   will be **бу́дет** (see ¶ 11-2)
beautiful day **хоро́ший день**
beautiful girl **краса́вица**
beauty (person) **краса́вица**
because **потому́ что**
become, to **стать** (**I**) *pf.*
beet soup **борщ**
before **до** (*with gen.*)
begin, to **начина́ть** (**I**)
better (*adv.*) **лу́чше**
   I feel better **мне лу́чше**
big **большо́й, -а́я, -о́е;** *pl.* **-и́е**
bird **пти́ца**
black **чёрный, -ая, -ое**
Black Sea **Чёрное мо́ре**
blackboard **доска́**
blue **си́ний, -яя, -ee**
   (of) blue (color) **си́него цве́та**
book **кни́га**
Boris **Бори́с**
borshch **борщ**
both ... and ... **и ... и ...**
bought **купи́л**
boy **ма́льчик**
bread **хлеб**
breakfast (*noun*) **за́втрак**
   to have breakfast **за́втракать** (**I**); *pf.* **поза́втракать** (**I**)

bright, it is **светло́**
brother **брат**
Brown **Бра́ун** (*surname*)
building **зда́ние**
but **а, но**
butter **ма́сло**
by **у** (*with gen.*)

C

California **Калифо́рния**
carefully **внима́тельно**
cat **ко́шка**
Caucasus **Кавка́з**
ceiling **потоло́к**
certainly **коне́чно**
chair **стул**
chalk **мел**
chat, to have a **поговори́ть** (**II**) *pf.*; **побесе́довать** (**I**) *pf.*
cheerful **весёлый, -ая, -ое**
    it is cheerful **ве́село**
cheerfully **ве́село**
Chicago **Чика́го** (*not decl.*)
chief (*adj.*) **гла́вный, -ая, -ое**
children **де́ти**
chocolate **шокола́д**
city **го́род**
class **класс**
clear **я́сный, -ая, -ое**
clever **у́мный, -ая, -ое**
    how clever he is **како́й он у́мный**
climate **кли́мат**
coffee **ко́фе** (*m.; not decl.*)
cold **холо́дный, -ая, -ое**
    it is cold **хо́лодно** (see ¶ 16-1)
color **цвет**
composition **сочине́ние** (*n.*)
comrade **това́рищ**
Coney Island **Ко́ни-А́йленд**
continue, to **продолжа́ть** (**I**)
converse, to **разгова́ривать** (**I**)
country **дере́вня, страна́** (*land*)
course, of . . . **коне́чно**
cow **коро́ва**
Crimea **Крым**
    in the Crimea **в Крыму́**
cry, to **пла́кать** (**I**)
    to begin to cry **запла́кать** (**I**) *pf.*
cultured **культу́рный, -ая, -ое**
cutlets **котле́ты**

D

dance, to **танцовáть (I)**
dark, it is **темнó** (see **¶ 16-1**)
day **день** *ⁿ*
    beautiful day **хорóший день**
    good day **дóбрый день**
daytime, in the . . . **днём**
dear **мíлый, -ая, -ое; дорогóй, -áя, -óе;** *pl.* **-íе**
depart for, to **уéхать (I)** *pf.* **+ в**
department store **универмáг**
deserted **пустóй, -áя, -óе**
dessert **десéрт**
    for dessert **на десéрт**
diary **дневнíк**
dictionary **словáрь**
difficult **трýдный, -ая, -ое**
diligent **прилéжный, -ая, -ое**
dine, to **обéдать (I)**
    to have dined **пообéдать (I)** *pf.*
dining room **столóвая** (see **¶ 20-9**)
dinner **обéд**
    to have dinner **обéдать (I)**
    to have had dinner **пообéдать (I)** *pf.*
dislike **не любíть**
divan **дивáн**
do, to **дéлать (I)**
    to have done **сдéлать (I)** *pf.*
doctor **дóктор**
dog **собáка**
door **дверь** (*f.*)
draw **рисовáть (I)**
    to have drawn **нарисовáть (I)** *pf.*
dress oneself, to **одевáться (I)**
drink, to **пить (I)**

E

each **кáждый, -ая, -ое**
    each other **друг дрýга**
    with each other **друг с дрýгом**
early (*adv.*) **рáно**
easy **лёгкий, -ая, -ое;** *pl.* **-ие**
eat **есть** (*irr.*) (see **¶ 15-2**); **кýшать (I)** (see **¶ 15-6**)
egg **яйцó** (*pl.* **я́йца**)
eight **вóсемь**
eighteen **восемнáдцать**
eleven **одíннадцать**
Empire State Building **Э́мпайр стейт бíлдинг**
empty **пустóй, -áя, -óе**
end (*noun*) **конéц** *ⁿ*
end, to **кончáться (I)**

energy **энéргия**
engineer **инженéр**
England **Áнглия**
English **англи́йский, -ая, -ое;** *pl.* **-ие**
    in English **по-англи́йски**
Englishman **англичáнин**
enter, to **входи́ть (II)**
entire **весь, вся, всё**
entirely **совсéм**
Europe **Еврóпа**
European **европéйский, -ая, -ое;** *pl.* **-ие**
even **дáже**
evening **вéчер** (*pl.* **вечерá**)
    good evening **дóбрый вéчер**
    in the evening **вéчером**
every **кáждый, -ая, -ое**
everybody **все**
everywhere **всю́ду** (*adv.*)
examination **экзáмен**
excellent **прекрáсный, -ая, -ое**
excellently **прекрáсно**
exclaim, to **закричáть (II)** *pf.*
excursion **экскýрсия**
exercise **упражнéние**
explain, to **объясня́ть (I);** *pf.* **объясни́ть (II)**
eye **глаз** (*gen.* **глáза,** *pl.* **глазá,** *gen. pl.* **глаз**)

F

face **лицó** (*pl.* **ли́ца**)
factory **фáбрика**
fall, in the . . . **óсенью** (*adv.*)
family **семья́**
far (*adv.*) **далекó**
    not far **недалекó**
farm **фéрма**
    at the farm **на фéрме**
fast (*adv.*) **бы́стро**
father **отéц**ᶠˡ (*gen.* **отцá**) (see ¶**9-5**)
Fedya **Фéдя** (*dim. of* **Фёдор**) Teddy
feel, to
    I feel better **мне лýчше**
    I feel worse **мне хýже**
few, a **нéсколько**
fifteen **пятнáдцать**
final **послéдний, -яя, -ее**
finish, to **кончáть (I)**
first **пéрвый, -ая, -ое**
    at first **сначáла** (*adv.*)
    for the first time **в пéрвый раз**
fish **ры́ба**

five   **пять**
floor   **пол**
fond, to become . . . of   **полюби́ть (II)** *pf.*
foot, on . . .   **пешко́м**
    to go on foot   **ходи́ть пешко́м**
for   **за** (*with acc.*); **для** (*with gen.*)
foreign   **иностра́нный, -ая, -ое**
forest   **лес** (*pl.* **леса́**)
forget, to   **забыва́ть (I)**; **забы́ть (II)** *pf.*
fortunately   **к сча́стью**
Foster   **Фо́стер** (*surname*)
four   **четы́ре**
fourteen   **четы́рнадцать**
France   **Фра́нция**
French (*adj.*)   **францу́зский, -ая, -ое**; *pl.* **-ие**
    in French   **по-францу́зски**
Frenchman   **францу́з**
frequently   **ча́сто**
    more frequently   **ча́ще**
Friday   **пя́тница**
    on Friday   **в пя́тницу**
friend   **друг, това́рищ**
from   **от** (*with gen.*); **из** (*with gen.*); **с** (*with gen.*); (see ¶ **25-1**)
fruit, stewed . . .   **компо́т**
funny, it is . . .   **смешно́**
further   **да́льше** (*adv.*)

G

gaily   **ве́село**
garage   **гара́ж**
garden   **сад**
gay   **весёлый, -ая, -ое**
    it is gay   **ве́село**
gentleman   **господи́н**
geometry   **геоме́трия**
German (*noun*)   **не́мец**^{fl}; (*adj.*) **неме́цкий, -ая, -ое**; *pl.* **-ие**
    in German   **по-неме́цки** (*adv.*)
get on, to   **пожива́ть (I)**
get up, to   **встава́ть (I)**; **встать (I)** *pf.*
girl   **де́вушка**
    little girl   **де́вочка**
give, to   **дава́ть (I)**
glad   **рад, -а, -о**; *pl.* **-ы**
glass   **стака́н**
go (by conveyance), to   **е́здить (II)** *hab.*; **е́хать (I)** *act.*; (see ¶ **13-3**)
go (on foot), to   **ходи́ть (II)** *hab.*; **идти́ (II)** *act.*; (see ¶ **13-2 & 13-3**)
go (set out), to   **пое́хать (I)** *pf.*
go in, to   **входи́ть (II)**
Gomez   **Го́мес**
good (*adj.*)   **хоро́ший, -ая, -ее**; *pl.* **-ие**; (*adv.*) **хорошо́**

good afternoon   до́брый день
good morning   до́брое у́тро
good night   споко́йной но́чи
goodbye   до свида́ния
governess   гуверна́нтка
grammar   грамма́тика
Grand Central Station   Центра́льный вокза́л
grandfather   де́душка
grandmother   ба́бушка
gray   се́рый, -ая, -ое
group   гру́ппа
guide   гид

H

happy   счастли́вый, -ая, -ое
hate to, to   о́чень не хоте́ть
have to, to   до́лжен, должна́, -о́
he   он
head   голова́ (pl. го́ловы)
headache   see aches
healthy   здоро́в (m.), здоро́ва (f.)
hear, to   слы́шать (II)
hello   здра́вствуйте, алло́
her   её
here   тут, здесь
here is, here are   вот
high school   сре́дняя шко́ла
his   его́
history   исто́рия
Hoffmann   Го́фман
home (homewards)   домо́й (see ❡ 10-6)
    at home   до́ма
    to stay home   сиде́ть до́ма
Hopkins   Го́пкинс
horse   ло́шадь (f.)
horseback, to ride . . .   е́здить верхо́м, е́здить на ло́шади, е́здить
        верхо́м на ло́шади
host   хозя́ин
hostess   хозя́йка
hotel   гости́ница
hour   час
house   дом (pl. дома́)
    summer house   да́ча
housekeeper   хозя́йка
how   как
    how are you?   как вы пожива́ете?
    how do you do!   здра́вствуйте!
    how long?   как до́лго?
however   же
hurrah   ура́
husband   муж

I

I   я
if   éсли
immediately   сейчáс же
impossible, it is . . .   не мóжет быть; нельзя́ (see ¶ 16-1b)
in   в, во (*with prep.*); чéрез (*with acc.*) (*lit.*, after the lapse of); по (*with dat.*)
instance, for . . .   напримéр
    as for instance   как напримéр
interest, to   интересовáть (I)
interesting   интерéсный, -ая, -ое
    it is interesting   интерéсно
interview   интервью́ (*n.*; *not decl.*)
into   в (*with acc.*)
Irene   Ири́на
is, there . . .   есть
Ivan   Ивáн
Ivanova   Ивáнóва
Ivanovich   Ивáнович

J

Joachim   Аки́м
junior   млáдший, -ая, -ее; *pl.* -ие
just now   тóлько что

K

Katya   Кáтя
kind, what . . . of   какóй, -áя, -óе; *pl.* -и́е
kiss, to   целовáть (I) (see ¶ 21-7)
know, to   знать (I)
know how, to   умéть (I) (see ¶ 19-3)

L

lady   дáма
lake   óзеро (*pl.* озёра)
lamp   лáмпа
language   язы́к
last   послéдний, -яя, -ее
    at last   наконéц
late (*adv.*)   пóздно
laugh   смея́ться (I)
    to burst into laughter   засмея́ться (I) *pf.*
leave for, to   уéхать (I) *pf.* + в
lesson   урóк
letter   письмó (*pl.* пи́сьма)
library   библиотéка
lie, to   лежáть (II); полежáть (II) *pf.*
life   жизнь (*f.*)
like, to   люби́ть (II), нрáвиться (II); (see ¶ 13-5, 14-4, & 18-1)

likely **наве́рно**
likewise **та́кже**
listen to, to **слу́шать (I); послу́шать (I)** *pf.*
literature **литерату́ра**
little (*adj.*) **ма́ленький, -ая, -ое;** *pl.* **-ие**
little (*adv.*) **ма́ло**
    a little **немно́го**
live, to **жить (I)**
London **Ло́ндон**
long **дли́нный, -ая, -ое**
    for a long time **до́лго** (*adv.*)
    how long **как до́лго**
look, to **смотре́ть (II)**
    to look at **смотре́ть на +** *acc.*
    to look at television **смотре́ть телеви́зор**
Los Angeles **Лос-А́нжелос**
loudly **гро́мко**
love, to **люби́ть (II)**
    to fall in love **полюби́ть (II)** *pf.*
lovely **ми́лый, -ая, -ое**
lunch, to have . . . **за́втракать (I)**

M

magazine **журна́л**
main (*adj.*) **гла́вный, -ая, -ое**
mama **ма́ма**
man **мужчи́на** (*m.*)**; челове́к** (person); *pl.* **лю́ди** (people)
many, how . . . **ско́лько**
many thanks **большо́е спаси́бо**
map **ка́рта**
Mary **Ма́ша**
Masha **Ма́ша**
master **хозя́ин**
mathematics **матема́тика** (*sing. in Russian*)
Maxim **Макси́м**
may, one . . . **мо́жно** (see ¶ 16-1b)
    one may not **нельзя́** (see ¶ 16-1b)
me, to . . . **мне** (*dat.*)
means (*v.*) **зна́чит**
meatballs (Russian) **котле́ты**
meet, to **встреча́ть (I)**
middle (*adj.*) **сре́дний, -яя, -ее**
milk **молоко́**
minute **мину́та**
Miss **госпожа́**
Misha **Ми́ша** (*m.*)
Mister **господи́н**
mistress **хозя́йка**
Mrs. **госпожа́**

Monday **понеде́льник**
    on Monday **в понеде́льник**
more **ещё, бо́льше**
morning **у́тро**
    good morning **до́брое у́тро**
    in the morning **у́тром**
Moscow **Москва́**
most **са́мый, -ая, -ое**
mother **мать**
movies **кино́** (*not decl.*)
much **мно́го**
    how much **ско́лько**
    too much **сли́шком**
museum **музе́й** (*m.*)
music **му́зыка**
must **до́лжен, должна́, -о́**
my **мой, моя́, моё;** *pl.* **мои́**

N

Nadya **На́дя**
nap, to take a . . . **поспа́ть** (**II**) *pf.*
near **о́коло; бли́зко** (*with* **от**); (*both with gen.*)
necessary **ну́жен**
    it was necessary **ну́жно бы́ло**
need, to **ну́жен** (*with dat.*) (see ¶ 13-6)
neither . . . nor . . . **ни . . . ни . . .**
never **никогда́**
new **но́вый, -ая, -ое**
New Orleans **Но́вый Орлеа́н**
New York **Нью-Йо́рк**
newspaper **газе́та**
nice **ми́лый, -ая, -ое**
    it is nice **ми́ло**
Nicholas **Никола́й**
night **ночь** (see ¶ 27-2)
    at night **но́чью**
Nikolaev **Никола́ев**
Nikolaevna **Никола́евна**
nine **де́вять**
nineteen **девятна́дцать**
no **нет**
no one **никто́** (*pron.*)
nobody **никто́** (*pron.*)
not **не**
notebook **тетра́дь** (*f.*)
nothing **ничего́**
notice, to **уви́деть** (**II**) *pf.*
novel **рома́н**
now **тепе́рь, сейча́с**
    just now **то́лько что**
nowhere **нигде́**

O

obliged to   **до́лжен, должна́, -о́**
occasion (time)   **раз**
odd   **стра́нный, -ая, -ое**
office   **конто́ра**
often   **ча́сто**
oftener   **ча́ще**
oh   **о, ах**
O.K.   **хорошо́**
old   **ста́рый, -ая, -ое**
Oleg   **Оле́г**
Olga   **О́льга**
on   **на** (*with prep.*); **по** (*with dat.*)
once   **оди́н раз**
    at once   **сейча́с же**
    once again   **ещё раз**
one   **оди́н, одна́, одно́**
oneself   **себя́** (*reflex. pron.*) (see ¶ **19-1**)
only   **то́лько**
or   **и́ли**
order, in . . . to   **что́бы**
Orlov   **Орло́в**
other   **друго́й, -а́я, -о́е; -и́е**
our   **наш, на́ша, на́ше;** *pl.* **на́ши** (*adj. & pron.*)
out of   **из** (*with gen.*)
owner   **хозя́ин** (*m.*), **хозя́йка** (*f.*)

P

papa   **па́па** (*m.*)
paper   **бума́га**
parents   **роди́тели** (*m. pl.*)
Paris   **Пари́ж**
park   **парк**
Paul   **Па́вел** *fl*
Pavlovich   **Па́влович**
Pavlovna   **Па́вловна**
peace   **мир**
pen   **перо́**
pencil   **каранда́ш**
people   **лю́ди**
perhaps   **мо́жет быть**
person   **челове́к**
Peter   **Пётр**
Petya   **Пе́тя**
Petrov   **Петро́в**
piano   **роя́ль** (*m.*)
    to play the piano   **игра́ть на роя́ле** (see ¶ **16-2**)
picture   **карти́на**
pity, it is a . . .   **жаль**
    it is a great pity   **о́чень жаль**
    what a pity   **как жаль**

plant (industrial) заво́д
play   игра́ть (I); поигра́ть (I) *pf.*
    to play tennis игра́ть в те́ннис (see ¶ 16-2)
    to play the piano игра́ть на роя́ле (see ¶ 16-2)
pleasant прия́тный, -ая, -ое
    it is pleasant прия́тно
please пожа́луйста
    to please нра́виться (II)
pleasing, to be нра́виться (II)
poorly пло́хо
portrait портре́т
position, to be in a . . . to мочь (I)
possible, it is . . . мо́жно (see ¶ 16-1b)
    how is this possible? как э́то мо́жет быть?
post office по́чта
prefer, to предпочита́ть (I)
prepare, to приготовля́ть (I)
presently сейча́с
pretty краси́вый, -ая, -ое
professor профе́ссор (*pl.* профессора́)
pronunciation произноше́ние
pupil учени́к (*m.*), учени́ца (*f.*)
put, to класть (I)

Q

question вопро́с
quiet (*adv.*) ти́хо
quietly ти́хо
quite дово́льно

R

radio ра́дио (*not decl.*)
railway station вокза́л
rain дождь (*m.*)
    it is raining идёт дождь
    it was raining шёл дождь
rapidly бы́стро
rarely ре́дко (*adv.*)
rather дово́льно
read, to чита́ть (I); прочита́ть (I) *pf.*
recently неда́вно
regret сожале́ние
relate (once), to рассказа́ть (I) *pf.*
remarkable замеча́тельный, -ая, -ое
remember, to по́мнить (II)
reporter репортёр
rest, to отдыха́ть (I); отдохну́ть (I) *pf.*
restaurant рестора́н
rich бога́тый, -ая, -ое

ride, to **е́здить (II)** *hab.*; **е́хать (I)** *act.*
    to ride horseback **е́здить верхо́м, е́здить верхо́м на ло́шади, е́здить на ло́шади**
right, all . . . **хорошо́**
rise, to **встава́ть (I); встать (I)** *pf.*
Rockefeller Center **Рокфе́ллеровский це́нтр**
room **ко́мната**
Russian (*noun*) **ру́сский, -ая;** (*adj.*) **ру́сский, -ая, -ое**
    in Russian **по-ру́сски** (*adv.*)
    Russian language **ру́сский язы́к** (see ¶ 10-2)

S

salad **сала́т**
same, all the . . . **всё-таки**
samovar **самова́р**
San Francisco **Сан-Франци́ско** (*not decl.*)
sandwich **са́ндвич**
Saturday **суббо́та**
    on Saturday **в суббо́ту**
say, to **говори́ть (II); сказа́ть (I)** *pf.*
school **шко́ла**
    high school **сре́дняя шко́ла**
scream, to **крича́ть (II); закрича́ть (II)** *pf.*
sea **мо́ре**
second (*adj.*) **второ́й, -а́я, -о́е**
secret **секре́т**
see, to **ви́деть (II); уви́деть (II)** *pf.*
seldom **ре́дко** (*adv.*)
self **себя́** (*reflex. pron.*) (see ¶ 19-1)
serious **серьёзный, -ая, -ое**
seriously **серьёзно**
seven **семь**
seventeen **семна́дцать**
several **не́сколько** (*adv. with gen. pl.*)
she **она́**
shore **бе́рег** (*pl.* **берега́**)
    on the shore **на берегу́**
short **коро́ткий, -ая, -ое;** *pl.* **-ие**
shout, to **крича́ть (II); закрича́ть (II)** *pf.*
show, to **пока́зывать (I); показа́ть (I)** *pf.*
sick **бо́лен, больна́**
sing, to **петь (I); запе́ть (I)** *pf.*
sister **сестра́**
sit, to **сиде́ть (II); посиде́ть (II)** *pf.*
situated, is . . . **нахо́дится**
six **шесть**
sixteen **шестна́дцать**
sky **не́бо**
sleep, to **спать (II); поспа́ть (II)** *pf.*

slowly   ме́дленно
small   ма́ленький, -ая, -ое; *pl.* -ие
smart   у́мный, -ая, -ое
Smirnov   Смирно́в
Smith   Смит
so (*adv.*)   так
sometimes   иногда́
song   пе́сня
soon   ско́ро
    as soon as   как`то́лько
soup   суп
    beet soup   борщ
south   юг
Spaniard   испа́нец *fl*
Spanish   испа́нский, -ая, -ое; *pl.* -ие
    in Spanish   по-испа́нски
speak, to   говори́ть (II)
specialist   специали́ст
sport   спорт
sportsman   спортсме́н
sportswoman   спортсме́нка
spring, in the . . .   весно́й (*adv.*)
Stalingrad   Сталингра́д
stand, to   стоя́ть (II); постоя́ть (II) *pf.*
state   штат
station (railway)   вокза́л
stay home, to   сиде́ть до́ма
steamer   парохо́д
stewed fruit   компо́т
still   ещё, пока́ ещё
store   магази́н
strange   стра́нный, -ая, -ое
street   у́лица
streetcar   трамва́й
    to go by streetcar   е́хать на трамва́е
student (*noun*)   студе́нт (*m.*), студе́нтка (*f.*); (*adj.*) студе́нческий, -ая,
    -ое; *pl.* -ие
studies   заня́тия (*n. pl.*)
study, to   изуча́ть (I) (see ¶ 10-1); занима́ться (I) *intrans.*; учи́ться (II)
    intrans.
stupid   глу́пый, -ая, -ое
subject (of study)   предме́т
such a   тако́й, -а́я, -о́е; *pl.* -и́е
suddenly   вдруг
sugar   са́хар
summer, in the . . .   ле́том (*adv.*)
Sunday   воскресе́нье
    on Sunday   в воскресе́нье
supper   у́жин
    to have supper   у́жинать (I); поу́жинать (I) *pf.*

surely **наве́рно**
surname **фами́лия**
    what is your surname? **как ва́ша фами́лия?**
surprise **сюрпри́з**
swim, to **пла́вать (I)** *hab.*

T

table **стол**
take, to **брать (I)**
talk, to **говори́ть (II); поговори́ть (II)** *pf.* ; **заговори́ть (II)** *pf.*; **бесе́до-
      вать (I)**
    to have a talk **побесе́довать (I)** *pf.*
Tanya **Та́ня**
tea **чай** (*m.*)
teach, to **преподава́ть (I)**
teacher (*m.*) **учи́тель, преподава́тель**; (*f.*) **учи́тельница**
telephone **телефо́н**
    on the telephone **у телефо́на**
television set **телеви́зор**
    to look at television **смотре́ть телеви́зор**
tell (once), to **сказа́ть (I)** *pf.*
ten **де́сять**
tennis **те́ннис**
    to play tennis **игра́ть в те́ннис** (see ¶ 16-2)
than **чем**
thank goodness! **сла́ва бо́гу!**
thank you **спаси́бо**
thanks **спаси́бо**
    many thanks **болшо́е спаси́бо**
that (*rel. pron.*) **что** (see ¶ 21-1)
that is **э́то**
theater **теа́тр**
    movie theater **кино́** (*not decl.*)
then **пото́м, зате́м, тогда́** (see ¶ 25-1)
Theodore **Фёдор** (*dim.* **Фе́дя**)
there **там**
there is **есть**
therefore **поэ́тому**
these **э́ти**
they **они́**
think, to **ду́мать (I); поду́мать (I)** *pf.*
thirteen **трина́дцать**
this (*pron.*) **э́то;** (*adj. & pron.*) **э́тот, э́та, э́то** (see ¶ 14-1)
three **три**
Thursday **четве́рг**
    on Thursday **в четве́рг**
time **вре́мя** (*n.*)

time (occasion) **раз**
    at that time **тогда́**
    for a long time **до́лго** (*adv.*)
    for the first time **в пе́рвый раз**
    for the time being **пока́**
    to spend time **проводи́ть вре́мя**
tired **уста́л, -ла, -ло, -ли**
to **на** (*with acc.*); **в** (*with acc.*); (see ¶ 25-1b)
to (towards) **к** (*with dat.*) (see ¶ 15-5)
to (up to, until) **до** (*with gen.*)
today **сего́дня**
together **вме́сте** (*adv.*)
tomorrow **за́втра**
    tomorrow morning **за́втра у́тром**
tonight **сего́дня ве́чером**
tourist **тури́ст** (*m.*), **тури́стка** (*f.*)
towards **к** (*with dat.*)
town **го́род** (*pl.* **города́**)
tragedy **траге́дия**
train **по́езд** (*pl.* **поезда́**)
    to go by train **е́хать по́ездом**
trip **экску́рсия, пое́здка**
true, this is not . . . **э́то не пра́вда**
truth **пра́вда**
Tuesday **вто́рник**
    on Tuesday **во вто́рник**
Tula (*industrial town*) **Ту́ла**
twelve **двена́дцать**
twenty **два́дцать**
two **два** (*m. & n.*), **две** (*f.*)

U

U.S.A. **США** (*pr.* **Сэ Ша А**)
U.S.S.R. **СССР**
ugly **некраси́вый, -ая, -ое**
Ukraine **Украи́на**
unattractive **некраси́вый, -ая -ое**
uncle **дя́дя** (*m.*)
understand, to **понима́ть** (**I**)
unfortunately **к сожале́нию**
united **соединённый, -ая, -ое**
United States **Соединённые Шта́ты**
university **университе́т**
usually **обыкнове́нно**

V

Vanya **Ва́ня** (*m.*)
various **ра́зный, -ая, -ое**

vase **ва́за**
Vera **Ве́ра**
very **о́чень**
village **дере́вня**
voice **го́лос** (*pl.* **голоса́**)
Volga (*river in the U.S.S.R.*) **Во́лга**
volleyball **волейбо́л**

W

wait, to **ждать** (**I**) (see ¶ 16-4)
walk, to **идти́** (**I**) *act.*; **ходи́ть** (**II**) *hab.*; (see ¶ 13-2 & 13-3)
walk (for pleasure), to **гуля́ть** (**I**)
    to take a walk **гуля́ть** (**I**); **погуля́ть** (**I**) *pf.*
wall **стена́**
Wall Street **Уо́лл-стрит**
want, to **хоте́ть** (*irr.*)
war **война́**
warm, it is . . . **тепло́**
was **был, -ла́, -ло, -ли**
wash oneself, to **умыва́ться** (**I**)
Washington **Вашингто́н**
water **вода́**
we **мы**
weather **пого́да**
Wednesday **среда́**
    on Wednesday **в сре́ду**
week **неде́ля**
weep, to **пла́кать** (**I**); **запла́кать** (**I**) *pf.*
well (*adj.*) **здоро́в**; (*adv.*) **хорошо́**; (*exclamation*) **ну!**
    very well (*adv.*) **прекра́сно**
    well then **ита́к**
went away (once) **ушёл, ушла́, ушло́, ушли́** (*past of pf.* **уйти́**)
what **что**
    what a, what kind of **како́й, -а́я, -о́е**; *pl.* **-и́е**
    what else **что ещё**
    what then **что же**
    with what **чем**
when **когда́**
where **где**
where to **куда́**
wherefore **заче́м**
which **кото́рый, -ая, -ое** (see ¶ 18-2)
white **бе́лый, -ая, -ое**
White (*surname*) **Уа́йт**
whither **куда́**
who **кто; кото́рый, -ая, -ое**
    who is this? **кто э́то?**
whole **весь, вся, всё; це́лый, -ая, -ое**
why **почему́, заче́м**
wife **жена́**

window **окно́**
winter, in the . . . **зимо́й** (*adv.*)
wish, to **хоте́ть** (*irr.*)
with **с** (*with instr.*)
without **без** (*with gen.*)
woman **же́нщина**
word **сло́во**
work **рабо́та**
work, to **рабо́тать** (**I**); **порабо́тать** (**I**) *pf.*
worse **ху́же** (*adv.*)
    I feel worse **мне ху́же**
write, to **писа́ть** (**I**); **написа́ть** (**I**) *pf.*

Y

year **год**
yes **да**
yesterday **вчера́**
yet, as . . . **пока́ ещё**
you **ты** (*fam. sing.*); **вы** (*pl. & polite sing.*)
young **молодо́й, -а́я, -о́е**
young man **ю́ноша**
younger **мла́дший, -ая, -ее;** *pl.* **-ие**
your, yours (*adj. & pron.*) **твой, твоя́, твоё, твои́; ваш, ва́ша, ва́ше,**
      ва́ши
youth (*person*) **ю́ноша**

INDEX